Limits of the Novel

Evolutions of a Form
from Chaucer to Robbe-Grillet

Limits of the Novel

Evolutions of a Form
from Chaucer to Robbe-Grillet

DAVID I. GROSSVOGEL

Cornell University Press

ITHACA AND LONDON

Copyright © 1968 by Cornell University

First published 1968
Second printing 1971

International Standard Book Number: 0-8014-0162-3
Library of Congress Catalog Card Number: 68-16381

PRINTED IN THE UNITED STATES OF AMERICA
BY VAIL-BALLOU PRESS, INC.

Per John

L'intero libro invece
di tante note

Acknowledgments

The following authorizations to quote are herewith acknowledged: James Joyce, *A Portrait of the Artist as a Young Man*, copyright 1944 by Viking Press, Inc. (also Jonathan Cape Ltd, for the Executors of the James Joyce Estate, and the Society of Authors), and *Ulysses*, copyright 1946 by Random House, Inc.; Franz Kafka, *The Trial*, translated by Willa and Edwin Muir, copyright © 1957 by Alfred A. Knopf Incorporated; Marcel Proust, *Remembrance of Things Past*, translated by C. K. Scott Moncrieff and Frederick A. Blossom, copyright 1941 by Random House, Inc.; Alain Robbe-Grillet, *The Erasers*, translated by Richard Howard, copyright © 1964 by Grove Press, Inc., *For a New Novel*, translated by Richard Howard, copyright © 1965 by Grove Press, Inc., and *The Voyeur*, translated by Richard Howard, copyright © 1958 by Grove Press, Inc.; and Laurence Sterne, *Tristram Shandy*, edited by James A. Work, copyright 1940 by The Odyssey Press, Inc.

Grateful thanks are also extended to the John Simon Guggenheim Foundation for time to read some of these authors.

And because they demonstrated my contention that the best reader is perforce a critic (though he may also be a helpful friend), my deepest appreciation to my colleagues: Professors Robert M. Adams, Dalai Brenes, Paul de Man, Jean-Jacques Demorest, Neil Hertz, Jean Parrish, Karl-Ludwig Selig, Michael Shinagel—and especially John Freccero and Judith S. Herz. *Qui aime bien corrige bien.*

D. I. G.

Ithaca, New York
November 1967

Contents

Limits of the Novel

Evolutions of a Form
from Chaucer to Robbe-Grillet

Introduction

Pero usai di dire tra i miei amici, secondo la sentenzia de poeti, quel Narcisso convertito in fiore essere della pittura stato inventore: ché giá, ove sia la pittura fiore d'ogni arte, ivi tutta la storia di Narcisso viene a proposito. Che dirai tu essere dipigniere, altra cosa ché simile abracciare con arte quella ivi superficie del fonte?

LEON BATTISTA ALBERTI, *Della pittura*

The intent and methodology of this essay are simple: they assume that the reader's response to the fiction of a novel will depend, according to the extent of his sophistication, on belief or appreciation. They assume further that belief is a more primitive response which becomes eventually esthetic commentary; that the first response supposes commitment, the latter detachment; that the first ingests the work of art through a form of osmosis, while the second turns it into a phenomenal object. And lastly, this theory relies on the heresy that the writer, however appreciative he may be of his reader's esthetic appreciation, will not be satisfied until he has reached the reader beyond that appreciation, until he has become that reader's truth.

But before examining the implications of this interaction between writer and reader, one must first be satisfied that the human instinct involves an urge to write or a need to read: since both activities suppose self-consciousness—an awareness of self that defines and situates—more rudimentary attempts at self-situation must be accounted for. In the beginning, there are many gods. When all nature manifests itself to man primarily as threat, gods are as widespread as are the evidences of danger that must be propitiated. But as man achieves control and the multiform danger is reduced to those refractory questions that will continue to elude him, pluralism becomes pantheism: nature speaks to man with one voice, responding with its oneness to his need not to feel incomplete. Notions of transcendency, unity, circularity, timelessness come to be associated with the godhead. A victim of irrationality, man sees his peace and fulfillment in control: against chaos, he opposes logos. For him order supposes the imposition of the mind upon the erratic or nonminded, for such a reality can exist only in his mind. Aristotle establishes all nature within the control of a superior mind—God's: nature is the realization of the thought of God, but of a God that exercises himself only in contemplation. This means that nature is a form of perfection (a conclusion that will affect all art for centuries to come) and God is perfect: he is an essence whose absolute purity is denoted by his single and self-defining act; he is the mind that thinks about thought. The God of Aristotle might be a man (thought being the most lofty attribute of man and his only absolute assertion), but a man without the god-creating shortcomings of man.

These considerations have a relevancy to the literature

that man devises for himself. But at a more superficial level, the fortunes of his divinities also suggest a symbolic analogue for his art. Art first appears as a way for him to identify and particularize nature. But as his exploration carries him beyond surfaces, he first represents through familiar equivalents that for which he no longer has an apparent image. Once he dwells at the heart of the mystery, he feels akin to a god—and when the godlike sense is in him, nature need not serve as a pretext or as a symbol for his representations; he assumes the proud name of poet and his representations become a guaranty of truth. In the end, his gesture is like that of Aristotle's God: since there is none more lofty or more significant, it becomes the only activity worthy of his concern or definition.

A poet like Valéry keeps returning to the image of Narcissus; for him, all art stems from, and is contained within, the poet's need to elucidate his creation. Since Narcissus was perfect beauty, he knew the perfection of that which the water reflected. His contemplation, since he was a perfect artist, could have no lesser object: he immobilized himself in his act of creation. One day, as an artist, he attempted to comprehend the perfection of his creation and moved into his reflection; it was then that the gods drowned him.

As the God of Aristotle turns into pure thought thinking about thought, pure art becomes for the pure artist the self-commentary that defines him in his creative gesture: action and creation are one. The poem by Mallarmé starts at the first rung of the Platonic ladder. The Idea is the only formulation worthy of the poet. It will always remain within his sight and forever elude his grasp, since he is endowed with but one of the divine attributes—God's vision. In his attempt, his necessary frustration describes the form of the eternally missing Idea; it contrives a poem tensed between the reality from which the poet is taking flight and the Ideal, the Azure, the Pure Whiteness, the Absolute, which, whatever it is termed, he cannot attain. The painter discovers that the object he is copying becomes on his canvas another object, the statement of pigments, of their thickness, their areas, their relations. No matter how faithfully he tries to submit his painting to its object-model, the canvas will always be a thing of colors, shapes, and lines of his making; its truth is its phenomenal reality and his authorship. Is he then not justified in creating that phenomenal evidence without the pretext of a model? And is not the musician answerable only to a structure composed of the tones he has created and the stress of these harmonic forces—"presentation" rather than "*re*presentation," to use the expression of W. J. Ong? [1]

The drama and the novel follow a similar development, but because they mediate reality for someone besides the author, their self-commentary also takes into account the presence of the one in whom that mediated reality assumes its ultimate definition. During the seventeenth century, Corneille writes *L'Illusion comique* in anticipation of Pirandello, Ghelderode, Genet, by contriving a play whose development is the questioning of the spectator's part within an action that is itself dramatic commentary. And when the novel can no longer tell a simple tale, it becomes the mode that notes the indifference of its reader and finds the new dimensions of its fiction in the relation of that reader to the author through the object between them.

The God of Aristotle, being a god, could limit his self-definition to thought thinking about thought. It was sufficient: no more is expected of a god for whom desire is

[1] *The Barbarian Within*, p. 33.

equivalent to deed. But man, no matter what his vision, remains frustrated in his doing. His attempts are tragic and magnificent; they measure his limitation and his utmost grandeur. God cannot not do; but, dying, man leaves behind him the imperishable evidence of his frustration—his art. And to speak for him in his desire and his vision, it is an immortal thing and absolute: pure art commenting upon itself. It is the one redemption of man's mortality and his single triumph over the immortals.

1

The Novel and
the Reader

Because the work of art exists in a public domain, its definition is generally dialectical and depends on more than itself. The artifact is a metaphor—something that stands for something else which it recalls—and is therefore, ultimately, a thing, though its objective tangibility varies according to its ontological mode. Being a metaphor, the artifact is also a sign: it comes into being at the moment of interpretation; the object is the creation of someone, but it exists also in the eye of the beholder. Its assessment is thus, in many ways, the outcome of the confrontation between artist and critic, creator and beholder.

From the point of view of the artist, the artifact must result from the impelling sense of a truth of which the artist feels himself possessed, a sense so strong as to compel its expression. Minor urges, such as the desire to play, to have fun, to decorate, and the like, may result in pleasant productions but will not involve the conscious artist sufficiently to define him through his work and, lacking the power to make such definition, will not allow him to define his artifact as art.

Viewed in this light, the artist is the poet, he who

makes, and is not unlike God, that other creator. Still, there appears to be at least one significant difference between the poet and God in their respective acts of creation: God has no model from which he proceeds and must be incontrovertibly an originator, whereas it is not always clear to what extent the poet is a free and independent agent. The question has been of interest for some time, the earliest speculation evincing already an uncomfortable ambivalence, if we leave out of account the opinion that the poet is primarily a copyist with nature as his model. Although such poets are not as derivative as Plato's (the hapless imitator whose very models turn out to be imperfect copies themselves), they hardly suggest comparison with a life-breathing God. They remain timid even in the statement of their emancipation. Horace, who begins by asserting that "Painters and poets [. . .] have always had an equal right in hazarding anything," is considerably less assertive in the next breath: "but not so far that savage should mate with tame, or serpents couple with birds, lambs with tigers" (*Ars Poetica*, 9-13). That Horace, who must have been familiar with centaurs, or at least with griffins, should have resisted such animal-pairing is perhaps less surprising when one considers that the very griffin derives its symmetrical supernaturalism from two familiar categories—the lion and the eagle. The parts of the supernatural are natural enough: even though called upon to fashion the poet's wildest fancy, they are originally found in nature. The poet's freedom may consist in a subversion of nature, but nature is still the ultimate reference.[1]

[1] Admittedly, one of the reasons why Horace rejects these couplings is that tame should not associate with savage. If a lamb and a tiger are brought into such a combination, what is known of

Such commonsensical madness was not likely to lead the
poet too far afield. But there have also been those who
placed the poet nearer to God by relating his inspiration
more closely to a divine source than to one that was (like
nature) equally apparent to all. Believing as he did in an all-
informing intelligence, the Neoplatonist could situate the
poet, if he felt kindly disposed toward him, in an especially privileged position. For Plotinus, the world soul
flowed from this intelligence (the *Nous*) which emanated
from the One or Absolute Being. Since man's soul was in
touch with the world soul, there was no need for Plotinus'
poet to be deceived, like Plato's, by imperfect replicas of
the Idea, and Plotinus substituted for Plato's artist (limited
by misguided concern with a bed made by a carpenter)
the example of Phidias, who fashioned a god (in fact,
many gods). Plato had failed to mention whether his carpenter had a better appreciation of essences than his painter, but the fact remains that even as imperfect copies of
some celestial couch, beds are relatively plentiful here, on
earth, whereas gods go to some pains not to appear as
promiscuously. It followed that Phidias must have
"wrought the Zeus upon no model among things of sense
but by apprehending what form Zeus must take if he
chose to become manifest to sight" (*Enneads*, V, viii, I).
Plotinus refers presumably to the giant statue at Olympia
which was considered to be the masterpiece of Phidias.

---

each inhibits the effect of the other, and instead of two threats
adding their individual awesomeness to the eeriness of their combination, an unwieldy and self-canceling object is produced, whose
effect is comic. This comic effect depends, however, on a prior
recognition of, and familiarity with, the component parts (against
which the unnatural coupling operates). Still, it is not expected
that a zoologist would be awed by even a griffin. He is more
likely to be incredulous or, at the very best, interested.

There is no surviving piece of statuary that can be ascribed with certainty to that sculptor, though certain other pieces, such as the Dionysus from the eastern pediment of the Parthenon (now in the British Museum), show a perfection of form in male and female shapes such as is tautologically attributed to Phidias. For the colossal statue in the Olympieion, our reference is Pausanias, who says of it: "The image is worth seeing. It surpasses in size all other images except the colossuses at Rhodes and Rome: it is made of ivory and gold, and considering the size the workmanship is good" (*Description of Greece*, I, xviii, 6).

Thus, the apprehension which Phidias had of a suprahuman being was to be conveyed through the huge size of the statue, far exceeding that of any mortal; the costly and exotic materials used in its making—ivory and gold; and lastly, though Pausanias appears less affected at this point than one might have hoped, the grace and noble bearing of an ideal human figure: here is familiar datum indeed—the crafted artifact and that which allows human cognition. So the Zeus supposedly wrought "upon no model among things of sense" seeks at least a part of its effect from matter and the material world of the senses which Plotinus believed to be at the source of all evil. Even the idealized beauty of the statue that attempts a more convincing departure from human limitations derives from the imperfect human body. The myths that examined the many aspects of Zeus's divinity forces a more drastic break between the reader's awareness of human possibility and the various incarnations of the god—such as a golden shower, a swan, or an all-consuming brilliance. Still it must be remembered that even these were metamorphoses—changes from a more recognizable form, for even a god must retain some human essence if he is to be apprehended by a human.[2]

Difficult as it may be to vouch for the divine inspiration of an artist by pointing to his material achievements, it is at least equally difficult to account for artistry on the sole basis of its imitative excellence. On the face of things, it would appear that for Aristotle, mimesis is the foundation of all art: "Epic poetry and Tragedy, Comedy also and Dithyrambic poetry, and the music of the flute and of the lyre in most of their forms, are all in their general conception modes of imitation" (*Poetics*, I, 2). The same, according to Aristotle, is true of the plastic arts, painting, and singing: "There are persons who, by conscious art or mere habit, imitate and represent various objects through the medium of colour and form, or again by the voice" (I, 4); moreover, "even dancing imitates character, emotion, and action" (I, 5). The reasons are that "the instinct of imitation is implanted in man from childhood" (IV, 2), one learns through imitation, and since "to learn gives the liveliest pleasure" (IV, 4), imitation is pleasurable.

For effective imitation, the external forms of a perceptible reality must be observed: "Within the action there must be nothing irrational" (XV, 7—instead of *irrational*, Wheelwright and others give *supernatural* as a translation); for example, the *deus ex machina* has no place in the action. For a similar reason, tragedians keep to real names because only "what is possible is credible" (IX, 6), and the iambic is used by them because it is, "of all measures, the most colloquial" (IV, 14).

Moral and didactic benefits ensue from such imitation.

[2] Phidias may have been more aware of the human dimension of his divinities than Plotinus cared to admit. One of the several, equally unreliable accounts of the sculptor's life says that he was ultimately condemned for impiety because he included the portrait of Pericles, as well as his own, on the shield of yet another epic statue of his—that of the goddess Athene.

The most important of the six aspects of tragedy, the structure of incidents, shows how men achieve happiness or misery according to their actions. One may distinguish between trivial and serious poetry in that the latter imitates "noble actions, and the actions of good men" (IV, 7). The pleasure people get from a painting "is, that in contemplating it, they find themselves learning or inferring" (IV, 5)—since "the most beautiful colours, laid on confusedly, will not give as much pleasure as the chalk outline of a portrait" (VI, 15).

Still, concerned though he is with the object of the artist's imitation, Aristotle finds himself acknowledging that the work of art itself is an object. Tragedians must follow the example of good portrait painters and "while reproducing the distinctive form of the original, make a likeness which is true to life and yet more beautiful" (XV, 8). That beauty, within the art form, becomes a matter of organic concern; for example, "beauty depends on magnitude and order" (VII, 4), and the function of the poet is, not to relate what happened, but "what is [dramatically] possible according to the law of probability or necessity" (IX, 1). The original definition of mimesis has been considerably expanded when Aristotle concludes about the poet that "even if he chances to take an historical subject, he is none the less a poet; for there is no reason why some events that have actually happened should not conform to the law of the probable and possible, and in virtue of that quality in them he is their poet or maker" (IX, 9).

It would appear then that the poet's truth, even though originally derived from an existing model and patterned upon that model, becomes in its formulation a new entity with a truth of its own. If mimetic perfection were adequate to convey the artist's vision, the artifact would need only to afford recognition through itself of a truth

that is external to it ("Ah, that is he!" exclaims Aristotle's
viewer of a portrait painting [IV, 5]). But if in the process
of imitation, the imitative object becomes distinct from
that which it is imitating, then its appreciation and recognition require other criteria (such as the aforementioned
standards of proportion, harmony, organic necessity), and
these criteria must be sought within the artifact itself.

The critical faculties of the viewer turn that to which
he is responding into an object. But "since the objects of
imitation are men in action" (II, 1), it follows that the response of the viewer will be forever dual, as will be the artifact itself, a part of whose truth must be found in its human evidence. Aristotle fails to distinguish between plastic
and other arts because he supposes that the human assertion of each is the same in that all intend to commit the
noncritical part of the viewer, reader, or spectator: "Pity
is aroused by unmerited misfortune, fear by the misfortune of *a man like ourselves*"; [3] unless the viewer is willing
and able to recognize himself in the object of the artist's
imitation, he cannot commit himself to it other than criti-
cally.

And so the expression of the artist's vision becomes a
subject of contention between the artist and his public.
Even though that vision is the impelling force that determines its expression, if simple mimesis is not sufficient for

---

[3] XIII, 2. Our italics. It is not altogether clear to what extent pity
can be bestowed on a fiction unless it too is "like ourselves." We
assume that the objects of both our pity and fear must be "like
ourselves" and that it is their dramatic circumstances that will determine whether pity or fear will be elicited. It is in this sense that
the Aristotelian motions of pity and fear should be interpreted:
they represent the utmost extent to which the viewer can be
drawn into, or repulsed by, the artifact to whose human truth he
has committed himself.

its understanding, new points of reference and new means of coercion must be sought by the artist who is now concerned, not only with the form of his creation, but also with the ways it can be fashioned so as to commit the reader to a reality that transcends the form. For those who use words as their medium, and more particularly, written words, the contest involves an author whose strategy is to entice his reader into giving his reality to the author's fiction and the same reader (especially if he considers himself sophisticated), who resists the author's strategy by being aware of it, and thus remains a critic for whom the author's creation is an analyzable object.

This critical detachment by the reader departs from the human impulse to tell and hear stories. If, according to the interpretation of some writers, poetry came before prose because the first utterance of man phrased an emotion instead of an idea—the latter depending for its formulation on a store of verbal symbols—it is at least equally true that story-telling is closely related to the development of the social structure: structure supposes continuation and continuation implies history; the tribe preserves its definition through ritual rote, part of which is the telling of what it was in the past—what it *was* being a major part of its justification for continuing to *be*. In that sense, the *Iliad* and the *Aeneid* are the distant and sophisticated echoes of a ritual whose purpose was once to preserve the form of a clan. The danger of listener alienation through critical distance can scarcely have been a matter of concern at such an early time. If historical man develops as does the child, the substance of the ritual tale conjured for its listeners a nearly visible reality and a sense of immediacy. According to Simon O. Lesser's preliminary formulation, "At the start [stories] are completely real. It is the capacity to distinguish between fiction and reality which must be acquired" (*Fiction and the Unconscious*, p. 1). One may assume for that reason that the tale itself was a much balder narration than the complex form into which it grew when its authors found the need to attach a more sceptical audience.

As individualistic concerns begin to loosen the ritual structure, we may suppose that lyric poetry comes into being, the collective vision becoming of less immediate interest to the individual than the recognition and rehearsal of a more private state of being. Therefore, later versions of even the primitive tale rely, for a part of their suasion, on the lyric—on an appeal to the intimacy of the reader, in his moods, yearnings, or perceptions, rather than on a presentation of surfaces, such as a description of external events. A reminder of some of the aspects of the *Song of Roland* may help to explain more precisely what is meant. In stanza cx, the chanted, self-contained lines of this assonanced verse turn into the cadence of a dirge in anticipation of the death of Roland—over a thousand lines before its actual occurrence. The thirty-line *laisse* turns away from the field of battle, where the French are slaughtering pagans by the thousands, to France, where an apocalyptic scene is presently described: the land is lashed by a storm of such intensity that darkness descends at high noon. The elements conspire to achieve a landscape of doom. The earth trembles; the heaviest walls, the very heavens are rent. And throughout, the strongly cadenced lament stresses in every line the single assonance whose climactic vocalization is the stanza's final word—*Rollant.* Or again, it is the re-echoing of *laisses similaires* that prolongs the agony of Roland, who, knowing that he is dying, attempts to destroy his sacred sword by striking it against the rocks of Roncevaux. As each stanza restates the hero's agony, the words repeated become the throbbing of his pain, and the motion visually analyzed is reconstituted as intensity within the reader.

Through a similar process, a number of key adjectives (*cler, halt, douce,* for example) accumulate an emotional charge through repetition and become the core of progressively more intense motives. "Halt sunt li pui" ("tall are the mountains") endures as a somber note even though the battle is being waged on the plain, since the doom of Roland and the French gives the landscape a psychological dimension that is more important to the poem than topographical accuracy.[4] *Douce* introduces a rare feminine term to this masculine epic, and once again the landscape is fashioned by thoughts about it, as the homeland ("douce France") becomes the tender personification of the past and of the good which death will now forever put aside.

Nor are these the only instances of poetic metamorphoses that change an object into an emotion. In this clash between the forces of Christendom (all rather stylized, except for the three heroes, Roland, Oliver, and Bishop Turpin) and the more particularized heathens (since evil must be specific under pain of losing its awesomeness), there appears the striking figure of Chernuble (stanza LXXVIII), whose Samson-like mane trails to the ground and

[4] Ramón Menéndez Pidal feels: "La description est fort mal amenée, car les mots *halt sunt li pui* ne conviennent pas au riant plateau de Roncevaux, fort éloigné de toute hauteur" (*La Chanson de Roland et la tradition épique des Francs,* trans. I.-M. Cluzel, [2d ed.; 1960], p. 325); he suggests a borrowing from a former version in which Roland died in a mountain pass where "la mort douloureuse de Roland avait lieu conformément à la vérité historique." But since the death of Roland is as agonized in the present form of the poem, can we not assume that the poet had to make his work conform to a poetic truth?

is like a banner to this knight of darkness who can, when he is so minded, carry the load of four pack mules. He comes from the devil's own country, a kingdom upon which the sun does not shine, where no wheat can grow nor dew gather—and where, prophetically, the very stones are black.

It is perhaps not overly surprising to find poetry informing a national epic that chronicles a national disaster and means to salvage patriotic pride from suffering. The intent of poetry is to speak directly to the precritical man that exists at the level of sensitivity and emotion: it is the language through which the grandeur of abstract concepts may achieve meaning as personal perception when a gesture of universal scope is enacted within the reader's consciousness. Poetry humanizes the objects and the landscape that surround Roland at a time when his audience is acquiring certain feelings and needs that he does not yet possess. In the epics that follow upon the *Roland*, it is a man that stands within the landscape and amidst the objects of his circumstances. Guillaume, the hapless warrior in the Garin de Monglane cycle, becomes increasingly a figure whose human dimensions are unequal to the battles he must wage and whose attempts to persist at a symbolic level sometimes reach the comic intensity of pathos—as when he is forced to carry his own arms, which his too feeble squire cannot bear, except very briefly through populated places where it is absolutely necessary to show at least a pretense of bravery. And that which links together the epics grouped in the cycle of Doon de Mayence is a hero to whom a wrong has been done, who turns traitor and apostate, but who in the hour of his revenge is torn between his desire and his fear of winning.

After the social structure of the tribe has disintegrated

and its lore has become meaningless, the reader seeks a private and recognizable figure to whom he may entrust himself, or seeks at least an inference of his human condition as poetry may fathom and suggest it. Lacking a recognizable projection of the reader or his human equivalent as poetry, the story is depersonalized—is merely an accounting of deeds for which there is no doer once the hero and reader no longer share a common ancestry. That such depersonalized fiction should exist at all appears imputable to a desire on the part of both reader and writer for a sustained mode of writing and to the emergence of a new interest in the reader—an interest in *pattern* (to borrow a term which Arnold Kettle has used, slightly differently, in his *Introduction to the English Novel*). Since intensity cannot be defined as duration, the effect of lyric suasion must be limited to short pieces or can operate only episodically in longer ones. And if the link of Aristotle's "man like ourselves" is rejected by either reader or writer, commitment to an extended form of writing becomes problematic.[5] Nor is the Aristotelian persona a guarantee of reader entrapment. For whereas poetry states the poet's truth as lyric immediacy and the tribal legend chronicles what is intended and received as objective truth, the creation of even "a man like ourselves" is the creation of a fiction—a game that proposes to the reader certain condi-

[5] It is interesting to speculate how much Christian ethics may be responsible for fostering the critical distance that rejects the Aristotelian persona. The awareness that only God can create a human being leads to a long-lasting suspicion of the dramatic actor who appears to be usurping the divine privilege and most likely accounts for some of the taboos against transvestites and sexual deviates, of whom earlier ethics were more tolerant. It is likewise true that the fictional character emerges only gradually, as literature becomes something more than a representation of facts or a didactic vehicle.

tions (such as the suspension of disbelief) which he may
or may not choose to accept. The only factual reality
about a fictional convention is the object which that fiction becomes as artifact, and it is on that reality that the
writer may attempt to ground his parafictional ties with
the reader. The writer knows that the self-distancing of
the reader moves him from identification to critical com-
prehension and can therefore engage his reader, in his very
withdrawal, by calling his attention to the work as *pattern*—an entity that is not dependent for its life on a human echo or on the affective cooperation of the reader but
on his intelligence. This is the allegorical form whose com-
prehension involves the deciphering of signs—as opposed
to symbolic writing that converts the reader through infra-
intellective associations (sounds, rhythms) or others to
which the reader responds with his feelings rather than
with his knowledge—such as colors and nonsymbolic objects.[6]

[6] Definitions of allegory differ. Angus Fletcher (*Allegory, the
Theory of a Symbolic Mode*) relates the whodunit and Zane
Grey's westerns, among others, to the allegory, in that the first
requires a solution, and in the second, "a surface texture of sublime scenic description is the carrier of thematic meaning" (p. 6).
As will be shown later, the whodunit would appear to be an instance of inadequate pattern, in that it commits the intelligence of
the reader to the trajectory of a nonexistent hero instead of to the
form which that trajectory creates. Fletcher would call the *Roland*'s scenery a *paysage moralisé*, as he does Zane Grey's in *Black
Mesa*. The point has already been made here that this form of
contamination is lyrical and seeks its being within the visceral
reader, proceeding as it does through affect rather than intellection. If the correlative object between reader and writer operates
through denotation—that is to say, if what it signifies is marked
off from its context and can be transposed without altering that
significance—the work that embodies it is allegorical; if the correlative object operates through connotation, depending for its

During the Middle Ages, readers had become sufficiently sophisticated to be able to distance themselves from their reading, and writers had become skilled in the ways of forestalling, or attempting to forestall, their escape. Modern scholarship has made us aware of the complexity of their contrivances and of the problem of allegorical reading. For example, if we follow Professor Poggioli, the fifth canto of the *Inferno* has something new to tell us about Francesca da Rimini, whose brother-in-law Paolo won her affection and who was killed with her lover when her husband surprised the adulterous couple.[7] Our attention is now drawn to facts that may have been more obvious to the medieval reader: that Paolo and Francesca are, after all, in hell, and that the last sentences of Francesca bespeak an awareness of her fault; of the Arthurian romance that brought her and Paolo together she concludes, "A Galeotto was the book and he that wrote it." (The translation is by John D. Sinclair, who reminds us that Galeotto was the intermediary between Lancelot and Guinevere and that "his name became the synonym for a pander.")

We are first to note the courtly language spoken by Francesca:

"O living creature gracious and friendly, who goest through the murky air visiting us who stained the world with blood, if the King of the universe were our friend we would pray to Him for thy peace, since thou hast pity of our evil

---

specificity on a specific context, it is symbolic. The rose that stands for a dynasty is allegorical; the one that suggests sensuality is symbolic.

[7] Renato Poggioli, "Tragedy or Romance? A Reading of the Paolo and Francesca Episode in Dante's *Inferno*," *PMLA* LXXII (June 1957).

plight. Of that which thou art pleased to hear and speak we
will hear and speak with you while the wind is quiet, as here
it is. The city where I was born lies on the shore where the
Po, with the streams that join it, descends to rest. Love,
which is quickly kindled in the gentle heart, seized this man
for the fair form that was taken from me, and the manner
afflicts me still" [verses 88–102, Sinclair translation].

She is a lady of good feudal breeding, not only in her
poise and the gracious forms of her speech to Dante the
character, but in her *Weltansicht* as well. For the unmen-
tionable divinity, as Professor Poggioli points out, she finds
a feudal euphemism, "the King of the universe," whose
blessing or curse is thought of "in terms of courtly grace
or disgrace." Even in hell, and from the very first description by Vergil, her world remains courtly, peopled as it is
with the figures of romances or with figures that are ro-
manticized: Cleopatra, Helen, Tristan, or "the great Achil-
les, who fought at the last with love"—not Homer's. Not
unlike what happens in the world of Don Quixote three
hundred years later, a world of books is being stigmatized.
In fact, Francesca herself is an Arthurian character whose
sin was the re-enactment, with Paolo, of Guinevere's with
Lancelot. And as we move from the allegory to its moral
lesson, from the book which informs this part of hell to
the poem that Dante is writing, we find that the poet is in
fact making a comment on a former self. Dante the character, who swoons with pity at the agony of Francesca, is
the younger Dante, rejected by the poet of the *Inferno*—
in proof of which her words ("amor ch'al cuor gentil
ratto s'apprende") echo the words of a sonnet of Dante in
the *Vita Nuova* ("amore e'l cor gentil sono una cosa"),
the courtly book of a younger poet disowned by his ma-
turer self.

Such is the allegorical Francesca, the one we discover with our intelligence—or at least with the help supplied by specialists. Why then the misreadings so prevalent among even enlightened readers in more recent times, against which the efforts of the specialists have been directed—readings that make of Francesca the noble victim of a tragic love rather than a carnal sinner lost through the influence of poor literature? Part of the fault rests with Dante the character who sees Francesca as a victim whose "torments make [him] weep for grief and pity." But the main responsibility is that of Dante the present poet. The first view he gives us of the second circle is far more hellish than is ultimately warranted: at the start, it is a noisy place presided over by an unpleasantly loud custodian, "horrible, snarling" Minos, who uses an ugly tone of voice, according to Vergil. The notes of pain that reach the visitors' ears are a "bellowing as of a sea in tempest beaten by conflicting winds [. . .] smiting and whirling," into whose "fury" enter "shrieks" and blasphemy. The first of three bird images that will be used to describe the damned shows the helplessness of starlings in a winter storm: so does infernal torment "blast the wicked spirits [. . .] hither, thither, downward, upward." The second bird image, designating the shades that approach with long-drawn wailing "borne on these battling winds," is that of cranes "chanting their lais." While this last word certainly stands as a first allusion to a form of courtly literature, the expression in its more common meaning designates the lamentation of the damned, and the harsh sound of the Italian word *lai* reminds us that the noise of cranes is guttural and resonant.

Driven by their lust on earth, the lost souls are still hounded in hell—but this time with a vengeance, a divine

vengeance, a vengeance of such intensity that not only
does Dante the character need divine authorization to
speak to Paolo and Francesca ("if One forbids it not"),
but the fury of retribution must abate for mere intelligibil-
ity ("we will hear and speak with you while the wind is
quiet," says Francesca). However, in point of fact, the star-
crossed lovers have never appeared in the furious part of
the circle. They move about in their own aura, and from
the first it has been of quite a different kind. The raging,
battering, blasting storm has vanished at their entrance,
and the very elements are soothed as they "go together
and seem so light upon the wind." And this gentleness that
softens hell itself contrives the third bird image, that of the
dove, the biblical symbol of peace, the Christian symbol of
simplicity and gentleness, the lay symbol of love and love-
liness: "As doves, summoned by desire, come with wings
poised and motionless to the sweet nest, borne by their
will through the air, so these. . . ." Such is the poetic
spell of these lovers that the retributive frenzy is stilled:
long before Dante's request, they have gentled the wind.
The pain and aimlessness that are reflections of desire in
the world of Minos they alter as well; they are indissolubly a pair, stronger than rhetorical statements about
the tragic alienation of adulterers. And the frigid world of
anxiety and harshness that expresses this alienation becomes, through Dante's image of Paolo and Francesca—
one whose terms are warmth, security, and tenderness—as
doves, poised and motionless in flight, suggesting "the
sweet nest" toward which they tend. The allegorical mind
of the elder Dante may have dealt harshly with the poetic
follies of the young man he once was, but finding himself
anew in the damnable world of the *dolce stil nuovo* whose
sin is its seduction, the wiser poet relapsed and sinned

again through poetry. Thereafter, what chance was there for those who were ignorant of the allegorical castigation? Poetic suasion has led generations of subsequent readers romantically astray.

At the allegorical level, the game played by writer and reader is an exclusive one: only a few have sufficient ability and interest to recognize and piece together the separate parts of the puzzle that is being proposed to them. As more people who have less specialized knowledge begin to read, reader attachment through puzzle-piecing becomes increasingly unsatisfactory and begins to go out of favor. Bearing in mind that this discussion supposes a writer possessed of a truth—therefore a writing that begins with the needs of the writer—receptivity rests nevertheless with the reader. If the writer's need requires an extended form that is beyond the capacity of lyric poetry to bear, and if total *pattern* can no longer find a large audience, the author will seek for his statement new forms of prose. Alongside the category he labels *pattern*, Kettle, in *An Introduction to the English Novel*, suggests the classification he calls *life*, denoting attempts to involve the reader in forms of writing that are "life-communicating." Kettle would seem to mean that "life" writing contrives existential circumstances in a manner so compelling that a reader senses them as his own. Lyric poetry seems to be the best example of this kind of writing, since it depends to a major extent for its realization on its physiological translation within the reader, whereas allegory would seem to be the most thorough example of *pattern*. But there is a paradox in this distinction: *pattern* writing is so defined because it cannot be absorbed as sentience by the reader, and though it can be perceived, it remains external and unassimilable. It is thus objectively real. But Aristotle's "man like ourselves," who

is such presumably in order to be *life*-communicating, remains mere fiction until he *is* ourselves and has therefore
no objective reality.

The author for whom the lyric and allegorical modes
are inoperative may thus hesitate to depend for his contact
with the reader on the Aristotelian persona. The sort of
writer with whom we are not concerned here, the one
whose writing is primarily subordinated to his reader's
needs, will usually attempt to meet his reader halfway between his own and his reader's detachment from the writing by partially preserving *pattern*—that which I have
termed inadequate *pattern*. The picaresque and the detective story can be examples of the kind of writing in which
the reader's attention is kept by means of an algebraic process (the Arabic root of the word *algebra* referring to the
operation that effects the reunion of broken parts). Such
an operation presumes to engage (but not to overtax) only
a part of the reader—his intelligence—in the gradual eluci-
dation of a design or a series of designs. The fictional protagonist acts, not as the Aristotelian persona, but as a master of ceremonies, since there is little in him of concern to
his reader that might either affect, or be affected by, his
adventures. These exist for their own sake and would not
be substantially altered or lessened by his demise or his replacement. Both genres have been used on occasion, however, to situate a hero with dimensions of his own: the
hero's ultimate dimension being within the reader, it need
have but little to do with his fictional circumstances.

Moreover, it is nearly impossible for any writing to exist
as only the limited *pattern* provided by the circumstances
of a nonexistent hero. When the protagonist is reduced to
merely his trajectory because of a deficiency of features
which the more complex reader might discern as his own,

that reader will simply lose interest; but the more primitive reader will endow even that trajectory with his own dimensions and, to that extent at least, will rehabilitate the hero. Even the garden variety of detective or adventure story recognizes this need in that it seeks to mythologize the very cipher at its center so as to relate the hero's intricate motions to at least a semblance of human necessity. It is significant also that the picaresque evidences, at the very least, a concern with moral questions and uses the itinerary of its hero to satirize society. The entrapment of the more complex reader will thus necessitate the kind of hero that might encourage even that reader's propensity to identification; but the hero will be situated within a *pattern* of sufficient scope to keep the reader engaged even if he moves from identification to a critical distancing. The first extended examples of prose technique to evolve such elaborate and self-conscious awareness of reader response are the first that can be properly called novels: they are Rabelais's *Pantagruel* (1532) and Cervantes' *Don Quixote* (1605).

Had Rabelais carried out only what he first intended, *Pantagruel* would not be a novel as here defined. The Prologue tells us of a very recent best seller, *Les Grandes et Inestimables Chronicques de l'énorme géant Gargantua,* of which the printers sold more copies in two months than they will sell of Bibles in nine years. Wishing to add to that public's enjoyment, Rabelais now offers it a book of the same kind. At least that part of the Prologue may be taken at face value: colportage lists of the times show that there was a great demand for repeats and adaptations of the courtly romances of the thirteenth century; the *Pantagruel* Prologue notes that *Fierabras* and *Robert le Diable* still possess "magic properties," and the *Chronicques* to

which it refers placed its giant, derived from the Morgante
and Margutte of Luigi Pulci's *Morgante Maggiore* (1483)
and the Fracasso of Teofilo Folengo's *Baldus* (1517 and
1521), in an Arthurian setting. At the start, Rabelais intends only to take advantage of a well-established success.
While waiting to take over the main characters of the
Chronicques in his own *Gargantua* of 1534, he invents for
them a son, Pantagruel, but here too he is drawing from
current mythology. Abel Lefranc, in "La Genèse de Pantagruel" (reprinted in his *Rabelais*), has shown that the
name and character existed in popular literature as early, at
least, as the fifteenth century, Panthagruel being one of
the four devils of Lucifer's escort, whose provinces are the
four elements. Panthagruel rules the briny deep and is thus
the demon of thirst. When cause and effect become confused, the name designates popularly any severe dryness or
affliction of the throat. Episodically, at least, Rabelais's hero
is a great drinker who provokes great thirst in others.

Quite clearly, the book is taking no chances at the onset.
Moreover, it will dispense only the most effortless sort of
fun: it is loosely constructed, ever ready to go out of its
way for the sake of some unrelated ribaldry, be it a story
or merely a side-glance. It is full of spoonerisms, jokes,
proverbs, and similarly childish games. It holds as a general
moral truth, and exemplifies as a fact, that the highest
good is in making love, overeating, and carousing. Up to
this point, it would be altogether the most common sort of
potboiler if it were not for the author's own gusto: the
sweep of Rabelais's verve becomes such that he loses sight
of his reader and creates through sheer virtuosity a lyrical
object.

Curiously, Rabelais will achieve lyricism of another sort
when he returns to his reader. Pantagruel is the folk leg-

end of thirst, but he refers to the great drought of the spring, summer, and fall of 1532, and the land he walks is the land that Rabelais had walked before him—the Touraine and Poitou regions, Lyons and Paris: familiar times, familiar sights to a less abstract and less prurient reader—their voice is both deeper and more intimate.

The sweep of Rabelais's style acts as a centrifugal force in yet another way to frustrate its original reader and intent. The huge accumulation of food and drink, the endless undoing of women, move his reader from titillation to amusement. What might have been participation becomes understanding at the level of disbelief: the reader no longer shares in the downfall of a woman; his knowledge of her becomes, more metaphysically, that of the downfall of women in general. At such moments, and even at a primitive level, the contact of Rabelais with his reader turns into a dialogue *about* his writing. But, unconsciously perhaps, Rabelais is going to enlarge and uplift that dialogue: he will eventually find himself talking as a humanist, and to humanists.

In chapter viii, Pantagruel receives from his father, Gargantua, a letter which is, among other things, a hymn of praise to the new dawn in the arts and sciences. The letter also makes a curious plea for filial duty: it urges Pantagruel to become a bottomless well of knowledge. As for Rabelais himself, he has already heeded that exhortation. His very ribaldry has scientific overtones, reminders that he is, after all, a doctor of medicine. When he scoffs at obscurantists on the bench, in the pulpit, in the university chair, it is as one who knows the law, the Gospels, the classics well enough to cite his sources. What Henri Lefebvre has called a violence to know (*Rabelais*, 1955) becomes subversive; the hunger for information turns into a

war against glosses in lay and sacred books alike. And
Rabelais joins once again the battle against the detractors
of humanism, from which battle this writing might at first
have been intended as a diversion. But such concerns are
too specialized: they do not remain within the scope of
the fairgrounds audience to whom the Prologue addresses
itself.

As he enters into this dialogue, Rabelais changes what
might have remained a pleasurable indulgence into the creation of an abstract *pattern*. This does not give his writing
novelistic form (if anything, it represents a step in the opposite direction—even though it does help to explain one
of the many differences between a story about a giant as
Rabelais tells it and the tradition which he alleges). *Pattern*
alone serves no purpose, being no more than the net which
the author stretches to avoid losing his reader if that
reader should fall from the human level at which the writing finds its information as novel. But *pattern* and the dimensional vicissitudes of his giant help to establish that
human level in *Pantagruel*.

Pantagruel is frequently forgetful of his size. In fact, he
is most keenly aware of it only when he has not yet attained it, as a child exhibiting in surprising deeds the heroic
promise common to chivalric childhoods. But once he is
full-grown and starts on his *tour de France*, he does so as a
student man-sized—proportioned to the pasture lands, the
towns and taverns that were Rabelais's, and these are humanizing grounds. It is a man, not a giant, who berates the
Limousin student for using Latinate verbiage, who de-
ciphers the scholastic cant of the Librairie Saint Victor,
who meets another student, Panurge, "whom he loved all
his life"—for these are human rather than mock-epic gestures. In fact, for quite a while, Pantagruel disappears

completely behind the figure of Panurge. (When the giant emerges again, it is toward the end of the book, in the climactic war against the Dipsodes; even here, however, he is contrasted at least once with Panurge to indicate that craft is better than might.)

Panurge is the vagabond student and, as such, though certainly man-sized, he would hardly be more than a stock figure of the medieval repertoire, reminiscent of *Pathelin* or the Pseudo-Villon's *Repues franches*. But much of his buffoonery is performed in the service of the idea which Rabelais himself has introduced in his dialogue with the humanistic reader. At such times Panurge is more than a stock figure, for his purpose is identifiable with Rabelais's and suggests therefore a human truth. Panurge meets Pantagruel and addresses him in many languages, in imitation of *Pathelin*; but whereas in the latter these verbal disguises devise an elementary trick, no such purpose is served here: Panurge merely knows how to say in ten languages that he is starving to death. And as Panurge talks, Pantagruel will forget even such student tools as Greek, Latin, and Italian to allow the humanistic Panurge to show that he indeed knows them all, along with more esoteric ones. Similarly, the argument of Panurge against Thaumaste becomes more than the obscene gestures of the street farce as they mime the scholastic debate that is being mocked. Is it surprising thereafter to find even the great thirst of these people interpreted symbolically?

Admittedly, this is slender evidence for the claim that such an "enormous Feast of Mirth" (D. B. Wyndham Lewis, in his Introduction to *Gargantua and Pantagruel*) is in fact a novel. Still, possessed with the land, its people, a cause, an unquenchable thirst to know, and a torrential language to match and phrase his boundless concerns,

Rabelais could not *not* write something very like a novel. He himself was aware of it by the time he was through with *Pantagruel*. Two years later, *Gargantua* stressed deliberately these adumbrations of a novel and the Foreword draws attention to them; in Urquhart's translation:

Therefore is it, that you must open the book, and seriously consider of the matter treated in it. Then shall you find that it containeth things of far higher value than the box did promise; that is to say, that the subject thereof is not so foolish, as by the title at the first sight it would appear to be.

Even without taking into account the obvious "humanity" of Don Quixote and Sancho Panza, the case for the *Quixote* as a novel is an easier one to make. The more complex the analysis, the more the book's complexity may become apparent. But that complexity becomes evident as well through the failure of any attempt to read it as a simple book. If one assumes, for example, that it proposes to laugh knight-errantry tales out of existence, Don Quixote is a man whose mind has become muddled with reading such tales to the extent that he sees himself as one of their characters. Comedy then would stem from the disparity between his vision, shaped by the *Amadis of Gaul* and other romances, and his own considerably more cumbersome efforts. A Don Quixote of this kind would have only a fitful existence and, at times, would indeed disappear altogether. In chapter iv of Book I, Don Quixote encounters the sheep boy, Andrés, whose master has bound him to a tree and is flogging him soundly. This is the Don's first adventure in knight-errantry, and he is able to effect the boy's release. However, once the champion of the oppressed has ridden away, the farmer ties up the boy again and starts beating him with renewed vigor. If there is humor to be found in this incident, it derives largely from abstract speculation about human conduct and the ineffectuality of moral gestures. At any rate, it has little to do with the figure of Don Quixote as such. It is different from the images of Don Quixote charging on a horse that collapses in mid-career, of the knight missing his stirrup in a ceremonial descent from his steed, and the like. Such images demand from the reader a visualization of the scene and a recollection of the ideal with which the scene contrasts. Thus visualized, Don Quixote must possess at least sufficient reality to be dismissed. But even though the character will exist briefly as the insignificance that laughter dispels, that existence is hardly commensurate with the amount of reader involvement required by a novel.

Mindful of the criticism of his interpolated tales in Book I, Cervantes explains toward the end of the second book why he has dropped them and requests "that he be given credit not for what he writes, but for what he has refrained from writing" (chapter xliv). The sentence that introduces this digression is curious:

They say that in the original version of the history it is stated that the interpreter did not translate the present chapter as Cid Hamete had written it, owing to a kind of grudge that the Moor had against himself for having undertaken a story so dry and limited in scope as is this one of Don Quixote.

The passage elicits the remark from John Ormsby (in his own translation) that "The original, bringing a charge of misinterpretation against its translator, is a confusion of ideas that it would not be easy to match." [8] Whether or not this passage represents a genuine "confusion of ideas,"

[8] Even if, for the sake of logic, we translate the Spanish to read, "Cid Hamete having finished this chapter, [he later claimed that]

there was at least justification for that which led up to it.
Until chapter ix of the first book, Don Quixote is represented as the central figure in a narrative vouched for by
Cervantes ("In a village of La Mancha the name of which
I have no desire to recall . . ."; the author introduces
himself as narrator in the very first sentence of the book).
But in chapter ix, the fight between Don Quixote and the
gallant Biscayan is deliberately held up ("with swords un-
sheathed and raised aloft") while Cervantes looks for further records of the history which he is relating. At this
point, the narrative is no longer given as Cervantes' own
but as that of an Arabic historian, Cid Hamete Benengeli,
whose work Cervantes asks an anonymous Moor to translate; the authenticity of Don Quixote which derived hitherto from that of Cervantes the narrator is weakened at
this point by Cervantes himself, who changes the Don into
merely the reference of a fictional character. Still, after
thus breaking the fictional continuity with this aside to the
reader, Cervantes allows Cid Hamete Benengeli to recede
and returns to his former narrative mode.

It is in Part II that the Arabic scholar is revived by Cervantes as a means of separating himself from his story.
Many of the chapters are given specifically as Cid Hamete's view of them; in fact, he is occasionally more distinct
than the figure of whom he is writing, as in chapter viii:
" 'Blessed be the mighty Allah!' exclaims Hamete Benengeli at the beginning of this eighth chapter; and he repeats
it three times: 'Blessed be Allah!' " In distancing himself
from his fiction, Cervantes is deliberately encouraging the
reader's disbelief in the story in order to conciliate that

---

the interpreter did not translate it as he had written it," we must
suppose that Cid Hamete somehow became acquainted with the
subsequent translation.

reader personally: Don Quixote is discredited that Cervantes may be more creditable. The ultimate purpose is to consider as more important the questions which the author is debating—and more particularly, the literary questions —as in the previously quoted reference to the emendations of the second book. In this manner, the reader may remain committed to a fiction which he might reject if he did not sense that its author was using it as a pretext for the discussion of matters that involve only the author and his reader.

Nor is the objectification provided by the Arabic historian a mere device: the comments of the second book were written with reference to more than a fiction—Don Quixote now exists as the incontrovertible reality of Book I, and many of the literary problems that concerned Cervantes as he was writing Book I were now given a wider scope and a more personal cast by the publication of that book ten years earlier. In fact, the first part was largely engulfed by the swell of the literary debate. During the ten-year interim, and from the very start, many pirated editions appeared, capped by the "sequel" of Alonso Fernández Avellaneda in 1614. The second book was written in part to right the record (only Cervantes could write a genuine *Don Quixote*), in part also to disclaim the mere figure of Quixote (anyone can create the approximation of such a figure stripped of the concerns out of which Cervantes created him). It is at this level of concern and contempt that must be read the passage which either supposes that Cid Hamete knows as much about the literary circumstances of the *Don Quixote* as the nonfictional Cervantes (and this is frequently the case) or refers to a feigned author setting down in his writing his criticism of that writing's translator. Either interpretation indicates the

distance to which the fictional construct has been rele-
gated: if it has not been simply absorbed by the author
speaking for himself, it is turned into an amused parafictional aside to the reader—nonsense reminiscent of an introductory comment to the literature of knight-errantry
that notes how fair maidens rode through the hills and
dales of Romance until they were eighty and remained to
the end (if they were not raped) as virginal as their moth-
ers (I, ix).

These considerations do not enhance the claim that Part
II is a satisfactory novel. Though Cervantes courts the
reader through his disavowal of Don Quixote, he does so
at the expense of the human center—the defining core of
the novel. In proportion as he slights Don Quixote, Cervantes relies on the reader's critical interest—the mode of
the essay rather than that of the novel. As previously suggested, this is the consequence of the author's *engage-
ment:* the literary debate has become essentially personal
for him. According to the theory first propounded by Salvador de Madariaga, in *Don Quixote: An Introductory
Essay in Psychology,* Cervantes was concerned originally
with writing an *Amadis* of his own. If this is so, he chose
for himself a paradoxical way of achieving his aim: his
Amadis-supplanting hero had to convince the reader that
he was more worthy of belief than Amadis, while at the
same time discrediting lesser romances through the ludi-
crousness of his actions; somehow, the reader had to believe in the clown or madman at whom he was laughing.

Cervantes is able to achieve this tour de force in part by
making the literary debate a more integral part of his fiction. He entrusts these matters to such relatively cultured
people as the barber, the curate, or the Canon of Toledo.
Inasmuch as these people are represented by their theses,

the reader remains with them on the plane of debate: he is not asked to make a human commitment to fiction, and the question of his alienation does not arise. However, a number of figures become fictional within the debate; this occurs when they turn the voicing of their literary concerns from the reader to the character Don Quixote. When this happens, the reader-as-critic becomes a participant through the very impulsion of his critical momentum.[9] And since this entire debate is centered upon Don Quixote because he attempted to be a man turned book, it is not only the man Quixote who benefits from the reader's concern with books: the book turned man constructs the object that Cervantes wished. The reader has been drawn through his endowment of the protagonist into giving human shape—the shape of a novel—to the discussion about the book which he has just finished reading.

If Defoe, Richardson, and Fielding represent the earliest forms of the English novel, it came fully a century after its Spanish predecessor. Ian Watt (*The Rise of the Novel*) justifies the choice of these authors in that, in contrast to their predecessors, "they accepted the general premise of their times that, since Nature is essentially complete and unchanging, its records, whether scriptual, legendary or historical, constitute a definitive repertoire of human experience" (p. 14). Their enduring reputation must rest on something more, since, had they created only novels particularized according to the experience of their readers with reference to their own time, their works would sur-

---

[9] Proust does something similar when he moves Igor Stravinski into the world of his fiction through the patronage of Princess Yourbeletieff, or when he has the Goncourts visit the Verdurins at their *hôtel* on the Quai Conti.

vive, at best, as historical documents. Instead, modern readers have been able to find in them an intimate projection of their present mood. As an epigraph for *La Peste* (1947), Camus chose a quotation from Defoe (not from *A Journal of the Plague Year*, as one might have expected, but from the Preface to the *Serious Reflections of Robinson Crusoe*): "It is as reasonable to represent one kind of imprisonment by another, as it is to represent anything that exists by that which exists not." Such a prefatory statement by Defoe would appear to be an invitation to look for more in *Robinson Crusoe* than the economic or Puritan individualism to which Mr. Watt refers, and which would make of the hero's adventure little more than the fortuitous jeopardy of certain social and ethical circumstances and their material righting. Instead, Camus views the castaway as the symbolic statement of existential isolation, of man's sense of metaphysical loss and abandonment, and of his ability to project only the fact of self upon the world [10]—a statement which *Le Mythe de Sisyphe* (1942) phrases in the following ways: "Understanding the world for a man is reducing it to the human"; "Between the certainty I have of my existence and the content I try to give to that assurance, the gap will never be filled."

If the first novels were the first works to create characters in the image of their readers by individuating their traits, their names, their circumstances, the social and physical world within which they evolved, and the very form

[10] One would imagine that Mr. Watt would have allowed that the individualism of Robinson Crusoe is more than a sociological fact, since at this point in his book he quotes André Malraux as saying, in *Les Noyers de l'Altenburg*, that only three works (*Robinson Crusoe*, *Don Quixote*, and *The Idiot*) retained their truth for those who had experienced concentration camps.

and nature of that evolution, there would be no need to wait until Defoe appeared: Cervantes had already demeaned a figure of romance to such contingencies in order to show what happens to the dream of romance when it is brought down to earth. But had Cervantes done only that, he would have merely inverted the romance and been left with thin satire. His claim to novelistic complexity derives from his ability to redeem the satirized buffoon as a human being capable of commenting on his own action in a way that involves the reader in a more intricate weave of emotion and argument than would the simple parallelism of satire.

The criteria of Mr. Watt have a familiar ring: their theoretical premise sounds rather like Aristotelian mimesis, and his authors' "greater attention to the particular individual" (p. 18) is reminiscent of "a man like ourselves." If Defoe and Richardson created a hero conformable with the expectations of their reading public, and did so thanks to their minute detailing of the contemporary scene and its actors, it was in order to effect more than simple recognition: the familiar surfaces were supposed to be emblematic of the human predicament which the reader was also to recognize as his own.[11] Familiar surfaces do not give the reader enough with which to identify, since he is not likely to consider himself as a mere surface. But that reader may well accept a character whose human quandary is like his own, regardless of how alien that character's circumstances may be. If, as Mr. Watt suggests, Richardson was able to make tears flow "as no one else and as never before" (p. 174), it was because his book referred

---

[11] Fielding has been left out of this listing because his novels seem to bear a closer resemblance to the picaresque. For that reason, the picaresque author of *Moll Flanders* should be similarly omitted.

the reader to something in him that called for tears. If this
happened only because, for example, the segment of Richardson's reading public that was made up of servant girls
found it difficult to wed, then the human predicament becomes restricted indeed, and it is understandable that
"modern readers [may find] Clarissa too good and Love-
lace too bad to be convincing" (p. 212). But if the tears
were to be drawn from readers with more enduring problems, then the characters had to be proportionally less simple, and their circumstantial description had something to
do with it, as did also the epistolary mode of Richardson
and the fictional diary of Defoe—intimate forms suggesting that attention should be paid to the inner portrayal of
the characters rather than to their outer detail.

Ian Watt has intentionally neglected to use a modifier in
his title, *The Rise of the Novel;* he means that Defoe,
Richardson, and Fielding define the novel for the Western
world. He therefore finds it necessary to place such works
as *La Princesse de Clèves* and *Les Liaisons dangereuses*
"outside the main tradition of the novel. For all its psychological penetration and literary skill, we feel [that this fic-
tion] is too stylish to be authentic" (p. 30). But authenticity—the reality principle—cannot reside in fiction,
whose very meaning is feigning and invention: fiction can
only activate the reality principle, and that principle remains in the reader; whatever work of fiction will induce
the reader to grant it *his* authenticity will be a novel, regardless of whether it is written with careful regard for
surfaces or according to formalistic traditions. The rejection by Mr. Watt of the latter possibilities so narrows his
justificatory definition as to suggest that in the eighteenth
century the English novel innovated but little.

The achievement of Cervantes was not the writing of a

tale whose references were familiar to his readers; it was the contrivance with intangible words of an argument to which his readers could give their flesh and substance. The argument attains two dimensions: it is incarnate within the reader and objectified within the book. That book, for that reader, is a real object, and if the argument is pursued, it must be as part of a new cycle within which *Don Quixote* is transformed from fiction into objective reality.

The artifact is either a thing or a sign. If, as Aristotle suggests, its function as sign is to allow knowledge of man, its success depends on a prior acceptance of its function: it can then awaken within its object (whether reader, spectator, or listener) moments of that object's self-awareness. If, on the other hand, as the *Quixote* suggests, every successful artifact encourages a movement back from the thing signified to the signifying object, it becomes a matter of importance for the conscious artist to preserve in some measure the objective reality of his creation. A too facile assimilation of the work of art does not draw the assimilator out of himself and allows a reversal of functions: the assimilator affects the object, making it a part of himself without being affected by its defining separateness. This process is the more important for the conscious writer in that, as noted previously, the reader most likely to appreciate the writing as artistic object is also the one most likely to resist the human form that it suggests as sign. It is thus not surprising to find a growing awareness among artists and theorists of the artifact as object. In the twentieth century, that awareness is given its first and most dramatic statement by the surrealists.

In retrospect, it would seem that the surrealists' revolution was intended primarily to shock people out of motions that were habit-dulled and dehumanized: the repetition of empty gestures induced by moral, political, or religious systems, social or esthetic constructs, logic as it becomes tautological, and so on—not only because these are categories (therefore antithetical to man defined as growth and flux), but because man persists in such beliefs beyond his moment of awareness. The surrealist's concern is centered on this loss of awareness and his efforts directed to its reawakening. The surrealist revolution had in common with all revolutions a desire to liberate humanity from a previous bondage; once the world could be seen anew, the human condition might be transcended: the blinders would fall from the eyes of men and free a latent, godlike vision; universal synthesis could be effected.

Inasmuch as they were writers, the surrealists applied these principles to words—their effort coinciding in this respect with the poets'. The idea was to rediscover the word, to separate it from its familiar husk like a diamond from the rough. It is not the more extensively publicized experiments with automatic writing that are important here (these efforts were less concerned with the emergence of words than with freeing the mind from them altogether); reference is made instead to the ways in which a word can be made new again, as by dissociating its sound from sense [12] or by converting it to a less familiar usage, for example an earlier sense closer to the root meaning of the word.

So treated, words are no longer formless and disembodied stimuli that exist only collectively as the so-stimulated, but otherwise unrelated, mental process that assimilates them. Stripped of its denotative and connotative as-

[12] The experiment has a do-it-yourself simplicity: the most familiar word can be voided of meaning by repeating it until it becomes pure sound.

pects, the word becomes an object. For this, as for other articles of faith, the surrealists referred to Lautréamont, and in particular to the following phrase: "beautiful [. . .] as the fortuitous meeting on a dissection table of a sewing machine and an umbrella." [13] Although the simile is first of all evidence of the fantastic and cruel world projected by a schizophrenic mind [14] (male and female symbols of diverse kinds meeting on a bed which is actually the place where analysis destroys the human organism), there can be little doubt that because of their unusual juxtaposition the sewing machine and the umbrella are objectified: they achieve an irreducible identity that would not normally be theirs in the sewing room or the umbrella stand.

Objects themselves are similarly voided of their substance when caught up in the utilitarian stream of human existence, and the surrealist proposes to redeem it in the same way. When the nonsurrealistic artist copes with the object, his artifact becomes the metaphor that brings into proximity two realities: that of the world in which the object exists originally and that of the assimilative world of the one in whom the object is recreated mentally as reference to, or rearrangement of, past experience. But in so doing, the artifact becomes a distancing factor, since the direct relation of assimilative world to phenomenal [15] world must now be effected through the artificial construct of the artist. The surrealist eliminates this separating object by making it part of the phenomenal reality—an ultimate object with no metaphorical function, with no

[13] *Les Chants de Maldoror*, Canto VI.
[14] Such is at least the diagnosis of modern psychology. *Vide*, e.g., Jean Pierre Soulier, *Lautréamont: Génie ou maladie mentale?*
[15] The term is used here and elsewhere in the sense of "noumenal" or "ontic"—generally to denote the reader's world outside the book.

purpose but to signify itself. The ambiguity of the artifact that starts with Aristotelian mimesis, part object and part sign, is finally resolved: the object no longer has the power to signify. It thus stands separate and unassimilable, reacquiring its original properties of mystery and awesomeness. The artifact is then freed of its former dependency on the willingness of the assimilator to find it assimilable: the human fact of the assimilator becomes one of the two terms of the metaphor through which the surrealist experience is effected; the other term is the artifact itself as phenomenal evidence.

This being said, it is noteworthy that in practice the surrealists seldom objectified their world. Those who did were mainly painters and sculptors (Chirico, Magritte, Giacometti, among others) from whose midst came *objets trouvés* (like Duchamp's) [16] or collages (such as those of Max Ernst or the Picasso of the early 1930's) whose *things* subvert the form in which they are set in order to assert themselves and that form as objects. But because the surrealists did not allow for the peculiar stereochemistry of the written word which can be objectified as sound or sense only within the reader's ear or experience, their writings generally turn from the phenomenal world to an exploration or representation of inner states of being: their poems grow mostly out of the free association of images, and their novels are usually no more than mood creations, polemics, or humorous fantasy (e.g., Louis Aragon's *Le Paysan de Paris*, André Breton's *Nadja*, Raymond Que-

---

[16] Since the pristine vision of the artist is sometimes sufficient to render the object pristine. Breton defines found objects as "manufactured objects promoted to the dignity of art objects by the choice of the artist" (*Position politique du surréalisme*).

neau's *Pierrot mon ami.*[17] When *Don Quixote* becomes an object within the phenomenal reality of its reader with reference to the argument that originated as fiction, Cervantes comes closer to achieving the surrealists' aim of objectification than do most of their novels. It was only after the death of surrealism that the experiment was to exert its influence in shaping along entirely new lines the novel of mid-century France.

[17] There are of course moments in the novels when the occult mood is rendered effectively enough to become hermetic. The same is true of their poetry—and in particular of that written by the man who was perhaps their greatest poet, Pierre Reverdy. The work of others associated with the surrealist movement seems less relevant. The abstractions of Miró, for example, are primarily decorative. The mixed metaphors of Lautréamont or Dali do not construct an irreducible object any more than does the classical griffin. A Dali watch melting off the side of a table still refers to watches, tables, and the everyday process of melting, whereas the horizon line of a Chirico painting states its wasteland barrenness in the mood of the viewer.

Chaucer: *Troilus* and *Criseyde*

There is something in Chaucer's *Troilus and Criseyde* that repeatedly leads us astray from our expectation: it is a poem, but somehow we are caught up more in the intricacy of the tale as it is told than in the modulations of its telling; it is a courtly romance, and as such it presents the usual rigors of courtship, the prefatory refusals of the lady, the sighs and pallor of the lover, the constant threat of jeopardy that induces constancy on his part, etc.; but in this romance, the lady turns unfaithful, and the lover ends in heaven, looking down upon the scene of his earthly tribulations and laughing. It also has the necessary go-between of romance, efficient, loyal and discreet—but the discretion, loyalty and efficiency of this go-between attain disconcerting proportions: even though originally described as a lover himself, Pandarus turns into a force of such magnitude as to cast doubt on his human essence.

Courtly love is one of the forms of the periodic quandary that entraps man in the process of defining himself as something different from the animal. The silk and spice trades that will open twelfth-century Provence to new modes coming from beyond the Mediterranean through

Spain are the exotic symptoms of man starting to contemplate himself with an attention which he owed formerly to God. One day, the refinements which he now claims for himself devise the complexities of courtly love—a way of rendering ambiguous the simple act of physical love. Love is either a god or a problem (the formula belongs to Denis de Rougemont, in *Love Declared*): both are manifestations of a force that an ordered society must channel in order to be able to cope with it. But if policing the sexual act is a constant, whether through ritual or regulation, it is a fact that in the Western world such policing tends to view the act as an abstraction, so as to constrain it within an externally imposed framework. Christianity borrows from the Roman state the utilitarian notion of procreation, but it does not place the moral burden on the woman alone: adultery is a sin that extends to both sexes. Still, woman is regarded with suspicion for her part in the fall of man, and the dogma that honors her as a moral equal, sexually, is honored frequently through infraction. But courtly love represents a complete break with all externally imposed criteria: its ways are devised by those who have felt a need for such new ways (i.e., the policing is sought by one of those to be policed, rather than by the policing agency), and these needs are, for the first time, woman's (within the code, the woman will be, in fact, the policing agent).

By the twelfth century there is a sense of constraint within the world of Christendom. The pursuits of the masculine aristocrat—essentially those of a warrior—take him far from home, harden his ways, or at least change them according to modes that are alien to the ones that circumscribed him within the household. Meanwhile, even as the aristocratic woman remains at home, the world which her husband is gradually enlarging contributes to

her own sense of constriction; though extended in the
name of a traditional spirituality, this broadened world
yields economic benefits first of all, and she is the conspicuous consumer. Within horizons thus widened, the
Christian ethos no longer defines satisfactorily the relationship between the medieval man and woman of the privileged classes: as seen by the man, former boundaries seem
to be limiting; within the new ones, the woman too acquires new standards by which to judge her world. One of
the first to be judged (and found wanting) is her husband.
Add to this her memory of the chivalric code that protects
the weak, and the form into which she will project her
new world becomes fairly predictable. It remains for the
troubadour, who has never left home either, to become the
pro domo theorist of this new code.

Thus evolved a spiritualization whose stated purpose
sometimes paralleled the Christian ethic, but whose processes and ultimate purpose were considerably different; it
was a convention which, in the words of R. Briffault, "allowed the favored class to denounce, in terms approximat-
ing those of Christian morality, licentiousness, vulgarity,
disorder, and dissociate itself from any 'dishonorable' conduct while preserving for itself the benefits of that conduct." [1] Both moralities fuse to a certain extent when, in
the thirteenth century, the courtly love of the twelfth
contributes to the replacing of a Christ who looks too
much like an Old Testament figure by the Virgin.[2]

By the end of the twelfth century, Andreas Capellanus,
writing at the court of Marie de Champagne, was able to
codify the prescripts of Provençal *fin'amors*. His *De deo*

[1] Quoted by Moshé Lazar, in *Amour courtois et fin' amors dans la littérature du XII* siècle*, p. 83.
[2] For an amplification of this theory, see Lazar, *op.cit.*

amore was presumably to enjoy a long life: it was the subject of a special condemnation in Paris by Etienne Tempier a century later.[3] Capellanus commented upon a mode of behavior that had already left its mark on the work of another writer at the same court: the paths that Cligès, Lancelot, and Yvain traveled through the occult worlds of Chrétien de Troyes were largely determined, as was their bearing, by elaborate deference to such ladies as Fenice, Guinevere, and Laudine.

For Capellanus, love, as he defines it, is the supreme good whose efficacy engenders other goods: it gives a man the kind of character that renders his bodily defects insignificant; it confers a nobility of soul that transcends class distinctions; it commands the virtues of generosity, obedience, humility, and discretion in the lover. (The loved one—the lady—is presumably already possessed of these virtues.) Marriage belongs to another code; it is irrelevant to this one: "Causa coniugii ab amore non est excusatio recta" ("The fact of marriage is not a genuine hindrance to love"). The lady rules: "Dominarum praeceptis in omnibus obediens semper studeas amoris aggregari militiae" ("In all matters obeying the commands of the ladies, always add to the service of love").[4] The lover will al-

[3] Admittedly, some time must be allowed for the code, like the mores, to reach northern France, and it is also a fact that the condemnation by Bishop Tempier was but an afterthought in his fight against the Averroist heresy in general and Thomas Aquinas in particular; still, the attention which he gives the book in 1277 seems to vouch for its enduring influence.

[4] Though here the convention may have been due more to the social pressure of the Provençal court than to the written commands of its theorists. Chrétien is frequently ironic when he places the knight within the absolute power of the woman, and it may be more than a coincidence that when "Madame de Champagne" gave him the "matière et sens" of the *Lancelot*, in which submis-

ways be possessed of the loved one, anxious, affected in
sleep and appetite; he will tremble in the presence of the
beloved and generally exhibit a characteristic pallor. The
rewards for this behavior are ill-defined: voluptuousness is
discouraged, and such an exclusive quest certainly hinders
promiscuity. However, in distinguishing between *purus
amor* ("true love") and *amor mixtus* ("in extremo Veneris
opere terminatur"), Capellanus recognizes that even
though it is a dangerous sort of love, *amor mixtus* is still a
form of *verus amor* and thus cannot be condemned.

Written some two hundred years later, *Troilus and
Criseyde* is still a romance—though it is also more. After
seeing Criseyde in postures that define only her conventional role throughout Book I (the attractive and reserved
widow, the suppliant to Hector after her father's defec-
tion, the perfect figure that seduces Troilus), we first see
her as a particularization on the occasion of the initial visit
that Pandarus pays her at the start of Book II. Here she
appears in a setting belonging to Chaucer's own Middle
Ages: a young girl is reading to her and two companions
the Theban saga.[5] As in many other instances throughout
the poem, a specific kind of anachronism contributes a
medieval flavor to the scene. The book being read is presumably Statius' account of the *Thebaid* in twelve parts;
this would represent a first anachronism but it is vouched
for by Pandarus:

---

sion to the lady was so total as to be infamous, he was unable to
conclude the work. Moreover, the fact that one cannot make a
gender distinction in Capellanus between *amans* and *coamans*
tends to remove the woman from too central a position.
[5] For the medieval aspect of this scene, which is not in the *Filostrato*, see F. N. Robinson, *The Works of Geoffrey Chaucer*, p.
818, II, 80. Also consider the very form of the *Troilus and
Criseyde*, in which the poet describes himself as reading his work
to an audience.

> Quod Pandarus, "al this knowe I myselve,
> And al th'assege of Thebes and the care;
> For hereof ben ther maked bookes twelve"
>
> [II, 106–108].

But Crisyede seems to be referring to another work, which she terms a "romaunce": the picture she creates and the term she uses suggest the *Roman de Thèbes*, which had been composed about 1150 and was based on Statius. If this assumption is correct, the widow whose discretion reduced her to a mere personification of states of mind in Book I becomes particularized for the first time in Book II as a young lady interested in love stories, since, to the extent that the *Roman de Thèbes* departs from Statius, it does so as an early vehicle of courtly love.[6]

The very form of Chaucer's poem demonstrates throughout that the book being read to Criseyde reflects not only her own interest in a social ritual regulating sexual courtship, but mirrors as well that which changes Troy into a court of love. Pandarus has suspected from the very first that Crisyede's book may well be a romance:

> For Goddes love, what seith it? telle it us!
> Is it of love? O, som good ye me leere! [II, 96–97].

But Criseyde, laughing, chooses to refer to the formal structure of the poem (the death of Laius at the hands of Oedipus), and it is only then that Pandarus takes her cue and accepts her speaking of the book as if it were Statius'. The scene is a paradigm of the way in which the seeming

[6] For example, in the *Roman de Thèbes*, Ismene and Antigone no longer weep as in Statius over the tragic fate of the Labdacidae but converse instead about the problems of their loves. (As further evidence that Criseyde has the *Roman de Thèbes* in mind, see her reference, to "the bisshop [. . .] Amphiorax" in II, 104–105, on which, *vide* Robinson, p. 818, II, 104.)

of classical antiquity discloses the substance of a medieval
world. Troilus first catches sight of Criseyde at the temple
of Pallas Athena; however, the scene is actually that of the
parvis and the cathedral square, the hub of public social
life in the Middle Ages and the traditional place for lovers
to meet.[7] It is a world in which Cupid and Venus rejoice
over the lovers who are about to be united, but for their
joy Christian church bells perform the miracle of ringing
"withouten hond"; a world in which the day-staying love
of Alcmena and Jove becomes the inspiration for a medieval aubade sung by Troilus; a world whose warriors are
referred to as knights and barons and whose ladies make
music in tapestry gardens, after which—the passage is
reminiscent of Marie de France—

> A nyghtyngale, upon a cedir grene,
> Under the chambre wal ther as she ley,
> Ful loude song ayein the moone shene,
> Peraunter, in his briddes wise, a lay
> Of love   [II, 918–922].

It is in this world that Pandarus describes Troilus to
Criseyde as going through acts of Christian contrition for
having slighted a pagan Eros and where, in his grief, Troilus meditates on predestination and refers to the opinion of
tonsured heads; and it is here also that Venus is invoked as
might be the Virgin Mary, agency of grace (III, 1267).[8]

[7] See Robinson, p. 814, I, 162. At this point Criseyde is a figure in
black, not the color for mourning in the pre-Christian Mediterranean world. Her widow's clothing is deliberately medieval; note,
e.g., in II, 110, the advice of Pandarus: "Do wey youre barbe"
—referring to the pleated linen worn from chin to waist by wid-
ows.

[8] Venus not only combines her traditional attributes and the
Christian concept of love; she also becomes a part of medieval as-
trology. See Robinson, p. 822, III, 1–49.

This atmosphere is due in part to Chaucer's reminiscences of other romances. In addition to the *Filostrato* by Boccaccio which he follows in the main, Chaucer is indebted to a work which may have been the original source of Boccaccio, the *Roman de Troie* by Benoît de Sainte-Maure (1165), for the traits of some of the traditional figures such as Antenor and Diomede and for a number of details connected with the Trojan story. Chaucer also borrows from the already mentioned *Roman de Thèbes* and seems to have read *Le Roman d'Enéas* (see F. N. Robinson, *The Works of Geoffrey Chaucer*, p. 819, II, 611–644), while the song of Antigone, which is the musical accompaniment to the awakening love of Criseyde (II, 825, *et passim*), is reminiscent of the *Paradis d'amour* by Guillaume de Machaut.

At two levels, the poem remains an instance and an exemplar of courtly love: it is first of all, and largely, a copy of Boccaccio's tale; second, it frequently amends Boccaccio according to the formal conventions of the code. Chaucer makes of Tròilus a more considerate lover and a warrior of greater daring, giving him the twin visages of the ideal hero of courtly romance, who is meek in the bedroom but masterful on the battlefield. (The second of these traits goes beyond Capellanus and derives from a feminine ascendency which not only seeks compliance in the particulars of the lover's relations with his lady but which extends the lady's sway into areas that concern her only because she chooses to be concerned with them—as in Lancelot's treatment at the hands of Guinevere *after* he has saved her.) Troilus evidences a more patient adoration than Troilo: he is more gracious to his lady, even after her betrayal, and to the world in general (in conformity with the ennobling virtue of courtly love); he keeps a more

civil tongue, rants less in his amorous triumph and his ultimate defeat, giving the impression that his love is more
spiritual than his Italian counterpart's. Tropes such as
those of the Boethian *De consolatione philosophiae* in the
mouth of Troilus may serve to accentuate his feeling that
there is no free will and contribute to the ideal posture of
helplessness required of the courtly lover.[9] Needless to
say, over and above these instances of courtly orthodoxy,
Troilus loses sleep, knows he will die without his love, becomes a quivering mass in her presence but reveals no sign
of his love to the outside world—all this, once he has de-
cided to serve the god of love and live as his lady's servant;
or, to put it more precisely, having once agreed to live by
the refinements and niceties of the art of love—after "took
he purpos loves craft to suwe" (I, 379).

Up to a point, Criseyde herself is more the perfect
image of the courtly mistress than was Boccaccio's heroine—a difference marked, in a sense, by the contrast of her
"widewes habit black" with the "bruna vesta" of Criseida;
there is more reserve, more discretion, and less fleshly reality in Criseyde, and, at the start, this state is compatible
with the woman-centered view and rhythm of a courtly
affair. Chaucer himself vouches for the fact that she will
not fall rashly, but only after Troilus, "by proces and by
good servyse, / He gat hire love, and in no sodeyn wyse"
(II, 678–679)—that is to say, according to the ritual
code, by a process which the subsequent development of
the story will document. Whereas Criseida wants Troilo
clearly enough to make the animal spirits of both appear
to be more pronounced, Criseyde takes the courtly view
that her wooing represents an ultimate jeopardy of self
that can be redeemed only to the extent that she is able to

[9] See T. A. Kirby, *Chaucer's Troilus*, pp. 260–264.

retard its process. But her insistence on her honor involves sufficient grace and decorum to encompass Troilus within its consideration: quite clearly, Criseyde is the ideal object of Capellanus who knows that "Facilis perceptio contemptibilem reddit amorem, difficilis eum carum facit haberi" ("facility renders love contemptible; difficulty makes it held dear"). It therefore stands to reason that Criseyde is also the Petrarchian compendium of perfections (verbally stated but not necessarily evidenced), that she knows all about the love philters of romance (II, 651), the qualities to be looked for in a courtly lover (II, 661–662), the limits within which, and the tone according to which, the affair will proceed, and ultimately, with her breach of the code, she is fully aware of the appalling consequences of that breach:

> She seyde, "Allas! for now is clene ago
> My name of trouthe in love, for everemo!
> For I have falsed oon the gentileste
> That evere was, and oon the worthieste! . . ."
>
> [V, 1054–1057].

But even before the ultimate dereliction of Criseyde, Chaucer has shown that something is wrong with her courtly world. The doctrine of courtly love is not unlike any other mystique or ritualistic formalism: its efficacy depends on an unquestioning acceptance of its dogma as a whole. Writing after 1380, Chaucer is addressing an audience familiar with the prescripts of courtly love, but one whose familiarity may be, by this time, a matter of learning rather than of unconditional social compliance.[10]

[10] J. Huizinga (*The Waning of the Middle Ages*) questions whether such compliance was ever achieved in fact and sees at best a coexistence of the refined literary form and mores whose

When Criseyde assures Pandarus, "Myn honour shal I kepe, and ek his lif," she is following the correct chronology of courtly love that makes of the woman's honor something more important than her lover's life. But when Chaucer allows us to know the unspoken thoughts of Criseyde, the very definition of courtly love as unquestionable dogma is subverted by his analyzing the personal reasons of its principal officiant. As we go from Criseyde, the high priestess of this ritual, to Criseyde the woman, we move from a concern with form to a concern with particulars, from pattern to personal experience. Criseyde the woman places little reliance in the efficacy of the code: instead, she is a shrewd female assessing her particular circumstances in terms of her own well-being—which well-being may even envisage the well-being of Troilus to an extent that the courtly code would not; after Pandarus has threatened that Troilus might kill himself for love of her, she reflects:

> "Unhappes fallen thikke
> Alday for love, and in swych manere cas
> As men ben cruel in hemself and wikke;
> And if this man sle here hymself, allas!
> In my presence, it wol be no solas.
> What men wolde of hit deme I kan nat seye:
> It nedeth me ful sleighly for to pleie"   [II, 456–462].

---

crudeness sometimes dates back to primal mysteries. In literature itself the ethical qualities of courtly love are being replaced by the social virtues of the landed aristocracy by the time Jean de Meung completes *Le Roman da la rose* (1280), and in the courts of love at the start of the fifteenth century Huizinga senses a disparity between the literary salon ideal into which the chivalric form has evolved and the actual practices of its members. He notes at about the same time reactions against the formalism of the courtly code, such as the pastoral ideal, and quotes from the poetry of Eustache Deschamps, who, it will be remembered, knew and admired Chaucer.

It is the woman and not the courtly heroine who falls in love with Troilus. Although less quickly and less carnally than her Italian predecessor, Criseyde loves Troilus with a passion and instincts that courtly love reproves: on her first confrontation with Troilus, she prefaces her acceptance of him with a quick summary of his courtly duties (her honor must be safe, all formalities will have to be observed, Troilus is received "to my servyse," but even though he is a king's son, she will set the bounds of their love [III, 159 ff.]); however, she seals her words with a spontaneity whose feminine charm robs them of a good deal of their formality: "And hym in armes took, and gan hym kisse." Thereafter, Pandarus is able to invite the lovers to his house and to encourage them in their love:

> "And eseth there youre hertes right ynough;
> And lat se which of yow shal bere the belle,
> To speke of love aright!" —therwith he lough—
> "For ther have ye a leiser for to telle" [III, 197–200].

Her lip service to the code apparently forgotten, Criseyde does not see fit to react to words whose haste and pointedness subvert her own.

Although Criseyde opposes the coercive urgency of Pandarus with verbal references to courtly etiquette, she never delays his schedule, and at such times as circumstances allow her to shift from words to action, she is guided by her instincts rather than formal criteria. When, for example, Pandarus contrives a jealous Troilus, he knows that Criseyde will respond as a woman and not according to Capellanus ("Ex vera zelotypia affectus semper crescit amandi"—"The affection of a lover is always increased through true jealousy"), and he is confirmed: Criseyde precipitates her courtly doom by breaking the rules twice; she assures Troilus that she is anxious to relieve his distress, and she denounces jealousy.

In the same way as her rising love for Troilus broke through the constructs of courtly love, the love of Criseyde will wane according to human dictates, without the safeguards of courtly love to preserve it. After the Greeks and Trojans agree to exchange her for Antenor, Criseyde is submerged for a while by despair. But afterward, and with a purpose that far outdoes her Italian counterpart,[11] she begins to plan again: she will find ways of eluding her father and will return to the Trojan side before the tenth day is out. And by the time of her departure, she is composed enough to revert to the relative impersonality of the code:

> Ne pompe, array, nobleye, or ek richesse
> Ne made me to rewe on youre destresse;
> But moral vertu, grounded upon trouthe,
> That was the cause I first hadde on yow routhe!
> [IV, 1670–1673].

She and Troilus are therefore bound beyond the power of "remuable Fortune" to undo. Thus end her lamentation and the fourth book.

On riding out, Criseyde meets Diomede, who has come to escort her to the Greek camp. This Diomede is a self-assured and assertive man: whereas his Italian counterpart waited until Criseida had been four days in camp, this one

---

[11] Belying what might have been Christian resignation when she thought of starving herself to death, "syn neither swerd ne darte / Dar I noon handle, for the crueltee" (IV, 771–772). However, if this was not intended as Christian deprivation of suicide, it was a first indication that even at the height of her despair Criseyde did not lose complete sight of herself.

falls promptly in love and declares himself forthwith. His declaration will follow the courtly mode, but as he has only the distance between the two camps in which to declare himself, his haste subverts the ritual whose mainstay is lengthy duration. Nowhere else does Chaucer's irony stand out so clearly with reference to the artificiality of courtly love, and nowhere else does he so clearly show how perilously frail a construct it is to contain the human animal.

Diomede will use the code, as he will use any other means that will achieve his ends (and what these are is plain enough), even if those means should run counter to the most basic prescripts of the code:

> "certeynlich I am aboute nought,
> If that I speke of love, or make it tough;
> For douteles, if she have in hire thought
> Hym that I gesse, he may nat ben ybrought
> So soon awey; but I shal fynde a meene,
> That she naught wite as yet shal what I mene"
>
> [V, 100–105].

Diomede is opportunistic, self-willed, and in a hurry: he is the antithesis of the courtly hero who must reach his ends through paths mapped out by his lady. Even his courtly language shows that, alongside the Troilus lately described by Criseyde, Diomede appears to belong to another species. He swears to do her service, quite properly "as a knyght," but being unsure of such ethics, falls back upon the virtues of his clan: "Iwis, we Grekis kan have joie / To honouren yow, as wel as folk of Troie" (V, 118–119), thereby echoing the shift from ethical to social values already noted by Huizinga in *Le Roman de la rose*. Chaucer allows the present circumstances of Diomede to

make a further mockery of his words as he assures this
woman whom he has just met that never before has he
loved another and never shall he hereafter; but the author
turns his full irony upon the art of love by allowing
Diomede to allege the very code as his pretext:

> For I have herd er this of many a wight,
> Hath loved thyng he nevere saigh his lyve.
> Ek I am nat of power for to stryve
> Ayeyns the god of Love, but hym obeye
> I wole alwey; and mercy I yow preye [V, 164–168].

Out of the convention of the code, Criseyde replies that
she accepts Diomede's friendship, even though "in effect,
she naught his tales herde / But her and ther, now here a
word or two" (V, 178–179). To Diomede, for whom the
courtly pose is the sheerest of superficial veils, this acceptance represents encouragement enough to sense victory.
And since the code is flimsy containment indeed, he is of
course quite right.

Halfway through Book V, Chaucer pauses to describe his
principals, "as bokes us declare" (l. 799) and finds, amidst
a panoply of superlatives, that Criseyde was "Tendre-
herted, slydynge of corage" (l. 825); he thus departs from
Boccaccio in order to emphasize the human imponderable
contending with the fixity of abstract ethics. At the same
time, Chaucer makes the further pledges of Diomede less
emphatic than the Italian: the ever ill-concealed woman in
Criseyde is now sufficiently emergent to make all but the
most perfunctory references to the code of love quite useless. Where her Italian ancestress remains ambiguous and
guarded in her replies to Diomede, Criseyde soon finds
herself lying to him: on the tenth day (a moment significantly chosen) she will tell her new suitor that after

her husband's death she had no other love. Every step Criseyde retreats from the code into instinctual womanhood enables Diomede to take a step forward; his progress is more rapid than that of his Italian counterpart. The height of Criseyde's dilemma occurs when the conflicting exigencies of the woman and of the code contend most assertively in her: the woman is drawn to Diomede while feeling guilt and pain for the fate of Troilus, but these feelings of guilt and pain are exacerbated by the awareness that Diomede is not the equal of Troilus as a courtly figure. Criseyde is, not unlike Francesca, a woman corrupted by literature. Her peace of mind returns after she finally gives up the code; if there is a tragic moral to this tale, it must be sought in the plight of Troilus rather than in hers.

When Criseyde writes her first letter to Troilus (the one which the *Filostrato* requires), she has still not resolved her dilemma, and her words are little more than an effort to temporize. But by the time she writes her second letter (Chaucer's insert), even though she may still feel guilty enough to tax Troilus with thinking only of his own "pleasaunce," her indifference to him and to the code of love has become such that she is now able to manipulate that code for her own ends: she insinuates that she has heard uncourtly rumors about Troilus for the sole purpose of being able to dismiss the insinuation ("But now no force, I kan nat in yow gesse / But alle trouthe and alle gentilesse" [V, 1616–1617]) in such a manner as to prevent Troilus from importuning her further while at the same time allowing herself to remain with the image of a Troilus contained by, and relatively at peace within, the artificial construct of the code.

Troilus is one of the great figures in literature that are

brought down through virtue in love: he loses the object
of his affection because of too great a submission to that
object. In *Andromaque,* Racine has Oreste go mad, after
Hermione berates him for having killed the man she bade
him kill—but whom she loved, nevertheless. Troilus dies.
He begins as an ironical critic of love, knowing full well
"which a labour folk han in wynnynge / Of love" (I,
199–200), but once he has met Criseyde, he defers to her
mode and becomes an exemplar of the conduct she
preaches but is unable to practice. The paths of these lovers are divergent: the man subordinates himself to an ethical construct for the sake of the woman, but her ethical
construct gradually gives way to human assertions. It was
necessary thereafter for Chaucer to cap this irony by following Troilus after his death into the eighth sphere of
heaven, from which he could look down upon such tragic-
ally cross-purposeful trajectories and laugh.

In his final summation, the author comments:

> Lo here, of payens corsed olde rites,
> Lo here, what alle hire goddes may availle;
> Lo here, thise wrecched worldes appetites
>   [V, 1849–1851].

The words suggest that, at this moment, the author views
his tale from the same moral point of view as Troilus, rejecting the vanity of human effort expended on "worldes
appetites," high amongst which is, presumably, profane
love. This view appears to contrast with the opening
stanzas, in which the author sees himself as a "brother" to
all who are in love, urging the successful ones not to forget "the adversite / Of othere folk." [12] In a narrative that

[12] I, 25–26. This should not be construed as more than sympathetic
understanding. As for the apparent identification of the author

superimposes the ways and values of the Middle Ages upon a spurious antiquity, the prime pagan ritual (as op- posed to the teachings of Christian dogma) is the practice of courtly love, in contrast to the Christian concept of love—an idea twice remiss in that it not only strays from a spiritual orthodoxy but pursues its material object through mundane practice. It would therefore appear possible to be a sympathetic "brother" to all who suffer in love while de- crying the false and frustrating paths along which men are led in quest of it.

In a sense, there are two Troiluses, and both are unable to come to satisfactory terms with the dilemma of love. The first Troilus is the one who avoids the danger by pre- serving an ironical distance. His irony amounts to a form of hybris, and Chaucer will mock him for falling just as hard as any other mortal (I, 206 ff.). But the author is not content simply to counter irony with irony: he turns seri- ous in order to praise love immediately thereafter—"For alderwisest han therwith ben plesed" (I, 247); love is com- fort, it appeases the cruel heart, it makes the worthy worthier and causes mankind to turn away from vice and shame—shorn of its forms, these are the teachings of courtly love. The second Troilus defers to the woman who has drawn him into the dreaded world of "lewed ob- servaunces" (I, 198), in the belief that through such prac- tices he can most loyally secure his love against the dan- gers that first moved him to irony and detachment. But

---

with courtly love ("I, that God of Loves servantz serve"), elab- oration of that line in *The House of Fame* makes it clear that the servant of servants is the one who writes about the devotees of love, his role being "To make bookys, songes, dytees, / In ryme, or elles in cadence, / As thou best canst, in reverence / Of Love, and of hys servantes eke" (ll. 622–625).

because the courtly ritual ultimately fails the woman who
had compelled his abdication to it, Troilus is caught up in
an intricate and mundane ballet that misses its spiritual purpose. He will have but a brief moment of fulfillment—the
brevity of which serves to emphasize the vanity of the
elaborate process through which it was attained. Until the
moment of his subsequent grief, Troilus never achieves
human immediacy: his irony at first and his mannerisms
afterward keep him in artificial postures. His transformation into a lover transforms him in fact into a literary figure. And to dramatize this truth, there is Pandarus.

Pandarus is a force. He enters the scene unexpectedly at
the height of Troilus' need and from that moment on contrives events in such a way as to achieve for Troilus what
the latter cannot achieve himself. In fact, alongside Pandarus, the principals take on the wan and stylized appearance of the figures that illustrate medieval romances. It is
only after the moment of his triumph, when the human
dilemma returns the principals to human dimensions, that
Pandarus recedes as a force and ends, by the side of Troilus, as a faithful but helpless friend.

Pandarus is not as particularized as the Italian Pandaro,
the latter acting very much at the level of the other characters, although he is obviously a young man more vig-
orous and persuasive than the rest. Pandarus is of unspeci-
fied age but is older than the principals (he is also the
uncle of Criseyde), having that additional ascendency over
them. He also plays a much larger role than Pandaro. He
is first seen as he bursts in on Troilus' passive dejection in a
torrent of words. Like everything else about the Pandarus
of the first three books, his loquacity is primarily a form
of energy. He taunts, wheedles, makes jokes, speaks in
aphorisms—without ever giving the impression that his

words convey any human truth about him. Chaucer explains at this point that such talkativeness is meant to nettle Troilus out of his lethargy, but it soon becomes apparent that this is the normative mode of Pandarus. Troilus is determined not to speak, having already subscribed to the code that requires discretion as one of its principal virtues. But there is no holding out against Pandarus: in the long run, the strongest mettle is no match for his words; after his verbal barrage has been mercilessly trained on Troilus for sufficient time, the latter not only confesses the nature of his illness but reveals its details.

Some points in the foregoing are worth noting. Even though he is much more decisive than Pandaro on behalf of his friend, Pandarus does not convey the same impression of solicitude. Pandarus bullies and overwhelms Troilus: when the young man dozes off into morbid daydreams, Pandarus yells him back into consciousness ("And cryde 'Awake!' ful wonderlich and sharpe" [I, 729]). He turns aside every argument and makes light of what Troilus views as the most fearsome obstacles: when Troilus bemoans that Fortune herself is his foe, Pandarus dismisses even this agency. In the process, Pandarus is able to articulate and justify the code of courtly love, even while ridiculing its leisurely pace which is scarcely compatible with his own kinetics:

What! many a man hath love ful deere ybought
Twenty wynter that his lady wiste,
That nevere yet his lady mouth he kiste.
What? sholde he therfore fallen in dispayr.
    . . . . .
Nay, nay, but [. . .] thynk it is a guerdon, hire to serve,
A thousand fold moore than he kan deserve   [I, 810–819].

It is this argument, that practice of the code is its own reward, which finally affects Troilus, who considers his folly in yielding to despair and begins, instead, yielding to Pandarus.

When Pandarus senses the imminent collapse of Troilus, he greets it as if he has sensed a kill: " 'A ha!' quod Pandare, 'here bygynneth game' " (I, 868); and when he hears that the lady is Criseyde, he is even more delighted ("Lord, he was glad"), conveying once more the impression that his joy derives not so much from the concern he feels for his friend as from the purpose now being given his own energy. His reaction contrasts sharply with that of his Italian counterpart, who assures Troilo, on hearing the name of the lady, that matters will not be easy. In rapid fire, now, mixing aphorisms and Christian terminology, Pandarus places in the mouth of Troilus a prayer of contrition to the god of love, urges him to stand fast as a pillar of courtliness, and begs his leave to begin "to serve his fulle frend."

At the start of Book II, there appears to be a brief loss of momentum as Pandarus is seen abed in the haze of Maytime love. But this is a deceptive moment: in the next, he is at his niece's palace about his purpose, and the effect of his lethargy remains only to the extent that, like wind-driven pollen, a breath of sensual and active love enters the marble parlor of Criseyde with him, stirring the scene of courtly romance already referred to (see above, p. 48). "Do wey youre book, rys up, and lat us daunce," he urges Criseyde, "And lat us don to May som observaunce" (II, 111–112). But Criseyde resists this burst of life, responding instead according to the decorum of her role: she is a widow; is that the way she should behave? Checked in his action, Pandarus reverts to his more familiar weapon—

words: "Yet koude I telle a thyng to doon yow pleye" (II, 121), and having aroused her curiosity, he brings the talk around to Troilus by way of Hector, Troilus' brother and the hero of Troy.

Pandarus gathers momentum: his motions and acts begin to rival his speech. He moves between the lovers "as streyght as lyne," conjures up the threat of Poliphete before Criseyde, gives her a reaction when hers proves to be inadequate, overwhelms Troilus with his plan so as to forestall objections, enlists the aid of the house of Priam against the supposed wrongdoings of Poliphete, and at last, pushing people in and out of the way, achieves the purpose of this overly elaborate scheme: to have Criseyde visit Troilus alone in his bedroom. Even without being compared to Pandarus, Troilus is ineffectual: at the approach of his beloved he gives every indication of having indeed fallen prey to the illness he is supposed to feign.

"Pandarus, to quike alwey the fir, / Was evere ylike prest and diligent" (III, 484–485); as he becomes more and more purposeful, his very cheerfulness turns to energy. He sheds the last remnant of the unsuccessful lover ("I have a joly wo, a lusty sorwe" [II, 1099]). His moments of deepest compassion for Troilus leave him unaffected in his actions: 'Pandare wept as he to water wolde" (III, 115), but nevertheless he "poked evere his nece new and newe" (l. 117). He deliberately flouts the too leisurely code[13] and breaks down, through his willfulness, the mask of Criseyde ("Refuse it naught," he orders Criseyde, concerning the letter he has caused Troilus

[13] "Biennalis viduitas pro amante defuncto superstiti praescribitur amanti" ("A widowhood of two years for a dead lover is prescribed for the survivor")—in memory of which Pandarus comments: "this nyce opynyoun / Shal nought be holden fully yeres two" (II, 1297–1298).

to write, "And in hire bosom the lettre down he thraste"
[II, 1154–1155]). It should be noted that as his impetus
grows, Pandarus, who has been at best only a distant
image of Pandaro, becomes entirely the creation of Chaucer. But even as he creates this dynamic and successful
manipulator, the author shows his disapproval of the various postures through which he himself puts his people.
When love asserts itself in spite of the protective mask
worn by Criseyde, Chaucer interrupts his tale with an in-
terjection whose animus shows how much the mask has ir-
ritated him too:

> And how so she hath hard ben here-byforn,
> To God hope I, she hath now kaught a thorn,
> She shal nat pulle it out this nexte wyke.
> God sende mo swich thornes on to pike!
>
> [II, 1271–1274].

And in Book III, just before the climax of his endeavors,
Pandarus pauses to comment on his role and hints at the
ultimate sordidness of the courtly game: if people knew,
he would be looked upon with contempt. In so doing, he
does not give himself the protection of the courtly code
("Amoris tui secretarios noli plures habere") [14] but judges
himself by noncourtly standards of morality. He therefore
urges secrecy, reverting to the orthodoxy of the code, but
after having cast doubt on it because of the reasons al-
leged, especially when one considers with what alacrity,

---

[14] "You should not have many confidants for your love"—which
supposes that one at least is fitting and proper, in the tradition of
Tristan's Gouvernal and Lancelot's Galéhaut. For a further study
of the type in medieval literature, see Karl Young, *The Origin and
Development of the Story of Troilus and Criseyde* (London,
1908); also Kirby, *op. cit.*, pp. 107 ff.

extensiveness, and force Pandarus carries out his scheme.

Still, this is but an aside. In point of fact, Pandarus now contrives a favorable zodiac, a moonless sky, and propitious elements for the climactic meeting of the lovers. Troilus is less and less assured as the moment approaches, while Pandarus is more and more brutally assertive. He rides roughshod over the fears of Troilus ("Thow wrecched mouses herte, / Artow aghast so that she wol the bite?" [III, 736–737]) and nearly physically forces this timid lover into bed. (The scene, starting to verge on comedy, puts one in mind of some of the more sensational passages in the opening pages of Zola's *La Terre*.) It is not until well after Troilus and Criseyde are under the sheets that Pandarus finally dams his torrent of words and departs with his light to read a book. This should have been his final exit, but since the tale has now reached the level of comedy, Troilus suffers a final collapse and faints. Pandarus must once more enter the picture in order to right it. Only then, after recommending to Troilus that he not faint again, does Pandarus take his final leave.

After this, Chaucer remains much closer to his source, and Pandarus recedes. He will cry at the decision of the Trojans to trade Criseyde for Antenor, but he can do no more. Circumstances now trap the one who formerly manipulated them (V, 281 ff.). He tries to comfort Troilus and remains a faithful companion to the last, but his words no longer have the power to alter the course of events. This force of nature ends "as stille as ston" (V, 1729) and without being able to say a word. But by this time, he is little more than a man dwarfed by the agony of Troilus —hardly the one who brought the lovers together and created a world. That Pandarus had of a human being only the outward shape and certain mannerisms: he would

mock himself, as men do to show that they are human; he
would speak in proverbs, since, as Sancho Panza was to
know one day, these distill the essence of all human
knowledge; he would cry briefly or dance on an impulse,
take a solemn oath, and all the while exhibit a persistent
cheerfulness, for none of these human gestures ever revealed a human being: they merely clothed a purpose in
human shape. That Pandarus was the creature of a book, a
device imposing itself on human randomness, attempting
to discipline that randomness into a predetermined object.
Late in the fourteenth century, at a time when the human
gesture was becoming more interesting than the constructs
that modified it, the single-mindedness of Pandarus was the
fictile power of romance, the contrivance of literary and
social forms trying, sometimes with comic frenzy, to co-
erce the human response into artificial patterns.

The courtly code may never have been applied outside
of books; but if it was, it meant that a person acted in life
like a model character in a book. Criseyde gives early evidence of womanly instincts when she sees Troilus riding
by her window in one of the many scenes contrived by
Pandarus which are like model vignettes for a book of
courtly love:

> So lik a man of armes and a knyght
> He was to seen, fulfilled of heigh prowesse;
> For bothe he hadde a body and a myght
> To don that thing, as wel as hardynesse;
> And ek to seen hym in his gere hym dresse,
> So fressh, so yong, so weldy semed he,
> It was an heven upon hym for to see   [II, 631–637].

Clearly, it is the male she sees, and the effect on her is unmistakable: "Criseyda gan al his chere aspien, / And leet it

so softe in hire herte synke" (II, 649–650). But even her unspoken response borrows the mask of the code: "Who yaf me drynke?" (II, 651), which Robinson translates as "Who has given me a love-potion?"—the traditional evasion whereby the courtly hero may satisfy the high principles of his code while abdicating moral responsibility.

This contradiction is at the heart of the dilemma that begins as an ethical question and ends as a literary problem. If Criseyde acts as a courtly figure, she becomes a fictional object but loses her human truth. But can Chaucer, can his reader, can fiction generally, accept characters that have relinquished their human essence? Chaucer's answer is No. It must therefore be clear that at the level of romance, that which Chaucer creates is merely a literary object: not "real life" but a book, something as objectively external to the author as it is to the reader who rejects it. From the start, Chaucer reminds us that he is only transcribing Lollius: every time he himself appears as author, it is in order to draw attention to "mine author." In so doing, he follows Boccaccio, who stated that in the argument he was developing, he did no more than follow someone else's authority: he too was constructing an object that was supposed to look like its object-model—more than merely a conceit, as can be seen through the work of his mature years, the *Decameron*. There, he presents a collection of tales whose effect on the reader is mediated by those who relate them. But the tales that appear at first glance to be the meat of the book turn out to be tales which heighten the reality of the individual storytellers. This need to interpose a mediator between the reader and the story he is telling may explain why Boccaccio inscribed as a subtitle to the *Decameron* "Prince Galeotto." The identity of the subscript's author is a matter of some controversy—as recent a critic as Jean Bourciez thinks the words are someone else's commentary on the "influence pernicieuse" of the book. Still, if one considers that in his introduction, Boccaccio refers to the idle young ladies whose outward modesty conceals burning passion and thoughts of frustrated love, ladies for whom his book will come as solace, it is not farfetched to imagine that the author may have viewed his book from the outside, as an object—not only as a collection of tales that construct the identity of a number of storytellers, but as tales told through storytellers who are drawn from life and whose fictional existence returns to life as the tale they contrive becomes the real object, "the comfort," in Boccaccio's words, for "those whose distress seeks mitigation." The characters of Boccaccio go back, as he himself did, to the treasury of medieval love lore and present to specific readers the book that he, Boccaccio, is writing.

Chaucer's object, like Boccaccio's, is a consciously literary mode. Without Pandarus, that is to say without the power of fiction to mold (and the pretext of that fiction, courtly love), Troilus would be a man incapable of responding to the woman he loves and who pretends to live in that fictional world. But given the fictional resources of Pandarus, a garden grows out of the land of romance in which a woman reads the *Roman de Thèbes* and dreams a courtly dream; a song and its poetry (for Chaucer is also a poet) contrive the charm of bowers that never existed beyond the Hellespont—nor anywhere else perhaps, except in the now yellowing pages of a book—a nightingale, a cedar tree, and a lay of love. To speed the action of the romance along, no fiction is too implausible: Helen herself can be conjured up, and Antigone (out of some other legend?—it does not matter, since in the land of romance they are all more or less Greek, more or less in the same way), so that the lovers can be brought together for one brief moment. And if that does not suffice, there will be torrential rain to trap the couple under one roof, and a lightless world to shield them, and the enchantment of sleep to stay intruders and dispel their own attendants.

This is the part of the work that is what it claims to be: fiction—the conscious imitation of an object. This is the part that comes from Lollius, the *Roman de Thèbes*, the world of constructed artifact. It is the construction of Pandarus who, having contrived this book-as-book and brought about its climax, disappears into that from which he came:

> Quod Pandarus, "Now wol ye wel bigynne.
> Now doth hym sitte, goode nece deere,
> Upon youre beddes syde al ther withinne,
> That ech of yow the bet may other heere."
> And with that word he drow hym to the feere,
> And took a light, and fond his contenaunce,
> As for to looke upon an old romaunce   [III, 974–980].

But if Chaucer were merely to create such an artifact, if he were not distinct from Pandarus, there would be no way for him to express his disapproval, nor would his object be distinguishable from the former objects he is casting aside. The artifact as book thus allows that its characters may be those who in the real world enact the literary ideal of courtly love and thereby achieves a first level of human density: when a human being attempts to pattern himself on a fictional creation, he gives up a part of his human dimension; but when a fictional character supposes a human being enacting it, that fiction draws upon a non-fictional reality.

Once the human element enters, the romance is substantively changed, even though its outer form may not appear to evidence the change: it becomes comic at first and tragic in the end. The comic aspect results from the uneasy confinement of the polymorphous human within the unbending conventions of the code. An already mentioned instance of the foregoing is that of the early Criseyde responding to her situation now as a woman, now as a convention. It might also be Troilus, going from contempt to orthodoxy and, thereupon, being preached to by Pandarus in the name of courtly love:

> "How often hastow maad thi nyce japes,
> And seyd that Loves servantz everichone
> Of nycete ben verray Goodes apes;
>
> .   .   .   .   .
>
> "Now bet thi brest, and sey to God of Love,
> 'Thy grace, lord, for now I me repente . . .' "
>
> [I, 911–933].

Troilus is only too prompt to repent, thereby, as the French might say, executing himself.

Pandarus himself amplifies this comic mode by subverting the already awkward structure into which these characters are attempting to shape themselves: he is a force too great for the object he proposes, and gives too swift an impetus to a ritual whose purpose and whose dignity are measured by the time it requires. Events happen too quickly, too smoothly, without sufficient effort. It is only the one person who should be interested in a speedy conclusion, Troilus, who proceeds in the manner prescribed by the code: all the others are eventually caught up in the frenzy of Pandarus—the woman in Criseyde is more and more in a hurry; Diomede is in a hurry; Chaucer himself is in a hurry (see, e.g., II, 1271–1274).

The comic moment occurs when the mechanical contrivances are so stated as to defeat the human being without any real effort. But when within the same construct the human being asserts himself against his constraint, the result is no longer comic. The first assertion of the person within the structure comes as he questions that structure. Sooner or later, every character in *Troilus* questions the postures through which he moves—even Pandarus, as he pauses to wonder whether his name may not be an ultimate analogue for panderer. As previously noted, a clear-eyed Criseyde soon analyzes her own self-interest within the courtly scheme; Diomede manipulates what he knows of the code to his own purpose; and finally, when after his death he is able to do so, Troilus provides the last commentary. However, these are merely moments when, through the rational part of his characters, Chaucer distances himself from his writing. But there is also the dramatic commentary. It is as people breaking loose from the bounds of courtly confinement that Criseyde and Diomede bring about the downfall of a human being, Troilus, who is insufficiently insulated through even the most rigid compliance with the literary commandments.

In an age when an ethical mode remains only as a literary form, Chaucer is able to use the requirements of that form so as to have it comment upon itself and involve in the commentary the reader ready to reject that form. In creating out of the formal structure of the romance an antiromance, he anticipates his reader in his withdrawal so as to use that very withdrawal as a new form of involvement. It is a structure that allows this sort of complex dialectic between the author and his reader that defines the novel.

3

Cervantes:
Don Quixote

Don Quixote is a book most of whose concerns are, sooner or later, with books. An early and extended indication of this fact is provided by the chapter entitled "Of the great and diverting scrutiny which the curate and the barber made in the library of our ingenious gentleman." [1] Those works of chivalry (and others) containing lies or instances of ignorance are summarily condemned to be burned, as are also those that sin through shortcomings of style—involved conceits, stiffness, or dryness. Considerations of language spare Ariosto in the original but indicate that he would be burned in another tongue—along with all other poor translations, especially those perpetrated on poetry. As the curate moves through Don Quixote's shelves and goes from romance to poetry, he becomes more permissive: it appears that good writing is able to redeem certain works, such as pastorals and poems (in Part

---

[1] I, vi. Unless otherwise indicated, all translations and pagination of the *Don Quixote* refer to the Samuel Putnam edition in two volumes (New York, 1949). The Spanish text is that of *El Ingenioso Hidalgo Don Quijote de la Mancha*, comentado por Don Diego Clemencín (Madrid, 1833–1839).

II, chapter iii, it will be discovered that Vergil and Homer establish literary standards not only for the bachelor but for Don Quixote himself).

In addition to requirements of style, a premium is placed on skill in contriving the book and its episodes, and on the entertainment it is able to provide. Boiardo is kept for his inventiveness. Books like *Palmerin of England*, and *The Fortunes of Love* by Antonio de Lofraso, are spared, the first because it is wise and witty, the second because it is droll and absurd. *Amadis of Gaul* is saved for being the first romance of chivalry in Spain and better than others of its kind—and so is the first part of Cervantes' own *Galatea*, even though its poetry is not up to its plot.

Aside from the book by Lofraso, which the curate discovers with more pleasure "than if they had presented me with a cassock of Florentine cloth," the book that fares best is *Tirant lo Blanch*, which the same curate describes as "a treasure of contentment and a mine of recreation." It is praised for its inventiveness, its fun, its style, and its realism: "Here knights eat and sleep and die in their beds and make their wills before they die and do other things that are never heard of in books of this kind." The curate is referring to the fact that unlike other romances, this one derives its perception from its middle-class point of view: its steadily unidealistic eye turns the traditional abstractions to parody and the aristocratic gestures to burlesque. E. C. Riley calls the book "one of the most disconcertingly ambiguous novels of chivalry ever written. The hero (perhaps the most realistic of all chivalresque heroes), [. . .] is involved, at the court of Constantinople, in a protracted bedroom farce that is very funny" (*Cervantes's Theory of the Novel*, p. 24). It is apparent that the book meets with clemency because it avoids the extravagances that condemn others while redeeming itself through comic excellence and believable characters.[2]

Halfway between the dangerous romances and the sometimes acceptable poetry (less acceptable as epic, more acceptable in its lyric form) is the pastoral. Nine pastorals are identified in Don Quixote's library, but, fewer than half are condemned outright: "They are not harmful like the books of chivalry"; and instead of being referred to as "lies" or "follies," they are called "works of imagination such as may be read without detriment." Besides its stylistic virtues, Cervantes appears to recognize in the well-written pastoral a poetic convention whose improbable mask is less important than the psychological or moral truth that it intends. Even though it disguises its characters and their circumstances, the pastoral attempts an accurate statement about life. One will recall that Huizinga notes in this form a first reaction against the artificiality of the courtly mode (see chapter x, n. 10); the aforementioned *La Galatea* (1585), by Cervantes, is of course a pastoral romance.

Throughout the chapter, the satire cuts both ways: the housekeeper's fearfulness and holy water, the priest's eagerness to burn, are reminders that the Inquisition re-established in 1478 by Ferdinand and Isabella was not abolished in Spain until 1820. This may account for a number of the self-contradictions that reverse praise through subsequent condemnation—an attitude that should be contrasted with that of the bachelor who cites Pliny: "There is no book so

[2] Its author is nevertheless condemned to the galleys by the curate. Riley dispels this apparent contradiction by suggesting that though "the book is commended for its undeniable high qualities [. . .] the author is severely judged for wanting clarity of purpose"—in Riley's translation, "because he did not perpetrate all those absurdities in a calculated manner [*de industria*]."

bad [. . .] that there is not some good in it" (II, iii). The literary comment is somewhat diminished as a result, stating little more than a desire for style, for entertainment through skillful contrivance, and for truth through portrayal—especially when such portrayal will serve to undermine a no longer believable convention. A more detailed analysis must wait until I, xlvii, when it will be furnished by the canon of Toledo.

As against "Milesian fables, which are nonsensical tales designed solely to amuse and not to instruct," the canon constructs an ideal epic which will be capable of both amusement and instruction. He draws on Aristotelian mimesis in asking that fiction be truthful:

And if you should answer me by saying that those who write such books offer them to us as fiction and hence are not obliged to observe the fine points of the truth, I should reply that the falsehood is all the greater when it appears in the guise of truth, and that as fiction, the more it contains of the pleasing and the possible the more it delights us.

But these are things which he cannot accomplish who flees verisimilitude and the imitation of nature, qualities that go to constitute perfection in the art of writing.

Just as sight responds to beauty and harmony, so must the author's craft allow the reader's imagination to respond to his style and plot structure: the first must be pleasing, the second ingenious. It is in these particulars that chivalric writings have failed. And yet, if the epic form is properly handled, it will allow a good mind to display itself and show its knowledge—in the same way as it will allow the virtues that would inform an ideal man to construct one or more ideal characters. As envisaged by Cervantes, the form is sufficiently extensive and supple to display the peculiar qualities of the lyric, epic, tragic, and comic genres, and might be written in either verse or prose.

For in works of fiction there should be a mating between the plot and the reader's intelligence. They should be so written that the impossible is made to appear possible, things hard to believe being smoothed over and the mind held in suspense in such a manner as to create surprise and astonishment while at the same time they divert and entertain so that admiration [*admiración*] and pleasure go hand in hand.

Thus is devised a fiction that instructs and delights, one that spans the centuries in that it combines Aristotle's pleasure in learning and virtues of surprise such as were advocated by Jean Cocteau at the start of his career.

From J. C. Dunlop (*History of Prose Fiction*) to E. C. Riley, commentators on Cervantes have pointed out that little is new or original in his esthetics. We will have occasion to note his conformity to Golden Age criteria with reference to his readers. "Admiración," the theory that the reader's pleasure must be in part a wonderment tinged with awe, is not unlike the theory that was being propounded in Spain at the time by such theorists as Alonso López Pinciano (*Filosophía antigua poética*, 1596) or Francisco Cascales (*Tablas poéticas*, 1617).[3] Mention has already been made of Cervantes' debt to the *Poetics*,[4] his

---

[3] See, among the references cited in this chapter, D. Clemencín's commentary and E. C. Riley's *Cervantes's Theory of the Novel* (especially pp. 88 ff.). Note also Riley's indications of other theories which Cervantes might have been acquainted with, such as the *Rhetorica ad Herennium* and Tasso on heroic poetry.

[4] Which although not translated into Spanish until 1626 had been given currency through such writings as El Pinciano's. Moreover, Cervantes was in Italy after the publication of Castelvetro's *Poetica d'Aristotele* (1570).

acknowledgment of Homer and Vergil among the classics, Boiardo and Ariosto among the moderns. Certainly, his formulations in the *Quixote* (or in such of his other writings as raise literary questions, for example some of the *Exemplary Novels*) fail to hint at the complexity or the devices that fashion his great novel. Other than general pronouncements about style, structural harmony, and inventiveness, one is left with a statement of subversion, for the sake of sanity and entertainment, of forms that have lost their significance, and in particular, the romance once it has degenerated, in the words of Menéndez-Pidal, from "heroic effort" to "arbitrary effort." [5]

Still, such terms as "entertaining," "pleasing," "instruction," "admiration" suppose the satisfaction of a public, and their exact meaning cannot be ascertained without ascertaining the nature of that public. It is an obviously considerable body: "Little children leaf through [the *Don Quixote*], young people read it, adults appreciate it, and the aged sing its praises" (II, iii). But the words of the bachelor fail to analyze qualitatively this body which the first Prologue had called "that venerable legislator." Since that same Prologue had stated that "the entire work is an attack upon the books of chivalry" but had admitted that these enjoy authority and prestige "among the vulgar," it follows that the "legislator" whom the author had in mind was not any public. Though he undoubtedly wished to be read by everyone (and presumably was), Cervantes appears repeatedly to sense the existence of two kinds of readers, one "vulgar," the other "discriminating." It will be remembered that when the canon of Toledo "was once tempted to write a book of chivalry," he submitted the

[5] Ramón Menéndez Pidal, "The Genesis of 'Don Quixote,'" in *Cervantes across the Centuries,* ed. Angel Flores and M. J. Bernardete.

manuscript "to certain individuals who are passionately fond of this type of reading. Some of these persons were wise and learned, while others were ignorant, being concerned solely with the pleasure they derive from listening to nonsense" (I, xlviii). As E. C. Riley suggests, Cervantes assumed "that there would be among his readers a privileged body of initiates and others, the majority, outside the secret [. . .] this corresponds to the usual division Golden-Age writers made between the two classes of the public, the *discretos* and the *vulgo*" (*Cervantes's Theory of the Novel*, p. 108). The words of the canon are interesting: for both kinds of readers the text is identical and, quantitatively, so is the pleasure. But the quality of the pleasure is different, and the passionate fondness, though felt by each, remains in one group at the level of wisdom and learning, while in the other it turns the same book into "nonsense." Though the implications of their judgments are far-reaching, these people are talking about books of chivalry; we must suppose that the enjoyment of each group is derived from the *pattern* of these books, the weave of their adventures, but the vulgar who perceive only such a surface (or the "Vulgar" book that allows only such superficial perception) achieve no more than "nonsense," whereas that surface *pattern* allows a more discriminating reader (assuming an equally discriminating book) to reach beyond it to what we have termed *life*. Thus is resolved the distinction drawn by the bachelor between poet and historian—"The former may narrate or sing of things not as they were but as they should have been; the latter must describe them not as they should have been but as they were" (II, iii). *Things as they should have been* refer to the noncontingent *life* of the individual; *things as they were* refer to the contingencies that may subvert him but are nevertheless the only record that *pattern* is allowed. However, if it becomes possible to discern *life* beyond the *pattern* of even a novel of chivalry, then the cognition of poetry has been achieved, and the work is not unlike the writings of Vergil and Homer. The strategy of Cervantes will thus be to write a tale of knightly adventures to capitalize on "the authority and prestige which books of chivalry enjoy in the world at large" (I, Prologue), but in such a way as to conciliate as well the *discretos*, the "discerning few" whose praise is important (I, xlviii).

An exemplary hero, performing in an esthetically unified fiction that allows the operation of the lyric and tragic modes in order to provide entertainment and instruction, puts a number of demands on the fiction and the reader. To be exemplary, that hero requires a superhuman dimension; but if his fiction is to afford a tragic view, the character's reality (*life*) must be endowed by the reader: the character must be such as to enable the reader to become him. (In Aristotle it is the tragic flaw that permits contact between the spectator and an otherwise superior hero.) Such characterization and fiction would provide "instruction" through exemplariness and acceptance. But Cervantes also equates learning and amusement. (The curate repeatedly uses with approval such adjectives as "witty," "droll," "amusing." And the canon includes the comic as one of the major genres of the epic.) Still, it is doubtful whether even a form as protean as the one envisaged by the canon would enable an exemplary hero to survive for any length of time if he had to perform within a comic context devised for the sake of a contrastive lesson (certainly the organic quality of the esthetic texture would be in jeopardy). It would therefore seem that if the moral les-

son is going to be achieved through comic effect, there is
every likelihood that the very hero will be ultimately comical—a contingency that the author may well wish to anticipate.

If these criteria are to be applied to the chivalric novel,
it will somehow have to draw attention to the shortcomings of its predecessors without giving evidence of
their flaws and devise for its purpose a character whose
comic gesture will mock the ill-conceived gesture of his
models without allowing it to destroy him. The traditional
hero of chivalry becomes literarily reprehensible in his
"arbitrary effort" when his superhuman dimensions no
longer convince the reader. As such, he is annoying, not
comical, since there is only the reader's feeling of nonacceptance to condemn him. This nonacceptance eventually incriminates the rest of the fiction, inasmuch as it separates the reader from his reading instead of separating him
from only a predelimited part of it. If the hero is to be deliberately comical—that is, if he is to perform roughly the
same gesture, but as self-criticism and without alienating
the reader—that gesture must be set against a normative
mode, against reproof *within* the book. The comic anti-
hero may remain roughly the same as his model, but he
must operate against a point of view: something in his
landscape must be altered (as, for example, in *Tirant lo
Blanch*); the author himself must appraise him differently
and in such a way as to let the reader know.

Don Quixote is in fact an exemplary hero. Though be-
moaning unseemly interests in books of chivalry, the
canon describes him as a man "worthy and respected and
endowed with so fine a mind" (I, xlix). When the gentleman from La Mancha defends his readings against the
canon, he points to their didactic and moral virtues. It is

certainly true that nowhere has Cervantes drawn his hero so as to cast doubt on what he says about himself: "I may say that, since becoming a knight-errant, I am brave, polite, liberal, well-bred, generous, courteous, bold, gentle, patient, and long-suffering" (I, 1). No more than Chaucer to the spirit of courtly love does Cervantes object to the essence of chivalry—both men are criticizing an overlay, the gesture that has grown distinct from the spiritual truth meant to inform it, and more particularly that literature which is the ultimate shape of this formalism. Like Troilus caught in the intricacies of a code that no longer matches a human reality because it has grown beyond its human purpose, Don Quixote performs gestures that have nothing to do with the exemplary human being which he is; this is the essence of his "madness." He cannot distinguish between the virtues that give him both his substance and his dignity, and an illusion created by the ritualization of those virtues—which ritualization he has chosen to accept as total, for it must be made clear that Don Quixote is never enacting a role: even when he decides to feign madness in the Cardenio episode, he is drawing from an inner landscape and his models exist within him; he had passed the stage of imitation before the book began. For him, as for the Caligula of Camus, there is no metaphor, there is no verbal world: his world can be formulated only existentially or not at all.

But in contrast to the conventional novel of chivalry, for which this absolute vision also represents the totality of the fictional world, Cervantes does not assume responsibility for the world of Don Quixote. In fact, the author is so concerned to establish his distance from his writing that he emerges as one of the main characters—or, more accurately, as many. For Cervantes, as for the reader, *Don*

Quixote is a fiction on which they both comment as they progress through it together. Cervantes remains the author only in that he manipulates the *object* of his creation; that object is never supposed to become, at the first level of its apprehension, a fiction whose autonomy and verisimilitude are such as to lure the reader into acceptance and belief. The most obvious instance of such control has already been alluded to; it occurs at the end of I, viii, when the author, "excusing himself upon the ground that he has been unable to find anything else to set forth," leaves his hero and the Biscayan as they are about to go at each other. Putnam, *Don Quixote's* translator, reminds us that "breaking off the tale between one part of a work and the following one is common in the romances of chivalry" (I, viii, n. 6; he is presumably referring to such works as *La Araucana* by Ercilla, an epic poem that uses the device). But this is not the breaking-off of a tale: this is the deliberate freezing of spirited motion for the pleasure of reducing two characters, including the hero, to the state of mere objects. (Is there not already a hint of parody in the anonymous *Oliveros de Castilla* when the author stays the sword raised over the head of Queen Helen?)

Contempt for the character is not so different in its manner from other, more overt intrusions by the author upon his own fictional progress. In II, v, as "translator," he steps aside from his fiction to surmise that the present development may well be apocryphal. (In II, xxiv, Cid Hamete similarly dismisses the entire Montesinos episode.) But this surmise is scarcely an argument for the truth of the rest. From the very first, when the author casts some doubt as to the sequence of the events to come ("Certain authors say that his first adventure was that of Puerto Lápice, while others state that it was that of the windmills" [I, ii]), through the numerous chapter headings that advertise their own veracity and the factual quality of the "history" they relate, it is obvious that Cervantes is in fact asserting the nongenuineness of the world he is contriving. As a theorist, he is too concerned with the need for esthetic, intellectual, and structural verisimilitude to assume that any part of the descriptive fiction can be anything but bad faith, and he insists on being the first one to point this out at all times. In fact, his intrusion is so constant that it constitutes a fiction within the fiction—one clearly distinguishable from moments when he appears as himself, as in the already noted passage in II, xliv, where in pride and some irritation he draws attention to the merits of a second part that does not contain the digressions of the first.

Presumably because his intrusion is in danger of being rejected by the reader as no better than a fiction within the fiction, Cervantes anticipates him once more and deliberately fictionalizes himself into several intermediaries. The author of the book is merely "that curious-minded one who was at pains to have it translated from the Arabic" (II, iii)—a reference to the passage (I, ix) where, following the interruption of the fight between the Biscayan and Don Quixote, an "I" intervenes who will discover the sequel and give a Spanish-speaking Moor the task of translating it (even though the narrative had begun with an unmediated "I" that sounded until the end of chapter viii like the single author). The sequel is given as no more than a transcription, this one by an Arabic historian, Cid Hamete Benengeli, whose varying fortunes are worthy of note. We have already had occasion to point out in Chapter 1 that Cid Hamete acquires gestures and a dimension of his own; these frequently bear a suspicious resemblance to the

"I" of Book I (the Moor's final address to his pen in II,
lxxiv, for example, uses words and thoughts from the Prologue to Book I). But he can be turned into a mere joke
just as easily, as when Don Quixote refers to him in the future tense ("the sage who is to write the history of my exploits"—as is done for all famous knight-errants) in order
to account for an event that has already taken place: Sancho Panza is informed by his master, "It must have been
that sage [. . .] who put it into your mind and on your
tongue to dub me the Knight of the Mournful Countenance" (I, xix). Such dismissal reduces the figure to no
more than a moment of the author's playfulness within the
narrative.

Cid Hamete serves, however, a more important function; once he is established as a fictional entity, he can be
laden with the sins of the author's fiction: he is after all an
Arab, "and that nation is known for its lying propensities" (I, ix)—and for good measure, the translator is an
Arab also. Thereafter, it will be simple enough to shrug
off the fiction by saying, as does Sancho, "The one who
wrote the story must have made a mistake" (II, iv)—while
at other times Cid Hamete can be given as the model of all
accurate historians (both assertations having roughly the
same meaning). And should even greater flexibility be
needed, the Arab historian is also a "wise enchanter," and
"nothing that they choose to write about is hidden from
those who practice that art" (II, ii).

These instances of the writer's detachment from his
writing can be thought of only as a parafictional conversation of the author with his reader: it is certainly not at the
level of verisimilitude, or "history," or epic exemplariness
that Don Quixote is secure. As the knight is riding out on
his first sally, the author has him speculate how the future

chronicler of his deeds will set them forth, and as he rides, he composes in words the first page which he is enacting;

"No sooner had the rubicund Apollo spread over the face of the broad and spacious earth the gilded filaments of his beauteous locks, and no sooner had the little singing birds of painted plumage greeted with their sweet and mellifluous harmony the coming of the Dawn, who, leaving the soft couch of her jealous spouse, now showed herself to mortals at all the doors and balconies of the horizon that bounds La Mancha— no sooner had this happened than the famous knight, Don Quixote de la Mancha, forsaking his own downy bed and mounting his famous steed, Rocinante, fared forth and began riding over the ancient and famous Campo de Montiel" [I, ii].

This dithyrambic quotation is immediately followed by the author's own affirmation: "And this was the truth, for he was indeed riding over that stretch of plain." Not only has Don Quixote composed his fiction too late and in a style that is hopelessly out of keeping with its context, but the author (while confirming his hero) cancels even the fictional value of Don Quixote's words through his parafictional comment.

It is thus at the level of the parafictional comment that the illusive author must be sought: the subversions of the knight's fancies, the words of the canon on literature, the author placing a supposedly factual blame on his printers (II, xxvii), his remarks on the essential quality of the novelettes of the first part and their "fine craftsmanship" (II, xliv) most likely represent the moments when Cervantes is writing with least guile. Similarly, it might be assumed that he drops most of his literary disguises in the fictional inserts, those same novelettes, which, since they do not exist

wholly for the purpose of commenting on the hero, may
well represent for the author parentheses of a more gratuitous nature.

Among the longer inserts of the first part is the Cardenio episode. It begins with an extended account of the
mad hermit's doings and, as such, is closely interwoven
with the progress of Don Quixote. But it links up subsequently with the otherwise less necessary story of Dorotea
in order to form a romance in pastoral setting with a
happy ending. As early as the curate's inquisition upon the
books of Don Quixote, it has been shown that the pastoral
enjoys a position of relative immunity among literary genres. This one exhibits many virtues of the genre: the shepherds are plain (as plain as Sancho, the latter tells us), but
they are neither coarse nor droll—they act with dignity
and understanding; they are not covetous (as is Sancho),
they share their food and attempt to help Cardenio. Attention is repeatedly called to the fact that Cardenio himself is
"wellborn and well reared" (I, xxiii): he once was "a
youth of well-bred manners and appearance"; he writes
"in a very good hand" (I, xxiii), sings well, composes
fine sonnets (at least one of which was good enough for
Cervantes to use again in another work,[6] and after six
months in the wilderness of the Sierra Morena, he is still
amber-scented, as befits a young man of quality. He has
been driven mad by what he believes to be the unfaithful-
ness of Luscinda and the treason of his friend Fernando,
but when he is sane, he is very sane: although once interrupted by Don Quixote, it is he who tells the story leading
up to his madness in an acutely perceptive way; he notes
the envy of the servants in the household of Duke Ricardo

[6] In his comedy *La Casa de los Celos y Selvas de Ardenia.* (See
Putnam, ed., *Don Quixote*, I, 23, n. 8.)

(I, xxiv); his observations about young love and pleasure are accurate; he is aware of the mercy of heaven and the unreasonableness of his ways (I, xxvii). The disguise of the pastoral is outlandish, but its psychological portrayal is accurate, and this is especially important because Cardenio is also mad.

Cardenio's madness is active and factual. Its object, Luscinda, is real, as the story of Dorotea will confirm—the vision of Cardenio can be substantiated by that of another human being. When a fit seizes him, he knocks down Don Quixote, Sancho Panza, and the goatherd, thus not only marking sharply the discontinuity between his sane and insane moments, but giving evidence that the insane moments can affect the world around him. Significantly, his madness is related to Don Quixote's world through the interference of literature. In the sane recounting of his story, Cardenio reaches the moment when Luscinda asked him for a copy of *Amadis of Gaul*—at which point Don Quixote interrupts, praises Luscinda for enjoying such literature, and thus jeopardizes her as a serious figure. Cardenio then goes mad (not because of the book, but because of the interruption) and shows his insanity in the usual way —through assault; this time, however, he directs it against the novel: "I am convinced that great villain of an Elisabat was living in adultery with the Queen Madásima" (I, xxiv).

Cardenio is a calculus within the imaginary world of Don Quixote and acts as a catalyst; he is a tangible proof that moves Don Quixote, within the fiction that is his madness, to enact a conscious fiction, an exemplary madness of his own inspired by the reality of Cardenio. As usual, the surface of forms will turn the knight away from his spiritual purpose—this time because the substance eludes him; Cardenio went mad because of Luscinda, but the Don, whereas he is mad in the eyes of the world, has never conceived the figment of his imagination as a Luscinda. When the logical Sancho points out that fact to his master, he receives a magnificent reply:

That is the beautiful part of it. What thanks does a knight-errant deserve for going mad when he has good cause? The thing to do is to go out of my head without any occasion for it, thus letting my lady see, if I do this for her in the dry, what I would do in the wet [I, xxv].

But over and above his character, Don Quixote cannot achieve genuine madness: he acts only *"as if* he really had lost his senses" (I, xxv—our italics). Aside from two or three desultory somersaults, he soon returns to declamatory affirmations; his insanity reverts once again to literature. In the end, he bogs down in a discussion of technicalities with Sancho, and the experiment fails.

The reality of Cardenio emphasizes the literary quality of Don Quixote. It has been pointed out already that one of his discrepancies within this fiction is that the *style* of his own fiction is out of place (I, ii). This is not a conventional madness, as has been shown by the author's "as if" (I, xxv); instead of representing the break with a reality that can be confirmed through someone else's eyes, his is the altogether personal vision of a man replacing that reality with the constructs of literature: "Everything that this adventurer of ours thought, saw, or imagined seemed to him to be directly out of one of the storybooks he had read"; "and so he went on, stringing together absurdities, all of a kind thath is books had taught him, imitating insofar as he was able the language of their authors" (I, ii). Other than his difficulties with language, his "imitation" should not be viewed as effort, or even as a conscious process; such a view would distort the nature of his delusion. Had it represented mere volition, he would have been an author (and had not authors been ultimately creatures of language): "Many a time he was tempted to take up his pen and literally finish the tale [of Don Belianís of Greece]" (I, i). But this vision has grown, before we ever encounter Don Quixote, from volition to existential perfection.

To what extent Don Quixote is a creature of his vision can be ascertained through the episode of the Montesinos cave, inasmuch as it represents, symbolically and analytically, a descent into the hero. Since, when Sancho and the bachelor's cousin pull Don Quixote out of the cave, "to all appearances, he was sound asleep" (II, xxii), the author is forced to give up at least a part of his subverting commentary in order to present a dream, affording a somewhat less mediated image of the inner hero than that which generally describes him from the outside. As might be expected, the gentleman from La Mancha constructs crystal-walled castles and magically delightful scenes out of the full sumptuousness of his literary imagination, and peoples them with all the requisite characters of fiction. But withal, he retains a surprisingly sharp eye and the attention to detail of a shopkeeper. He is interested to find out that Durandarte had his heart cut out with a poniard instead of a dagger as is generally believed; he is shown Durandarte in the traditional state of the *gisant*, but cannot help noticing that his arm is "somewhat hairy and sinewy"; he is told that the victim's heart weighed fully two pounds and was kept relatively fresh by being sprinkled with salt; he has some difficulty with the appearance of the heroine Belerma, who is missing a number of her pure-white teeth, has a flat nose and a distressingly poor complexion which will have to be accounted for by Montesinos himself as being due to sorrow rather than menstrual difficulty, "for it has been many months and even years since she has had that experience" (II, xxiii). While stumbling over nearly every detail of the story, he never stops to question the atrocious corruption of the over-all epic. Even in a dream, he confuses past and present, allows the interference of characters from other legends, intrudes Dulcinea, for whom he has to stand up as usual (though she acts in a rather equivocal way), and faces the same rebuffs as in life. He does not appear to allow any of this to cast doubt on his sense of himself, even when Montesinos introduces him as "the famous Don Quixote de la Mancha" to Durandarte and is able to elicit from the latter only, "And even if it be not so, O cousin, I say to you: patience, and shuffle." Don Quixote rejects even the suspicion of a dream, being able to vouch for the veracity of it all through "the coherence of his thoughts."

That dream cannot be said to portray the inner man accurately, since it is clear that, even in his sleep, Don Quixote remains the victim of Cervantes. But it helps to determine the limits within which the character has been drawn: although his vision of the world is wholly literary, he does not reject, as do his forebears in novels of chivalry, the evidence of a world whose detail is eliminated by the heroic vision; Don Quixote merely rearranges that evidence to suit his literary construct. It is he who turns out to be the "wise enchanter," since, under normal circumstances, he is able to transmute objects, situations, and people to his purpose, even when they are not already, like Cardenio, a part of the literary mode.[7]

It is at the level of words, his own and those of others, that Don Quixote is least successful: his is an assimilative eye and a creative imagination, but for as long as he plays a role he can neither formulate that vision nor cope with the verbal formulation of others, since language alone does not give him the substance on which to base his imaginings. His apostrophes to Apollo and the dawn are part of his definition within the author's fiction, but as the Don's attempt to create fiction they fail because they are merely inappropriate words. His other verbal attempts at literature—his letters and his verse—are likewise inappropriate (even though in imitation of the successful Cardenio's).[8] It is here that can be predicted the futility of his arguments with Sancho (who is highly successful in creating a texture of words, even though that texture does not necessarily express him),[9] as when the latter attempts to demonstrate the nonexistence of Dulcinea: at such moments, his efforts and those of his master amount to little more than the sterile confrontation of two verbal definitions;

---

[7] It is perhaps here that must be sought what R. Girard terms "ontological health," even though he is somewhat reluctant to grant it to the hero (*Mensonge romantique et vérité romanesque*, p. 147).

[8] E. Auerbach believes that Don Quixote is the direct beneficiary of Cervantes' "beautifully articulated and musical bravura pieces of chivalric rhetoric" (*Mimesis*, p. 300), as in his address to Sancho's materialization of Dulcinea (II, 10); but even then, his words contrast comically with the crude speech of the peasant girls and certainly fail to convey any meaning to them.

[9] The argument remains substantially the same if we accept Riley's view that the proverbs of Sancho represent his peasant wisdom, but his misuse of them shows his lack of formal education (*op. cit.*, pp. 69-70).

Sancho cannot reconstruct a figment of his master's making, and his master cannot interpret words that fail to penetrate those figments. It is with evident relief that Don Quixote returns from the shadow of verbal constructs to the substance of objects whose very being releases him from any responsibility for their existence: "This that appears to you as a barber's basin is for me Mambrino's helmet, and something else again to another person" (I, xxv). Over a long enough period of time, this tenacity constructs his character and becomes a defining truth; but it is doubtful whether, as merely the stubborn creator of a literary world that has been rejected, Don Quixote would be able to find acceptance in the reality of the reader. Cervantes will rely on a far more elaborate scheme in order to achieve that aim.

Answering an unspoken question of Don Antonio Moreno, the Knight of the White Moon says:

"I am well aware that you have come to find out who I am; and, seeing that there is no denying you the information that you seek, while my servant here is removing my armor I will tell you the exact truth of the matter. I would have you know, sir, that I am the bachelor Sansón Carrasco from the same village as Don Quixote de la Mancha, whose madness and absurdities inspire pity in all of us who know him and in none more than me. And so, being convinced that his salvation lay in his returning home for a period of rest in his own house, I formed a plan for bringing him back.

"It was three months ago that I took to the road as a knight-errant, calling myself the Knight of the Mirrors, with the object of fighting and overcoming him without doing him any harm, intending first to lay down the condition that the vanquished was to yield to the victor's will. What I meant to ask of him—for I looked upon him as conquered from the start—was that he should return to his village and not leave it for a whole year, in the course of which time he might be cured. Fate, however, ordained things otherwise; for he was the one who conquered me and overthrew me from my horse, and thus my plan came to naught" [II, lxv].

Like nearly any passage that might be taken at random from the book, this one repays a second reading. Carrasco is first encountered in Book II (chapter ii), through his report to Sancho Panza that Book I now exists in print. In II, vii, he represents himself to the housekeeper of Don Quixote as "a bachelor of Salamanca and that means the best there is"—"no hay más que bachillear"—a misuse for *bachillerear* and a *double-entendre*, since according to Clemencín (*Don Quijote*, p. 43) the *Bachiller* is "he who receives the first honorific rank granted by a University in recognition of achievement," though "familiar speech customarily uses the name in ill part, calling *bachiller* one who speaks a lot and with impudence, and using the verb *bachillerear* in the sense of talking a great deal, with boldness but little reason" (author's translation). The personage is thus verbal, intelligent, and unlikely to accept or respect that which his mind refuses. This means that like nearly everyone else in the book, Carrasco will be at least double—someone who does, and yet does not quite, live up in body and spirit to what his titles promise: "although his name was Sansón, or Samson, [he] was not very big so far as bodily size went, but he was a great joker, with a sallow complexion and a ready wit" (II, iii).

Appearing before Don Antonio disguised as the Knight of the White Moon, the bachelor removes his armor before conveying the truth, as if it were first necessary for him to shed the world of make-believe into which he had entered. He is convinced that Don Quixote is a creature of "madness and absurdities" ("locura y sandez") and is per-

suaded that he knows the best way to effect what he terms
the Don's "salvation." His disguises are necessary to enter
into Don Quixote's world, but they are also meant to
usurp the Don's significance within that world: in his first
sally, Carrasco went forth as the Knight of the Mirrors,
wearing over his armor a cassock "all bespangled with glittering mirrors that resembled little moons" (II, xiv), a disguise that revealed only the identity of the beholder—in
this case, Don Quixote's.[10] And as the Knight of the
White Moon, he once again takes on symbolically the
character of Don Quixote, the latter's well-known pallor,
his "mournful countenance," his prevailing mood—his
very lunacy (moons being a part of both disguises).

Once he has determined to save Don Quixote, the bachelor proceeds with the determination of his convictions:
this creature of dreams must logically yield to the power
of the mind. However, the world of Don Quixote does
not yield as effortlessly as the bachelor has hoped: "Dig-
ging his spurs with all his might into Rocinante's lean
flanks [Don Quixote] caused that animal to run a bit for
the first and only time" (II, xiv). And, through a combination of accidents, he is able to charge and overturn his
opponent, who has paused in his tracks (Carrasco's steed
being "no swifter nor any more impressive-looking than
Rocinante").

With reference to the world of Don Quixote, the bach-
elor has been in an ambiguous position from the start.
When Sancho informs Don Quixote that, according to
Carrasco, they now exist in print, his master first assures
Sancho that the miracle must be the work of "some wise

[10] For a modern version of the same idea, see, e.g., Georges-
Emmanuel Clancier, *Les Incertains.*

enchanter," but he urges his man to fetch the bachelor because of what appears to be a certain uneasiness: "I am astonished by what you have told me and shall not eat a mouthful that sets well on my stomach until I have learned all about it"(II, ii). When they meet, the bachelor demonstrates that—in the author's words—he is "fond of jests" by going down on his knees and paying elaborate homage to the Don. So doing, he assumes two curiously contradictory roles: he is the reporter of a fact that is accurate both within and without the fiction of which he is a part, while at the same time he remains sceptical in his present role within that fiction.

When their conversation turns to literature (as so frequently happens in this story), the bachelor's role becomes even more complicated. It is, as usual, Sancho who brings things down to earth: as they deplore the record of beatings suffered by Don Quixote, his perceptive and nonidealizing squire remarks that it is there that the truth of the story comes in—to which the master retorts that such unseemly details might have been omitted in all fairness, since "Aeneas was not as pious as Vergil would have us believe, nor was Ulysses as wise as Homer depicts him" (II, iii). The Aeneas of Vergil and the Ulysses of Homer are not characters drawn from the romances which Don Quixote admires and the author rejects; they are traditional figures of greatness in a noncontroverted literature whose dignity stems precisely from the author's ability to stylize along the lines of greatness. At this point, the student from Salamanca is allowed to make an important literary distinction: "That is true [. . .] but it is one thing to write as a poet and another as a historian." This picks up a familiar statement (see for example Don Quixote himself in I, xxv)

whose repetition appears to be more than inadvertence or
a casual part of the fiction.[11] The assertion informs the
reader that he is dealing with a chronicle (or a "history,"
as it will be called throughout) whose virtue is in its exact
notation. We have had occasion to indicate previously
how deliberately fraudulent are Cervantes' claims to historical accuracy. Still, the statement is a reminder that even
though this fiction can make no claim to historical truth,
there may yet be truth of another sort to be found in the
notation of *life* as it is, when contrasted with the fraudulence of a genre that attempts to impose upon this *life* the
mere pretense of things "as they should have been" (II,
iii); and that at one level at least, even though Cervantes
separates himself from his hero, his reader will have to find
a part of the novel's truth in the accurate surface notations
of a *pattern*.

As the discussion proceeds, its three participants continue their curious evolution. Carrasco informs them that
the "Story of the One Who Was Too Curious for His
Own Good" has been criticized as an irrelevant insert.
Upon hearing this, Sancho calls the author a "son of a
dog," and even his more circumspect master is moved to
change his mind abruptly, declaring that "the author of
this book was not a sage but some ignorant prattler." It is
the bachelor who is again given the serious comment: "It
affords the pleasantest and least harmful reading of any
book that has been published up to now." But his previous
words notwithstanding, the bachelor will eventually move

[11] The relative merits of poetic insight and historical truth are a
substantial topic of literary debate during the Golden Age: note,
for example, the already mentioned writings of El Pinciano (on
which, *vide* W. C. Atkinson, "Cervantes, El Pinciano and the
Novelas ejemplares," *Hispanic Review*, XVI [July 1948]). For a
detailed treatment of this question, see E. C. Riley, *op. cit.*

from his former convictions to entirely different ones and begin believing the present fiction over the former: "Although he had read the First Part of the history, he never would have believed that the squire was as droll as he was depicted there. But as he now heard him [. . .] he was convinced of the truth of it all" (II, vii); this change of belief represents the first step taken by Sansón Carrasco on the road that will lead him into the heart of Don Quixote's world as the Knight of the Mirrors and the Knight of the White Moon.

The bachelor is not the first one who must reach Don Quixote by entering into his world even though he rejects it—in fact, *because* he rejects it: the hero, who cannot contrive a verbal fiction, is so possessed of his existential fiction that even the pragmatist Carrasco must submit to it. But before Carrasco, such figures of sanity as Dorotea, Fernando, the priest, the barber, and even, to a certain extent, the canon of Toledo,[12] were forced to accept its modes in order to defeat it. In the second book, however, something happens that quickens the pace and the intensity of these intrusions. Sancho Panza, being unable to find Dulcinea, decides to create her on the spur of the moment. The bachelor disguises himself as the Knight of the Mirrors and comes riding into the Don's world. And at the center of the book, occupying by far the largest part, is the wholly staged and spurious world of the Duke and the Duchess. Here are impersonated for the knight his most

---

[12] The canon of Toledo, the most articulate spokesman for sanity in literature, does not fare too well when he comes up against the maddest representative of that literature. He is "amazed at the manner in which Don Quixote jumbled truth and falsehood" (I, 49) to the extent that he had to concede points in such a manner as to be thrown off the logical progress of his own argument and remained at a loss for suitable rejoinders.

sacred imaginings, from Merlin to Dulcinea. Magic is created and adventures are rehearsed; Sancho Panza's island is materialized. When Don Quixote is able at last to escape with his squire from the very real grip of this nonillusory world, he encounters people talking about the *second* part of his history, the one he is supposedly in the process of enacting. He meets a historical figure, the Catalan outlaw Roque Guinart (Roca Guinarda), known throughout Spain at this moment of the Don's wanderings (later on, to make things complete, he will meet a fictional character out of an apocryphal book—Don Alvaro Tarfe); he is thrown into contact with the crowds of Barcelona that cheer and mock him; he encounters a talking head that has some doubts about the Montesinos adventure. It is after all these adventures, and others of the same kind, that the Knight of the White Moon comes along to vanquish him.

It is not enough to say that the Knight of the White Moon forces his way as a tangible evidence into the world of Don Quixote. In so doing, he first determines to subvert a genuine vision through a fraudulent substance. But in addition, this substantial reality not only desires to destroy the personality of Don Quixote by defeating him, but, as noted, does so in the guise of a symbol meant to usurp the symbolism of the knight from La Mancha. In Volume II, as never before, the personality, the very being of Don Quixote, is challenged—and the substantive world that assaults his vision is both deliberate and malevolent. When Sancho Panza creates Dulcinea, he does so without expending any effort: the first girl he sees coming his way on a donkey will do as well as the next. Cervantes and Sancho Panza combine to make the vision as inappropriate as possible: "All that he could see in her was a village wench, and not a very pretty one at that, for she was round-faced and snub-nosed" (II, x). The Don opposes the combined evi-

dence of his exacting eye and his inner vision, but this is
not the first time that he has had doubts, and the scheme
of Sancho succeeds: "Don Quixote was deeply dejected as
he thought of the cruel joke which the enchanters had
played upon him" (II, xi). His exacting eye notwithstanding, he is now unsure of the evidence of his senses—it is
becoming difficult for him to integrate his outer and inner
landscapes. When the cart of the Parliament of Death rolls
into view, he is tempted to take the masks of the players at
face value. But the players give him "a most civil reply"
(II, xi) and re-establish a human reality that Don Quixote
might not have questioned formerly (the mask of a demon
was not sufficient to construct a demon for him prior to
this, when this evidence always came from within him); he
begins to wonder whether that inner vision suffices: "I
perceive now that one must actually touch with his hands
what appears to the eye if he is to avoid being deceived."

After he has defeated the Knight of the Mirrors, Don
Quixote forces him to confess that he believes in all the
trappings of the Quixotic vision, "just as I am convinced
that you, though you appear to be the bachelor Sansón
Carrasco, are another person in his form and likeness" (II,
xiv). But the victory leaves more doubt than elation, and
in the next chapter, the knight is still trying to dispel the
evidence of the bachelor through the process of a rational
argument with his squire. Viewed in the sequence of these
doubts, the Montesinos dream may be more than simple
fun on the part of Cervantes: it may show the persistence
of these questions in the Don's very dreams. (There is
some evidence for this speculation in that when, very
much later, he reaches Barcelona, the episode is still sufficiently on his mind for him to ask the oracle of the talking
head about it.)

The Duke and the Duchess provide, in the words of

Waldo Frank, "perhaps the ugliest episode in the book." [13] For their own entertainment, these two idle and affluent patrons will give their parlor games the gamier taste of the hunt: at the heart of their make-believe, they place a human being, Don Quixote, whom they will hound and corner mercilessly. Even when their guest must take to bed (for five days) as the result of wounds suffered in this sport, they will find ways of continuing their fun with him. When their victim goes forth at last, he is, according to Frank, "aware of the subtle poison of their praise" (p. 192), and the foundation of his worlds has been further unsettled. Sancho himself, literally crushed by evidence of the materialization of his dream, ends up sadistically "mauled and trampled." [14]

The inner vision becomes harder and harder to preserve. There are more and more intrusions from the outer world, and these are self-contradictory, capricious, illogical, transitory: they assert themselves but provide no secure basis for their assertion. As Don Quixote says, his "eye" now requires his "touch"; but what he touches (the many masks and disguises) may well be fradulent; when genuine, the evidence is even more disturbing: the Knight of the Mirrors has already spoken of strange reflections—he has supposedly defeated Don Quixote in the past; when Don Quixote wins the tilt, he can only make Carrasco confess that the spurious Don Quixote "was some other that re-

---

[13] "The Career of the Hero," in *Cervantes across the Centuries*, ed. Angel Flores and M. J. Bernardete.

[14] II, liii. It becomes increasingly difficult as one proceeds through Book II to understand Auerbach's belief that tragic complications are "completely lacking" (*Mimesis*, p. 303) and that, in the second part, "the gaiety is even more relaxed and elegant" (p. 305)—just as, in view of Cervantes' constant manipulation, it is hard to understand how "he does not take sides [. . .] he remains neutral" (p. 313).

sembled him" (II, xiv). But this is hardly satisfactory: this new eidolon becomes more and more troublesome; he is a fictional and a nonfictional reality, the hero of Book I. But he exists also as the fictional and nonfictional reality of a Book II, obviously an apocryphal work, since Don Quixote's present anguish is evidence of the fact that Book II is still in progress. More and more the planes of truth and falsehood, illusion and reality, historical fact and fictional construct are being shifted, interchanged, confused, subverted. Don Quixote has always had to cope with the demons and enchanters of his vision; now he must cope also with the meddlesomeness of a world that is aware of him and of his vision, and with an author who is intent on questioning the nature of seeming and substance, of fiction and reality.

The world has been turned into a frame of reference so frequently counterfeit and so deliberately manipulated that even Sancho, who has always been close to the Castilian earth, is ultimately at a loss to formulate his own being clearly; he identifies himself for the Duchess as "that squire of his that figures, or is supposed to figure, in the story, the one named Sancho Panza—that is to say, unless they changed me in the cradle—I mean, in the press" (II, xxx). Defeated physically, subverted in his vision, projected into a reality that is less and less predictable, the visionary Don Quixote is doomed. He attempts a compromise: he will give his vision another form, the pastoral, since that genre is more acceptable than the one which he exemplified against such manifest hostility. But his existential assurance is too badly shaken: the compromise is mere rationalization, the fraudulent imposition of his conscious mind; it cannot sustain him. He returns home and becomes ill.

Toward the end of his short illness, Don Quixote falls into a deep sleep; when he awakens, he has gone over to the other side—the side that the greater number accept as reality: "I would die in such a way as not to leave the impression of a life so bad that I shall be remembered as a madman" (II, lxxiv). When the three pragmatists—the curate, the bachelor Sansón Carrasco, and Master Nicholas, the barber—hear this, "all three [are] convinced that some new kind of madness must have laid hold of him." Are they so wrong? Have sanity and insanity not been shown to be practically interchangeable? If the sane world can so constantly take the shape of the insane world in order to subvert it, cannot the insane subvert the sane through the same process? Don Quixote would certainly have ample justification for subverting the sane world.

It is the literary evidence that gives Don Quixote his first doubts: Sansón Carrasco tells him that he exists in a book. It is a disconcerting truth: that book is not only fiction; it is a fact, and its characters exist, both in and out of fiction. To complicate matters, Avellaneda has written his own version of a sequel. That sequel, like Book I, exists in the world of empirical evidence and tangible objects, but its characters are of a different kind. Both fictions are real as material evidence, both are real as fiction, but one is genuine and the other spurious. Throughout Book II, these circumstances determine for Don Quixote an increasingly worrisome problem of identity (while the same complexities of fiction and fact turn into a problem of being, even for Sancho Panza). The principals are not the only ones who are caught up in this quandary; their problem has become a problem for the reader as well. Not only is Book I a fact for him too (as is also the sequel by Avellaneda— the validity of which the reader must ascertain through literary criteria), but he now finds himself deep in a discussion about the nature of sight and semblance, fiction and its modes, that overlaps the book he is reading in order to remain as an ontological question within his own being. He may well reject Don Quixote (since Cervantes has obligingly anticipated him), but whether or not he accepts as a character the madman from La Mancha, he is now participating in the very doubts and questions that are constructing the fictional hero. The reader is in the same relation to Don Quixote as the Duke and the Duchess: they have placed the reality of a suffering human being at the center of their parlor games; the fun which the reader has made of the hero now informs that hero with doubts that are his own.

Like Don Quixote, the reader has been trapped from the beginning: he may reject the beatings, the fantastic adventures, the unbridled imaginings, the unbounded and unbelievable world of chivalry—as he is expected to—but this act of rejection, centered upon the mad and incredible character Don Quixote, creates beyond the novel a void in the exact shape of the knight from La Mancha. From the start, the reader is encouraged by its conscious author to read the book as a literary discussion. A number of the characters appear mainly as characters of a literary genre— Don Quixote himself, Cardenio, Montesinos, for example. Don Quixote abandons madness at the drop of a literary hint. Whole incidents turn out to be merely extended literary discussions: when Master Pedro puts on his puppet show for Don Quixote, it is a historical play (once again, like the Montesinos episode, a variation on the Charlemagne epic), but one that is commented on literarily. Both Don Quixote and Master Pedro interrupt the action as they feel moved to, in order to correct its style and narrative structure while it is developing. When Don Quixote questions an item of historical accuracy (verisimilitude), Master Pedro stops the play to tell him not to be concerned with trifles. In spite of this objective commentary, Don Quixote is drawn into the illusion and wreaks terrible havoc on the puppets. Pedro, who is actually the galley slave Ginés de Pasamonte, loses through Don Quixote's action that which presently defines him (as puppet master rather than as galley slave) and steps forward to bemoan his loss, but he does so by quoting the lines of one of the Rodrigo ballads. What happens to Don Quixote within the world of Master Pedro is, in microcosm, what happens to the reader within the world of Cervantes: it is a tampering with the reader's sense of reality, through the discussion of an artistic construct, in order for that discussion to contrive a fiction of the author's choosing.

The reader has been encouraged to see only a *pattern:* the reader's thoughts and the pattern both belong to the phenomenal world. But Cervantes is able, while remaining in the phenomenal world of the reader, to shape the reader's thought (through his discussion of the modalities of *pattern*) into the precise forms of characters which, within the work of fiction, could construct only that *pattern*. Through its particular structure, the *Don Quixote* also becomes the ultimate redemption of the picaresque genre —by presenting a journey during which the author discusses literature and in the process of which a character develops within the reader, a character who is as real as was the discussion that fashioned the reader's journey. When the book is funny—and it is one of the most profoundly comical books ever written—it is because the *pattern* has become so blatantly a reduction of what has taken over so much of the reader's truth—a process that H.

Levin has analyzed as "the pattern of art embarrassed by confrontation with nature." [15] But this is hardly the laughter of parlor games: it is in resonant form the ultimate affirmation of the truth of the character within the reader.

[15] "The Example of Cervantes," in *Contexts of Criticism*, p. 79.

4

Lafayette:
La Princesse de Clèves

La Princesse de Clèves is a slight work but also a significant one in that it attempts to make the reader sense, through the mode of his reading, the otherwise disguised object of the author's analysis. As a work of fiction, it evolves out of a historical chrysalis. Its first pages particularize a moment, the last months of the reign of Henri II in 1559, immediately after the treaty of Cateau-Cambrésis that brought to a close the wars of Italy and the conflict between France and Spain that had begun under Francis I. There being no battles to wage, the court is clustered in its splendor around Henri, Diane de Poitiers (the Duchesse de Valentinois, his mistress of some twenty years' standing), and Catherine de Médicis, the queen. The historical frieze is rich; among others, it includes the Connétable de Montmorency, the Guises, Mary Stuart (Mme la Dauphine), the Prince de Condé, the Duc de Nevers—one of whose three sons is the Prince de Clèves—the Vidame de Chartres, of the house of Vendôme, and the Duc de Nemours, the only man to whom M. de Chartres might have been compared—Nemours himself being "a masterpiece."

Mme de Lafayette describes Catherine de Médicis: "The

ambitious nature of the Queen afforded her great delight
in ruling; she did not seem to mind the King's attachment
to the Duchesse de Valentinois, and she never showed any
jealousy; but she was able to dissemble with such skill that
it was difficult to discern her feelings." [1] In her can be
seen one of the facets of this court: it is a political world,
one in which power is sought, pursued with fascination,
ruthless skill, and, for as long as it will serve, the utmost
discretion. Beneath the handsome surface, it is a viper's
tangle of plot and counterplot, the doing and undoing of
schemes. The two principal factions are the group rallying
around the Connétable and the supporters of the Guises.
Both are anxious to win over the Duchesse de Valentinois,
who, at this moment, no longer looks with favor on the
Guises. This part of the story is a generally accurate
chronicle as Mme de Lafayette might have encountered it
in the writings of Brantôme or some of the minor histori-
ographers who documented the times of Francis I and his
descendants.[2]

But when Catherine chooses not to notice the inclina-
tions of her royal husband (who "enjoyed relations with
women, even those with whom he was not in love"), she
turns her back on another aspect of the court—and the
one that most interests the author, whose opening words
have indicated this interest: "Sumptuousness and gallantry
never appeared in France with such brilliance as during
the last years of the reign of Henri II." At the time Mme

[1] Here and throughout, translations of *La Princesse de Clèves* are
the author's.
[2] Madame de Lafayette's historical sources have been accounted
for in detail, especially by coauthors Henri Chamard and Gustave
Rudler, in "Les Sources historiques de la Princesse de Clèves,"
Revue du XVIᵉ Siècle, II (1914); and in "Les Episodes historiques de la Princesse de Clèves," *ibid.*, V (1917).

de Lafayette is writing, gallantry ("la galanterie") denotes those worldly assiduities which, by the seventeenth century, have reduced the art of courtly love to the dimension of the *salons*. The historical figures that she has created are intended to appear only in their boudoir battles: it is in this fashion that they will enter the world of fiction.

These figures serve one more purpose: they are also the purveyors of "sumptuousness." As consigned by Mme de Lafayette, sumptuousness ("la magnificence") will be no more than a set of relatively abstract terms intending to suggest that the surface of this court is endowed with the absolute attributes of a fairy tale or of any conventional genre whose particulars do not require further definition. Her performers have neither features nor mannerisms. In the aggregate, they are "the princes and great noblemen of extraordinary merit who were the adornment and the wonder of their generation." Even when they are strongly particularized, the figures of history are blended into this uniform magnificence: "The Prince de Condé had, in a body ill-favored by nature, a magnanimous and proud spirit, and a wit that made him pleasing to even the most beautiful women." As for the principals, they are individual, but not individuated, superlatives.[3] The distinctions between them are hierarchic and determined by the quantity rather than the quality of their descriptions. The Duc de Nemours, the aforementioned "masterpiece," was not only "the handsomest of men," but there was also "an agreeableness in his mind, his face and his acts that belonged to him alone." He excels at sports, sets the style in fashion, and is, through his gentle attentions, an irresistible

---

[3] This is less true of the interpolated stories, which, because they are in fact moral allegories, present what are for all practical purposes morality figures.

lady-killer. The adjective "bien fait" (here translated as "handsome") occurs at least seven times in these preliminary pages and benefits a number of people, including the Duc de Nemours and the Prince de Clèves; in addition, the latter is judged worthy of his fine family name, being "brave and munificent." [4] The member of this triangle who has no actuality in history, Mlle de Chartres, the future Princesse de Clèves, is "a perfect beauty," admirable even in a court accustomed to beauty. The discovery that she has blonde hair will thus be especially startling and enhance considerably the fictional statement to which it contributes. But aside from this notation, all three are mere paragons among paragons; vague lineaments of courtly ideals, such as generosity, courtesy, and reserve, are still apparent, but they are attributed with such lack of discrimination—along with other absolutes—that they afford no help in distinguishing one character from another and are ultimately noncognitive.

The stylization of these figures is, in fact, stylistic. *La Princesse de Clèves* appeared in 1678, four years after Boileau's *Art poétique*, in which can be found the norms of good taste derived from the writings of the time that conformed to such standards (none of these being a novel, since the genre was not a major one, and since its fortunes, during the seventeenth century, had been largely a matter of fashion). The recommendations of Boileau can be summarized as a deference to *bienséances*, which the *Dictionnaire de l'Académie* (1694) views as modes of speech or

----

[4] "Brave et magnifique": both words indicate, in the language of the seventeenth century, outer as well as inner characteristics; "brave" refers, in part, to that which is *visible* of the moral trait; "magnifique" denotes *prima facie* what belongs to the surface, but it also connotes liberality.

action best calculated not to alter the harmony of social conventions. These definitions are circular, since any closed system is tautological. The circle is the motive figure at Versailles, where protocol disposes the court in concentric rings around the Sun King. The influence of the court also extends outward, generating about it the orbital trajectories of worlds whose own solar systems reflect Versailles, as Louis XIV is able, for the first time in French history, to impose a unifying authority upon the nation. The writers and their readers belong to this court —which means that the critics and their norms belong to it also. All belong to a society made up of *honnêtes hommes* that equates its civilization with a form of agreeableness—a civilization whose excellence supposes strict hierarchies and the conformation of its members to a single set of unvarying rules. The reader expects from his books the sort of good breeding that he himself exemplifies: learning that stops short of boredom; only such people, actions, and occurrences as he might encounter in his own world (he calls this familiarity the "reasonableness" of plot and portrayal); a tone that will not jar that of his social modulation. To these ends he requires an economy of means in a functional structure. Proscribed will be writing that copies transient modes rather than the appointed ones; lapses from accepted standards of taste in characters, their ways, or the style that describes them; adornments or complications that threaten in any way to burden this economy of agreeableness. The integrity of the work of art is its conformity to these codes; formal perfection is best calculated to embody the intention of the author. This kind of stringency reduces size (Pascal apologizes to a friend for a long letter explaining that he did not have time enough to write a shorter one), stylizes the physical (if not the moral) topography, tightens syntax, and impoverishes vocabulary: Racine requires fewer than two thousand words for the corpus of his tragedies. Language becomes coded: what symbols remain are, like technical signs, the informants of a complex world. Only a relatively limited number of syntactical arrangements are possible; the style that accepts their recurrence is called baroque, that which attempts to diversify within these imposed limitations, preciosity.

There is reason to believe that Mme de Lafayette intended her novel to be a tragedy of no less intensity than Racine's *Phèdre*, which had first been performed a little over a year before, but the form she chose seldom allowed critics to so view it. Voltaire saw in *La Princesse de Clèves* the "natural" adventures of *honnêtes gens* (*Le Siècle de Louis XIV*); for Sainte-Beuve, Madame de Clèves and Monsieur de Nemours were "such pure and charming beings" (*Portraits de femmes*); Petit de Julleville described it as a novel "simply written, without contrivances" (*Histoire de la langue et de la littérature française*); Gide said that it was "without a secret, dodge or deviation." [5] And it will be recalled that Ian Watt found the novel too stylish to be authentic (Chapter 1, p. 38). The hero of French classical tragedy appears with only the mediation of his own language to constrain him within its social boundaries: his actions contend directly against his words. On stage, this tension within the mask is emphasized by his physical reality, which underscores the animal truth denoted and denied by his language. But in the novel, the same hero appears as part of a texture that is wholly literary, and he is robbed of even an external reference to suggest that which his own words are masking. Readers of

[5] Quoted by Michel Butor (*Répertoire*, p. 78).

Mme de Lafayette have thus been apt to limit her characters according to the formal limitations which she imposed upon herself. They allowed her to be little more than the painstaking eye able to observe infra movements within the stagnancy of a social convention in relating the sad tale of a justifiably jealous husband, a lover bereft of hope, and the constancy of a dutiful wife.

However, in *La Princesse de Clèves*, the convention is a clue even as it is concealment. The author is not the only one using the formal mode of the seventeenth century: her sixteenth-century figures use it also and perform within her world rather than their own. They are endowed with a way of talking, a social ritual, and a set of values that cannot be distinguished from the modes that conditioned the author's style. Utterly blended into their fictional texture, they are twice familiar to the seventeenth-century reader. They are his ancestors: as the patterning figures of the tapestry into whose making they were once assimilated and which now records their names, they are a moment of his personal recollection. The gesture that history alone vouches for is a limited one; they are a splendid myth, but without that which corrupts flesh—a hieratic mask whose significance exists only for the one who can identify it through kinship. Nevertheless, to such a reader, that myth is similar in every particular to the one into which he is attempting to solemnize himself through his social manner. The mask becomes a mirror: Mme de Lafayette makes her reader move back a full century into his own past—the one in which he is flattered to believe—only to discover within a historical abstraction his own present image. At this level, the discovery involves little more than a surface, but the author intends it merely as a first step.

After the opening pages have set the historical scene, an awareness of history remains—less as a fatal agency than as counterpointed comment. Mme de Chartres finds that political considerations will affect the choice of a husband for her daughter; at the end, as the personal tragedies of the principals culminate, Henri II dies and a reversal of favoritism dooms a number of the merely historical figures. But within the appointments of history and the formal limits of a convention that discourages judgment or the externalization of character, the main actors are able, nevertheless, to emerge according to their own defining rhythms and modes.

Mme de Chartres is first described through the customary and bland hyperbole that denotes her membership in this society: "[Mlle de Chartres'] father had died young and left her to be brought up by Mme de Chartres, his wife, whose endowments, virtue and merit were extraordinary." She cultivated not only her daughter's mind and beauty; she also went about "giving her a sense of virtue while making it seem agreeable." The author represents the mother as a progressive pedagogue in matters of love —not content to preserve her daughter's virtue merely through silence:

she often described love to her daughter; she would show her what is agreeable about it in order to impress more forcefully what she told her of its dangers; she would tell her about how seldom men are sincere, their deceits and infidelities, the domestic unhappiness that a love affair brings; and she would make her see, on the other hand, what peace there is in the life of an honest woman, and how much virtue enhances and elevates a person who has beauty and noble birth; but she also made her see how difficult it is to keep such virtue which is preserved only through self-vigilance and great care in maintaining that which alone can make a woman happy—to love and be loved by her husband.

There is, in this progressive pedagogy, a relatively strong indictment of love justified through instances of masculine misdoings, against which marriage is a refuge. Frustration and fear talking in a woman who became prematurely a widow might sound similar. Nor is it inconceivable that such is the sound that Mme de Lafayette intended.

Mme de Chartres has brought her daughter to court in order to find a husband worthy of "one of the most important among the marriageable heiresses in the realm." But even though the court is the only place where a young girl of Mlle de Chartres' rank might find a suitable husband, it is also a dangerous place for a virtuous person. When Mme de Chartres finds that because of political maneuverings she cannot have for her daughter those eminent figures upon whom she has set her sights, a sense of urgency allows her to settle for the one whom the quantitative description of the author has designated as next best —M. de Clèves, the first suitor to notice her daughter and the first to declare his love. Mme de Chartres remarks that the young man has fine qualities but elicits what is most likely the coolest acceptance of a proposal ever recorded: "Mlle de Chartres answered that she had noticed the same fine qualities in him; that she would even marry him with less dislike ["répugnance"] than another, but that she was not particularly attracted by his person." Lukewarm though it be, this answer is immediately followed by a four-line paragraph which is sufficient for Mme de Chartres to arrange the marriage and for the author to make a perfectly ambiguous statement about her: "She did not fear to give her daughter a husband whom she could not love by giving her the Prince de Clèves."

M. de Clèves is an exemplary victim: he is perceptive and ineffectual. He notices even before marriage "that Mlle de Chartres' feeling for him did not extend beyond esteem and gratefulness." As a husband, he will have occasion to repeat and document his complaint, since, in the words of the author, "though her husband, he could not cease being her lover because, beyond possession, the longing remained." Emile Magne, in his edition of the novel, and following Brantôme, comments that the historical Jacques de Clèves "passed like a shadow through the world of the sixteenth century" (p. 19, n. 1); in a sense, he is a similar shadow in the fiction of Mme de Lafayette.

M. de Nemours is a more forceful and assertive presence from the start, when the listing of his attributes places him above M. de Clèves. He enters the life of Mme de Clèves in a manner that clashes with the tone and ways of the courtier:

When [Mme de Clèves] arrived, her beauty and apparel were much admired. The ball began; as she was dancing with M. de Guise, there was a considerable stir near the ballroom door as if someone were entering for whom people were making way. Mme de Clèves finished dancing; as her eyes were casting about for another partner, the King called out to her that she should take the newcomer. She turned and saw a man who she thought, at first, could be no one but M. de Nemours; he was striding over some chairs in order to reach the dance floor.

The actions of M. de Nemours break the surface stylization and conformity of the novel. As for Mme de Clèves, she is aware of M. de Nemours' presence and identity before ever having been introduced to him.[6] The other actors, those who remain on the conventional surface, are not deceived: "When they began to dance, a murmur of applause went around the room." The others see a perfectly matched couple; their external sense confirms the privileged vision of the reader.

M. de Nemours is immediately smitten—his usual reaction whenever the possibility of a new conquest presents itself. But here the reader is given once again intimations of the character's state of mind—the formerly cavalier lover now has scruples: "Mme de Clèves seemed so precious to him that he resolved rather to give too little evidence of his passion than to risk having it known publicly. He did not speak about it even to the Vidame de Chartres, who was his intimate friend and from whom he had no secrets." At this point, in spite of her wise upbringing, Mme de Clèves is unable to understand that anything is happening to her. Her mother is more perceptive.

It is only a matter of time until the feelings of M. de Nemours become known to the members of a court whose principal activity and whose very survival consist in masking themselves and attempting to unmask all others. Mme la Dauphine (the historical Mary Stuart), who had been formerly the object of M. de Nemours' attentions, is among the first to notice that he has changed. Before, he had an infinite number of mistresses ("it was even a fault in him"), but since his return from Brussels, he does not acknowledge a single one of them. One day, the Prince de Condé reports startling news: M. de Nemours has been

---

[6] As a result of the author's deliberate strategy. In his notes on the book, Valincour questions whether M. de Nemours could have been kept so long in Brussels without even a brief sally back to Paris (*Lettres à la marquise* ***, pp. 17–18).

heard to say that nothing will make a lover so unhappy as a ball attended by his mistress. All the while, Mme de Clève's self-deception remains at a level of remarkable naïveté: after rumors start linking her with M. de Nemours, she refuses to go to a ball he will attend, while keeping uppermost in her mind what has been said by the man she is avoiding about the unhappiness of lovers whose mistresses go to dances.

The two words used by the author as she begins her story—"magnificence" and "galanterie"—indicate even before she makes evident the object of her concern the mode of its disguise: this society and its morals are largely a matter of appearances. Educated only with reference to social judgment, Mme de Clèves has remained blind to herself. It will be her mother who will open her eyes, and in a particularly forceful way—though too late: she dies and turns her deathbed admonition into a stinging moral lesson. She confronts her daughter with her love for M. de Nemours, telling her that if she were to fall like other women, her own death would be a blessing for obliterating such a sight. Mme de Chartres then brings the conversation to a close and refuses to see her daughter, even though she lives on for another two days. In a world where the inner and outer eyes are so radically separate, her statement is especially hard. She first places strong emphasis on visual aspects of her daughter's dilemma: "I had noticed this leaning long ago"; "I did not speak to you at first for fear of making you notice it yourself"; "If this calamity should befall you, I welcome death with pleasure in order not to have to see it." And then, in an act that amounts to a condemnation, she cuts off her daughter from her sight for the rest of her days. This part of Mme de Chartres' lesson conforms with the courtly etiquette of the seventeenth century and with the style that represents this etiquette in literature: the book whose form and content are related to that idiom allows little of its ultimate meaning to transpire through its bland and benign surface.

There is no other ethical reference than the social eye: when Mme de Chartres considers her daughter alone rather than as a social object, she reminds her that duty is an obligation to self and repeats once again that peace of mind can be bought only through virtue. She then prepares for a Christian death, giving even the casual reader a sense of how effortlessly the formulations of a conventional morality can be descriptively applied to any sort of conduct.

As the author's polite and dispassionate reflection of surface occurrences continues, the distance between these and their consequences grows. After the death of her mother, Mme de Clèves returns to a world that is, as usual, idle and decorous to the superficial eye but unaffected in its animal instincts so long as they can be kept beyond the reach of human sight. In one of the vignettes periodically inserted within the narrative, M. de Clèves tells his wife about his friend Sancerre, who discovered the treachery of his mistress, Mme de Tournon, only after her death and thus remained in absolute frustration, bereft of the solace either to hate or content his desire. The story affects Mme de Clèves but little: "Everything that Mme de Chartres had said to her on her deathbed, and the pain of her mother's passing had left her feelings in abeyance, causing her to believe that they were completely gone." But she cannot evade the truth much longer. His love continuing to intensify, M. de Nemours turns a deaf ear to the King's plea that he sue for the hand of Elizabeth of England and gives up his prospects of a throne: his love-induced acts are beginning to affect the world in which Mme de Clèves dwells. Hitherto, even though M. de Nemours never missed an opportunity to communicate his love to Mme de Clèves, his actions remained relatively innocuous; but as his love expands against a seemingly unaffected object, it will manifest itself more and more as aggression. On a day that Mme la Dauphine is having miniature portraits made of the court ladies, two such miniatures fall within his reach:

M. de Nemours had long wanted to have a portrait of Mme de Clèves. When he saw the one belonging to M. de Clèves, he could not resist the temptation of stealing it from a husband whom he believed to be dearly loved; and he thought that among so many people crowded together there, he would not be suspected more than another.

He steals the picture, even though the consequences of such a theft are equivalent to those of a direct assault upon the world within which Mme de Clèves has insulated herself. But his theft also serves to show how fraudulent that insulation is: it does not bring an end to the dialogue that has begun between them. Both know about the theft. He urges her, if she noticed him, not to resist his action; and Mme de Clèves, though she is aware that the decorum by which she abides has been breached, is able to give herself reasons for not forcing him to return the portrait: she justifies one breach of decorum through the fear of a greater one. Her reasoning follows the rationale of the courtesies that compose her social code; she uses a deference to outer forms in order to satisfy her desire, thus rejecting her desire when she is conscious of it as a moral abstraction, while invoking, for the part of her that strives to attain it, the preservation of outward appearances. The novel that describes her as she goes through this process preserves the same outward appearances and similarly makes of them the means by which a more animal truth is reached.

When caught off guard, Mme de Clèves' feelings break through her social masking. In preparation for the joust that is to be held later, M. de Nemours is thrown from a horse, and she is unable to hide her concern. But this is only a premonitory sign. Some time later, a lost letter falls into the hands of Mme la Dauphine, who believes that it belongs to M. de Nemours and that it will therefore provide a clue to the identity of the mysterious person who has so changed this Don Juan since his return from Brussels. She entrusts the letter to Mme de Clèves, who reads it and experiences the sort of pain and anger that only jealousy can account for.

As it turns out, the letter does not belong to Nemours; it was sent to the Vidame de Chartres, who made it public (before losing it on a tennis court) as evidence of the sort of beautifully written letter that love can inspire. The Vidame is in a precarious position, since the letter uncovers the tangle of his various love affairs and threatens to expose him to the most dangerous of his conquests—the Queen. He therefore urges M. de Nemours, his best friend, to claim as his own the lost letter. The latter must either abandon his closest intimate, whose very life may be in danger, or appear to have betrayed Mme de Clèves to other mistresses. M. de Nemours accepts the plea to help the Vidame but goes first to Mme de Clèves in order to justify himself. She refuses to see him. Determined to push his plan through, he tells the story to M. de Clèves: this enables him to gain entry into her bedroom, led by her husband.

Once he is there, M. de Nemours can plainly gauge the extent of her misery, and though he has come for the express purpose of reassuring her, "the bitterness that M. de Nemours could see in the mind of Mme de Clèves gave him the keenest pleasure he had ever enjoyed and balanced his impatience to absolve himself." He does absolve himself, however, and leaves with the incriminating paper. But the court is a place of intricate plotting, in which hardly any move can fail to concatenate others. The Queen has become suspicious; Mme la Dauphine is now the one in jeopardy and holds Mme de Clèves accountable for the letter. It is of more than passing interest to note the reflex self-justification that is elicited: "I am greatly afflicted, replied Mme de Clèves, by the embarrassment I have caused you. I believe that it is as serious as you say; but it was M. de Clèves' fault and not mine." A forged letter must now be produced for the benefit of the Queen. M. de Nemours and Mme de Clèves send their people away and lock themselves up in order to contrive the sham, but so enjoy their tête-à-tête that "twice already messages had come from the Queen-Dauphine urging Mme de Clèves to hurry before they were more than half-through with the letter."

After this heady moment, Mme de Clèves reflects in solitude; for the first time, she senses her feeling accurately: her recent jealousy is evidence, no longer dismissible, of her love. She tells her husband on his return that she feels an immediate need to retire to their country home at Coulommiers.

When M. de Nemours learns that Mme de Clèves has left Paris, he follows her, using as a pretext a visit to his sister, Mme de Mercœur, who is a country neighbor of the Clèves. There he is able to spy on Mme de Clèves and

overhear her husband pressing her to explain why she does
not wish to return to Paris. She confesses that she is trying
to get away from the attentions of a suitor. The long-
frustrated husband now becomes an openly jealous man.
He realizes how little she has loved him, and the name
which she will not divulge becomes an obsessive question.
M. de Nemours derives such joy from this scene that his
self-control is further weakened: though he does not name
Mme de Clèves, he cannot forbear sharing his rapture
with the Vidame de Chartres—thus allowing the reader to
gauge the extent of his change from a former moment
when the newness of his love committed him to silence. His
indiscretion eventually reaches the ears of Mme de Clèves.
Though she has every reason to guess correctly the identity of the culprit, she suspects her husband, and "M. de
Nemours, who saw Mme de Clèves' suspicions turning
upon her husband, was happy to confirm them."

These outwardly correct lovers never touch, but the dialogue continues between them. The joust at which the
King will lose his life is the historical moment which the
author has carefully manipulated for this purpose: Brantôme records that M. de Nemours' colors were yellow and
black. In Mme de Lafayette's fiction, no one knows why
he wears yellow, except Mme de Clèves: it is her favorite
color, and she once told him her regret that, because she is
a blonde, it does not suit her. The tourney which begins as
simply another effort to idle the time away ends as a national disaster. A lance enters Henri's eye and mortally
wounds him. But while he is in agony, the court preserves
the usual mask; the author, who allows herself to comment
only upon the historical parts of her novel, notes at this
point that "a court so divided and filled with contradictory interests was in no small turmoil on the eve of such a

momentous event; nevertheless, every motion was covert and all appeared to be concerned with only the well-being of the King."

Mme de Clèves, in another of her periodic withdrawals, decides not to follow the court to Reims for the coronation. Sudden and drastic motions such as this enable her obsessed husband to identify her lover. After the ceremony at Reims, the court moves south to the royal residences along the Loire Valley. There, M. de Nemours hears about Mme de Clèves' return to Coulommiers, in the presence of M. de Clèves, who is watching him with sufficient intensity to guess his thoughts. When M. de Nemours leaves a second time for Coulommiers, M. de Clèves has him followed by one of his men. The lover again spies on the woman he loves and again he is able to see her in a moment as unguarded as when he overheard her confession to her husband. M. de Clèves' man reports to his master; the latter falls gravely ill. His wife joins him at Blois. Nemours visits "M. de Clèves' residence daily on pretext of hearing how he was," but is unable to see anyone, because Mme de Clèves, greatly affected by her husband's illness, refuses to leave his bedside.

M. de Nemours was desperate to see her so afflicted; he could easily tell how much this affliction rekindled her friendship for M. de Clèves, and how much this friendship was a dangerous diversion from the passion in her heart. This feeling caused him for some time a mortal grief; but the extremity of M. de Clèves' illness gave him new hope.

One must assume either that the author is naïve beyond any sense of conscience or that she is depicting in her mild and mannered way a passion that has reached monstrous proportions.

M. de Clèves dies, "enlightened too late" by his wife, unwilling to believe her innocence ("I do not want to see anything that might make me regret life") and yet attempting to believe that she could have felt for him, had circumstances been different, what she felt for another. The lovers are now free. As M. de Nemours is prompt to point out, they can talk and act openly. Indeed, Mme de Clèves will confess her love to M. de Nemours, but neither his pleas nor his pain can persuade her to become his. She ends her days in seclusion, near the Pyrenees—symbolically, the part of France most distant from the court.

M. de Nemours completes his trajectory from masterpiece to monster without derogating from his code any more than the author derogates from her style. Their manners remain those their society expects: whatever human destruction M. de Nemours may inflict, his outward demeanor never damages the weave of ritual gestures that fashion a gentleman, and these never comment upon the animal they conceal. Mme de Lafayette, whatever human destruction she may describe, never damages the stylistic weave that fashions the fictional gesture and never comments upon the animal she is analyzing. The two worlds exist apart from each other:

Never was a court composed of so many lovely women and handsome men; and it seemed that nature had taken pride in bestowing her most perfect gift of beauty on the greatest princesses and the greatest princes. [. . .] Those I shall name were the adornment and the wonder of their generation.

Ambition and love affairs were the soul of this court and occupied both men and women. There were so many different interests and intrigues, and women were so actively engaged in them, that love was always mixed with politics and politics with love. There was peace for no one, nor indifference; each was concerned with improving his position, pleasing, serving, or harming; boredom and idleness were unknown, all being constantly taken up with pleasure or plotting.

Lust for power is rooted in the sex drive: this places the very heart of the social organism in such danger that another and completely different world must be imposed upon it, if for no other reason than to allow the freedom of motion which is necessary to the operation of the world thus concealed; in the world that masks, movements are predictable, for all subscribe to the same set of assumptions and rules. And the index of this security is provided by the eye.

Within the nonfictional world of this society, a gentleman may most likely step over a few chairs in order to reach the woman that attracts him, especially if he is doing so at the King's command. But within the fiction read by those whose outer gestures are regulated (and one of whose regulations is its fiction), the first appearance of M. de Nemours raises a doubt, on which the symbolic statement develops. Here is preliminary evidence of what will be a growing awareness in the reader: this perfect courtier will let nothing stand between him and his desire. The eye will hardly ever be allowed to detect such evidence of the inner world; on the contrary, future incidents will show the ways in which the eye is deceived.

Nothing in their social code prevents these paragons from enjoying pastimes which would be condemned by the religious ethics which they profess,[7] but which outrage them only when they are victims. A complex example

[7] Of the four main characters, only one is not considered until the moment of his death: in time, M. de Nemours simply forgets. But the author notes about the other three, and in generally parenthetical terms, that they died in the edifying way of good Christians.

is provided by the letter which the Vidame de Chartres loses. That love letter is, in fact, the statement of a human being's pain; nevertheless, its owner will first read it to an audience for the gratification of his own vanity. Thereafter the letter will be lost, stolen, read in private, forged, misrepresented, and used for various ends. But that is not all. The same letter shows how even human pain turns to vengeance in a world whose ethics is so divorced from its fundamental modes, and illustrates, once again, the complex devising of the eye within that world; it begins as follows:

I have loved you too strongly to let you believe that the change you see in me is due to my inconstancy; I want you to know that your own faithlessness is to blame. You are surprised that I should speak to you of your faithlessness; you had hidden it from me with such skill, and I was so careful to hide from you the fact that I knew, that you are justified in being surprised.

When the mask is penetrated, another mask will hide the pain inflicted by this penetration, in order for the mask-wearer covertly to prepare a vengeance: the cycle is endless.

It is as elements of this divorce between politeness and humanity that the acts of M. de Nemours, which never betray the niceties of his wordly manner, must be considered. He steals a portrait because he wants it, without giving thought to the consequences of his act: the woman he loves is as much a victim of his desire as might be any other standing in his way. In pursuit of his satisfaction, he hounds her, spies on her, lies to her, encourages her misjudgments of her husband. When he has driven her to confess her love for him, his joy makes him overlook her pain. The pain of her husband—M. de Clèves' jealousy—intensifies his joy. And that is not enough: he eventually finds a source of comfort in the man's dying, so intent is he on the possession of his object. These soldiers have discovered, away from the battlefield, a more essential game, one that is at least as intense and certainly as deadly. The only difference is that here, the sexual self is asserted *in camera*—you kill while pretending concern for only the orchestration of a set of completely unrelated movements.

Up to this point, the world of Mme de Lafayette represents a simple duality: the animal self and the surface that shields it from sight.[8] But even the eye grows perverted. Why does M. de Nemours so desire the portrait of Mme de Clèves? Why does he so enjoy the repeated spying on her at Coulommiers? It is in Mme de Clèves herself that the corruption of the eye will be analyzed in its intricacy.

When she first comes to court, even though she is supposed to be an exceptionally virtuous young lady because of the special nature of her education, Mlle de Chartres is in fact someone whose upbringing conforms to the modes of her society instead of rejecting them. Mme de Chartres wants the virtue of her daughter to be compatible with social grace ("a sense of virtue while making it seem agreeable"). Mme de Chartres is also a woman of great personal pride, who wants her daughter to have a similar sense of herself; virtue is not its own reward—it extends the privileges of birth: she tells her daughter "how virtue enhances and elevates a person who has beauty and noble birth."

[8] What Heinz Politzer, speaking in an entirely different context, will call the "total alienation of the physical from the metaphysical world" (*Franz Kafka: Parable and Paradox*, p. 13). Here, the physical worlds would be those of the mask and the animal; the metaphysical absence, that which allows the drastic separation of mask and animal.

One of her deathbed admonitions is "Think of what you owe your husband; think of what you owe yourself; and think that you will lose that reputation you had acquired for yourself and I had so desired for you."

The element of Mme de Chartres' teachings that is distinctly her own is suspicion of the male: a man is to be trusted only as a husband. She never dwells as strongly on the immorality of extramarital affairs as she does on their inconvenience: the culprit loses her well-being; "and she would make her see, on the other hand, what peace there is in the life of an honest woman." It is better to withdraw from the world than to be exposed to the evils of an affair —even though her social sense views this withdrawal as something of an evil in its own right: "Do not fear to take the most arduous and difficult steps, as horrible ["affreux"] as they may seem at first: they will be sweeter thereafter than the consequences of a love affair." Her worldly and self-centered morality fails to account for the single force and circumstance that will affect her daughter—having neglected to consider love, she does not envisage that it can be found outside a marriage of propriety.

M. de Clèves first sees Mlle de Chartres while she is buying adornments for herself, but he pays no attention to the symbolism of her act. Perhaps the reason why he fails to do so is that he has been described by the author as "brave and munificent" ("brave et magnifique" [see p. 111]); his own inner virtues do not neglect the outer ones. If Mme de Chartres is concerned with morality in the quest for a husband worthy of her daughter, she equates it with social standing: "Mme de Chartres, who was extremely prideful, found hardly anyone worthy of her daughter." She looks first to the House of Guise and then to the prince-dauphin, the Duc de Montpensier. As for her daughter, marriage is simply a social formality, the exigencies of which will be attended to by her mother. The "lack of repugnance" with which she accepts her mother's compromise choice has already been noted. In marriage, she can bring her husband only the formal courtesies that convention has taught her.

Nothing in Mme de Chartres' pedagogy was concerned with the senses; these will have made Mme de Clèves deeply aware of M. de Nemours by the time her mother dies; what her death thus emphasizes is a reproach against the flesh. As a result, Mme de Clèves' social masking will be innocent through ignorance: whereas the others hide in order to give their sexuality full scope, she will withdraw in order to enjoy a solitary sexuality of which she is not even aware. She will fulfill her hunger only in ways that do not violate the social rules that her mother has impressed upon her. When the letter of the Vidame de Chartres is forged, she enjoys her first moment of sexual intimacy with M. de Nemours:

They locked themselves up to work on it; orders were given at the main door not to let anyone in and M. de Nemours' people were sent away. Such mystery and secrecy held no small measure of charm for the Prince and even for Mme de Clèves. The presence of her husband and the interests of the Vidame were as an alleviation of her scruples. She felt only the pleasure of seeing M. de Nemours; she was full of an utter and unmixed joy such as she had never experienced; this joy gave her a freedom and vivacity that M. de Nemours had never seen in her and that redoubled his love.

The social eye is satisfied: her husband knows what she is doing (though he certainly has no idea of her "joy," nor would he be able to understand it, at this moment, if he were aware of it). There is also complete privacy: the servants have been sent away, the front door is guarded, their own is locked—such "joy" as she does experience will not be known to the husband who is her reference as the guarantee of her propriety.

The fact is that Mme de Clèves is in love with M. de Nemours and that she does not love her husband; the curious convolutions of her social world allow her to express these feelings while deferring to the requirements of the mask. But when her instinct speaks without the need to mask, it is perfectly clear: she has already blamed her innocent husband for the loss of the Vidame's letter; she will blame him next for M. de Nemours' indiscretion.

Whenever the senses of Mme de Clèves threaten to carry her beyond a posture that others will judge as conforming with the acceptable mien, she finds her single resource in physical withdrawal. She cannot adjust the mask as do the others who know exactly what they are masking: her attempts are so naïvely directed at a specific danger that they will betray her to M. de Clèves. In fact, she does not withdraw because of a clear sense of guilt or absolute morality; her departures are meant primarily to statisfy the social eye by which she feels threatened (and presumably not because of her own conduct—she maintains to the very last her complete innocence—but because of M. de Nemours'); once the threat of the eye is removed, she indulges freely in the only sexuality that she knows:

She left for Coulommiers; as she departed, she was careful to have sent there the large paintings which had been copied on her instructions from the originals which Mme de Valentinois had ordered for her lovely house at Anet. All the remarkable events that had taken place during the reign of the King were depicted in these paintings. Among others, there was the siege of Metz, and all those who had distinguished themselves there were portrayed in a very realistic way. M. de Nemours was one of these, and that was perhaps what had given Mme de Clèves the desire to have these paintings.

It is before these paintings, alone and at night, that M. de Nemours will discover her:

It was hot, and she had nothing on her head or throat but her loosely tied hair. She was resting on a couch with a table in front of her upon which were several baskets full of ribbons; she chose some of them, and M. de Nemours noticed that they were the same colors as he had worn at the joust. He saw that she was tying them in knots around an India cane of an extraordinary sort which he had carried for some time and which he had given his sister, from whom Mme de Clèves had taken it without seeming to recognize it as having belonged to M. de Nemours. After she had finished her work, with an expression of charm and gentleness that reflected the feelings in her heart, she took a torch and went up to a large table before the siege of Metz painting which had the portrait of M. de Nemours; she sat down and began to contemplate this portrait with the kind of rapt attention that only passion can inspire.

M. de Nemours has been reduced to his phallic symbol, and her sexuality to the fetishism that is the only expression her solitariness will allow it. In order to achieve this lonely pleasure, Mme de Clèves has resorted to considerable effort (as denoted by the size of the paintings, her foresight in having them copied, her care in synchronizing their departure with hers); her deception of M. de Clèves has become active and elaborate, though her replacement of any self-knowledge by a purely formal set of social ethics preserves her belief in her own innocence and most likely allows her to overlook the fact that she has become a thief as well.

Reduced by her mother and her world to a nearly total dependency on the eye and a quasi-mystical belief in its power, Mme de Clèves allows it to become the totality of her sexual life. Butor notes that her autohypnosis is such that she believes she *sees* M. de Nemours outside her window, even though the night is dark and reflection, if she were capable of it, would convince her that he cannot be there (*Répertoire*, p. 78). But of course, he *is* there. For him as well, sight has become sexual. It has turned him also into a thief, a fetishist, and a voyeur.

The sexuality of Mme de Clèves is such that at the death of her husband, she will not be able to see M. de Nemours as a sexual object sufficiently satisfying to overcome the guilt she feels over the fate of M. de Clèves. She rejects M. de Nemours, arguing perhaps what has been her most impelling concern throughout—her peace of mind, which is the most articulate assertion of her sense of self. She will not be his, because he would not remain faithful: he has had several love affairs in the past; he would have others. With her mother speaking through her, she casts doubt on men as a species: "M. de Clèves was perhaps the only man in the world capable of preserving love in marriage. My fate was such that I was unable to profit from this hap; and perhaps his passion endured only because he found none in me." This is the end of Mme de Clèves: the most brilliant heiress in the realm, and the most virtuous, has maintained her virtue in her own eyes and in the eyes of her world, while going from indifference for her husband to deceit, from an avowal that ultimately kills him to fetishistic sublimation, from the consciousness of the well-born to an undisguised concern for her own well-being.

The seventeenth-century reader who discovered himself as a social performer beneath the sixteenth-century mask could sustain a limited interest in the novel through his sense of history and caste. But just as his life beneath his own mask was of far greater concern to him than the mode of his deception, he needed to penetrate beyond these hieratic surfaces in order to turn his reading into more than a social gesture. Only monsters are worth writing about, since man cannot transcend his mortality if he cannot envisage, at least potentially, such fabulous departures for himself. This eminently moral book told its reader, in a stylistically moral way but without moralizing, about seventeenth-century masking and afforded him a descent from "magnificence" to "galanterie" that extended beyond the classical and occasionally precious form into his own animal depths through the very manner of the story's telling.

5

Sterne:

Tristram Shandy

An equal awareness of self and audience thrusts the author Cervantes into the book he is writing while keeping Mme de Lafayette concealed from hers; the intent of both is identical: to place the reader within a phenomenal situation shaped by their fiction rather than to allow the phenomenal world of the reader to absorb the book as simply another of its hermetic and externally perceived objects. But for Laurence Sterne, the problem of devising a fiction to provide a phenomenal reality for his readers seems less central than his concern not to allow his fiction to mask his own presence nor to let its phenomenal world usurp his world. What Cervantes does as part of his fictional strategy, Sterne does out of a desire to convey himself from the relative isolation of York to the more pleasingly fashionable salons of London: the first intends to produce a novel, the second an author. But for Sterne (just as for the author to whom he most frequently alludes) a fictional world separates itself from the extrafictional presence of the author because of the very dialectical involvement of the author in his fiction.

It is hardly more than a commonplace to say that *Tris-*

tram Shandy is an extended digression on the manners and virtues of digression: "Digressions, incontestably, are the sunshine;——they are the life, the soul of reading;—— take them out of this book for instance,——you might as well take the book along with them." [1] But the forms and implications of Sterne's digressions are many. There are of course the author's teasing, deliberate tangents away from an action that is seldom allowed to develop very far (in the manner of the commentator's intrusion which, at the end of I, viii, of *Don Quixote,* holds up the duel with the Biscayan). But more pervasive than this deliberate suspension of the action is the digression without which "you might as well take the book along"—that deriving from an enjoyment of discursiveness which is as evident in the author as in his characters. There is no need to document once again the extent of this enjoyment among Sterne's contemporaries during "the great age of English conversation," [2] nor is it necessary to demonstrate the proximity of the writer Sterne to the "brilliant talker" that Virginia Woolf could sense in the novelist: [3] the author himself has called attention to the similarity of both exercises—"Writing, when properly managed, (as you may be sure I think mine is) is but a different name for conversation" (II, xi). He dips his quill into the inkhorn with an anticipatory delight matched only by that with which Father Shandy, Uncle Toby, and the others light their pipes before a season-defying fireplace whose principal function is manifestly to provide a congenial *ambiance* for their talk.

[1] I, xxii; p. 73. All quotations from *Tristram Shandy* are from the edition of James A. Work (1940).
[2] William B. Piper, *Laurence Sterne,* p. 16.
[3] Virginia Woolf, *The Second Common Reader.* For others who have investigated this propinquity, see Piper, *op. cit.,* ch. i.

But such talk cannot contrive action by either the narrator whose commentary diverts him or by characters who dwell in the realm of words, the anti-realm of action. Each seems anxious to remain, whenever possible, within the confines of a private vision and to assume that this microcosm is macrocosmic: once the narrator (Tristram himself) or any of the characters takes over the conversational reins, he mounts his very personal "hobby-horse" and departs instantly from the collective doings. Uncle Toby rides a "hobby-horse" that has been given as the model of benign monomanias: consequent upon a groin wound suffered at the siege of Namur and the specialization he has acquired in attempting to explain the circumstances of the event, his mind can be turned away from the most serious as well as the most trivial discourse by a word whose mere homonymy kindles his military reminiscences. He moves through the perilous *double-entendres* of flanks, curtains, hornworks, without humor or self-consciousness, for "When a man gives himself up to the government of a ruling passion,——or, in other words, when his Hobby-Horse grows head-strong——farewell cool reason and fair discretion!" (II, v). But Toby is no exception: "Mr. *Shandy*, my father, Sir, would see nothing in the light in which others placed it;——he placed things in his own light;——he would weigh nothing in common scales" (II, xix). He too is a creature of words, able to abstract the most serious event from its actual context: "What is the character of a family to an hypothesis? [. . .] Nay, if you come to that——what is the life of a family" (I, xxi). For the sake of comic frustration, his two principal theories concern noses and names, because his son and heir Tristram will be deprived of his full due in both regards: the author establishes a considerable distance between the characters' words and their reality.

Words are used by the other characters in much the same way, to preserve the inalterability of their own worlds. Even Parson Yorick, who looks and acts very much like Sterne himself—or at least like the public image that Sterne conceived for himself—has remarkable gifts of verbal contrivance and self-abstraction: the *Rosinante* upon which he rides through his parish is such "a lean, sorry, jack-ass of a horse" as to represent a tongue-wagging "breach of decorum" among his parishioners, but one whose consequences Yorick is able to bear with "excellent tranquillity." He contrives "fifty humorous and opposite reasons for riding a meek-spirited jade of a broken-winded horse," which are as many refusals of dialogue, mere punning exercises and splendidly self-centered: "upon his steed——he could unite and reconcile every thing,——he could compose his sermon,——he could compose his cough,——and, in case nature gave a call that way, he could likewise compose himself to sleep" (I, x). Nor is this "affair of his lean horse" merely episodic: "All I blame him for——or rather, all I blame and alternately like him for, was that singularity of his temper, which would never suffer him to take pains to set a story right with the world, however in his power" (IV, xxvii).

Inasmuch as they have any delineation, the characters of *Tristram Shandy* all dwell in such small and relatively closed worlds of their own. In conversations with her husband, Mother Shandy echoes placidly whatever he says to her, but her words construct no more than the usual palisade within which she remains as unaffected as she evidently is in bed. Dr. Slop is alive only to the problems of midwifery and Roman Catholicism. In her brief appearance, Widow Wadman is a nearly abstract sexual force into whose field Uncle Toby must inevitably be drawn. As for Corporal Trim, Uncle Toby's man, he is very much like Uncle Toby himself, except for his use of deferential preliminaries required by his position. He has, like his master, a propensity for reducing most events to military terms; he shares in the general delight with words: "Set his tongue a-going,——you had no hold of him;——he was voluble" (II, v); and his character is rounded to the extent of including a secondary mania: he is periodically, and unaccountably, put in mind of the wretched fate suffered by his brother at the hands of the Inquisition.

A character's ability to subordinate consistently the outer world, whatever the magnitude or the unexpectedness of its intrusion, to the normal processes of his monomania, is the comic affirmation—the dominance of the idiosyncrasy over the event. To this end, the characters are specialized according to their function: they are remarkably learned, but not to the point of engaging in learned dialogue. The most flagrant case is that of Toby, who has amassed as many books on ballistics, fortifications, and tactics as (significantly) "Don *Quixote* was found to have of chivalry" (II, iii)—books supposing a reading knowledge of many languages (among them Dutch, Latin, French, and Italian) and dealing with such subjects as mathematics, physics, and philosophy, even though the narrator speculates (and the events confirm) that "his brain was like wet tinder, and no spark could possibly take hold" (III, xl) once he was put off his hobbyhorse.

But it is the unsaddled and rather dim Toby who provides a large part of the character's dimension, showing him to be something more than a perfect automaton (and different from the reminders of *Commedia* types in Smollett or morality figures in Ben Jonson). Infuriating though he may be when he delays Dr. Slop during the time of

Mrs. Shandy's labor with quotations from Stevinus and discourses on fortifications (II, xii, and *passim*), or when he raises a cloud of pipe smoke such as to nearly suffocate Father Shandy in his own home (III, xxiv), Toby has been forgiven by many for the relative ease with which he can be driven behind just such a cloud of smoke or into a whistling of "Lilliburlero" that have seemed sufficiently void of malicious intent for at least one commentator to have seen in him "the archetype of guileless good nature."[4] Even Slop, the papist doctor in whom Sterne may have caricatured his enemy, Dr. John Burton, is not wholly secure in his religion and calling, sensitive as his anxiety keeps him to slurs that might be directed at either the Catholic or the accoucheur. In the long run, it turns out that even the vegetal being of Mrs. Shandy has a purpose, since at least a part of it aims at the destruction of the sexual animal in her husband.

The unexpected discomfiture of a character that was thought to be wholly wooden is a humanizing event. But too many defeats may well turn him into an object of another kind. Such jeopardy threatens Father Shandy, a character on the destruction of whose world all others are intent, including the author. Walter Shandy is afforded less security in his monomania than anyone else: even his grandest flights on his hobbyhorse are fraught with danger—and to such an extent as to cast suspicion on Uncle Toby's whistling and pipe puffing. Father Shandy, the reckless hypothesizer (the "reason monger"), is never so enthralled by his lucubrations that Uncle Toby cannot infuriate him with his mistranslations of all values into his

[4] H. D. Traill, *Sterne.* See also more recently Ian Watt: "Toby is as much an embodiment of the eighteenth-century conception of ideal goodness as Clarissa" (*The Rise of the Novel*, p. 294).

own. (Nor is even his wrath assertive, since Uncle Toby's prompt retreat awakens just as promptly strong feelings of guilt in his brother.) The first weakness of Walter Shandy is certainly one that no caricature can brook: a human need to convince; his dominant passion requires for its enjoyment the participation of others. While those around him are generally content to assert their individual worlds, his calls out for their cooperation. He is never so funny upon his hobbyhorse as he is in the throes of indignities forced on him through the incomprehension or indifference of the ones whose assent he so badly needs but whose monadic unity is considerably less permeable than his. He fathoms the full extent of this exclusion when he turns in desperation from Toby to Mrs. Shandy: "That she is not a woman of science, my father would say——is her misfortune——but she might ask a question.——My mother never did" (VI, xxxix).

Father Shandy's private world is vulnerable even to the insidious subversion of objects. The transcendental harmony of his systems is jeopardized by a door hinge that cannot be fixed, a coach armorial whose bend sinister proclaims only the fame of Aunt Dinah (the conspicuous blot on the family name), a prize bull of questionable virility: his verbal constructs envisage a perfection that his circumstances deride. The conjuration of objects against Walter Shandy represents a perverse resistance similar to the object-like refusal of dialogue which he encounters among his fellow men; but whereas theirs follows from the nature of their respective self-engrossments, there is no inherent reason for the ill will of objects in either their own nature or that of Walter's world: the conjuration of objects against Walter Shandy must thus be seen as the author's.

Sterne contrives the systematic destruction of Father Shandy's world in a manner which the relative self-insulation of the others does not allow. After throwing Mr. Shandy into the midst of such unlikely fellow theorists as Didius [5] and Kysarcius (to whom Walter "listen'd with infinite attention" [IV, xxix]), Sterne drives him to the ultimate resort of the word, the writing of the *Tristrapœdia* that will somehow harmonize in a purely theoretical realm the terribly contradictory forces of his reality; but after "considering with what difficulty he composed books," the narrator reveals Walter's culminating failure—an inability to sustain even his private myth: in referring to "the most original and entertaining" chapter in the book, Tristram confesses, "In order to render the *Tristrapœdia* complete, ——I wrote the chapter myself" (V, xxvi).

The deliberate destruction of Walter Shandy's world does not make him less comical than the more automatic characters: such humanity as his frustrations suggest is inhibited in proportion as he is turned into a plaything of the author. In an age of conversation, the people of *Tristram Shandy* are perfect comic types: their vice is talk; they are funny because of the extent to which their digressions carry them away from reality. But the most immediate of these comic objects is Father Shandy, since he is the first victim of his own digressive propensities. While the others are nearly as immune to slights which the author might direct at them as they are to each other, Father Shandy provides Sterne with the means of making his way back from the novel to the sitting room by allowing the author to emphasize his own voice at the expense of his

[5] Dr. Francis Topham, the Yorkshire lawyer whose power in the Diocese of York Sterne resented (Work, *op. cit.*, p. xxvii).

creature's: Sterne's writing becomes the social exercise of his wit through an extended digression about a character brought down through digressions.

But the destruction of Father Shandy has been achieved in a curious way: the incarnation of his failures is the exemplary botch into which his offspring Tristram is turned. After he has lost his nose to Dr. Slop's overassertive forceps and his name to Susannah's mindlessness, the unavailability of a chamber pot will cause Tristram to suffer through the unexpected drop of a window sash ("nothing was well hung in our family") a mutilation which his father's frequently expressed suspicion of Jews and Turks renders especially ironic: [6] as Father Shandy is progressively objectified and derided by Sterne, the narrator Tristram suffers in his flesh the consequences of his father's literary abstraction. If Tristram could be turned into a similar abstraction, he would represent no more than another objectified victim of the author's wit. But for a number of reasons, this is not possible. Because of his position as narrator, Tristram is of course precariously close to Sterne, and as the latter is exposed every time he objectifies his own writing, a process of contamination turns the author into the bloody victim of his own wit.

Sterne exploits consciously his double role as author and conversationalist, alternately disappearing behind, and becoming visible to the detriment of, his characters. To a degree, all humorous writing depends on a collusion between writer and reader at the expense of the comic character and requires the emergence of the author from his fiction. And yet, its humor notwithstanding, *Tristram*

[6] An instance of what Sigurd Burkhardt called the "messy fatality" of *Tristram Shandy:* all things fall upon the genitals (*"Tristram Shandy's* Law of Gravity," *ELH,* XXVIII [1961]).

Shandy begins with the assertion of fictional concerns; Tristram is conceived under the augury of time for the benefit of his own circumstances rather than the author's:

Pray, my dear, quoth my mother, *have you not forgot to wind up the clock?*——*Good G—!* cried my father, making an exclamation, but taking care to moderate his voice at the same time,——*Did ever woman, since the creation of the world, interrupt a man with such a silly question?* [I, i].

From an unhappy association of ideas which have no connection in nature, it so fell out at length, that my poor mother could never hear the said clock wound up,——but the thoughts of some other things unavoidably popp'd into her head [I, iv].

Hence follow painstaking efforts by the narrator to date events scrupulously and to establish the strict chronology of their occurrence:

Now it appears, by a memorandum in my father's pocket-book, which now lies upon the table, "That on *Lady-Day,* which was on the 25th of the same month in which I date my geniture,——my father set out upon his journey to *London* with my eldest brother *Bobby,* to fix him at *Westminster* school;" and, as it appears from the same authority, "That he did not get down to his wife and family till the *second week* in *May* following,"——it brings the thing almost to a certainty. However, what follows in the beginning of the next chapter puts it beyond all possibility of doubt.

——But pray, Sir, What was your father doing all *December,—January,* and *February?*——Why, Madam,——he was all that time afflicted with a Sciatica [I, iv].

Time, thus elaborately fictionalized, allows for its own continuation as fictional mode. Piper has noted how its consequences "have visited the Shandys with cramped

backs, squeezed wigs, ruined hopes, and, of course distant
and imminent deaths" (*Laurence Sterne*, p. 52). Upon this
temporal course are set the characters on whom the author
has little hold because of the obstinacy of their individual
ways—Mrs. Shandy, Uncle Toby, Corporal Trim, Parson
Yorick, among others.

These fictional characters are able to contrive at times a
fictional *symbolique* that is relatively elaborate. Even as he
is shown to be a mechanical respondent to stimuli of a
purely verbal nature, Uncle Toby constructs out of books
(like his predecessor Don Quixote) the fictional world
which he superimposes upon the delinquency of his circumstances, thereby performing within the gestures of his
fictional role the symbolic gestures of a literary self-
commentary. This reflection of the fiction within literary
references is sustained throughout the nine volumes of
Tristram Shandy in a variety of ways. As noted, echoes of
Cervantes are frequent, as are the reminders of Burton's
Anatomy of Melancholy, Rabelais (whose *pantagruélisme*
is reborn as "Shandeism"), Montaigne, Voltaire, etc. The
fiction is further expanded through footnotes that occasionally reach elaborate lengths and whose purpose is to
confirm that the characters are creations of books, appealing for their existence to learned sources, whether plausible or apocryphal.

Even digression can serve a structural purpose. One of
the demises of the action in Book II, while all concerned
are waiting for Mrs. Shandy to give birth, comes about as
the result of a lengthy description of Corporal Trim; this
establishes Toby's man in a relatively serious light for his
subsequent reading of the sermon (Sterne's own, after all)
and enhances his stature in preparation for his forthcoming
confrontation with Dr. Slop (the reading of an anti-

Catholic sermon to a Catholic).[7] Inserted stories of the
kind that Cervantes so prized, though they never operate
as the intricately cross-reflecting mirrors of *Don Quixote*,
stand out with greater contrast in *Tristram Shandy*, since
they require a more sustained kind of narration: they are
set like more singly purposeful moments of fiction within
the looser and mixed fabric of Tristram's narrative. Because of their self-contained purposefulness, they sometimes attain a high level of literary abstraction, as does, for
example, "The Fragment" (V, i), in the long-promised
chapter on "Whiskers," that parodies stylistically the tone
of the French romance which it narrates in a way that
prefigures the method of James Joyce in *Ulysses*.

But such instances of a fiction that does not display the
author directly are relatively rare in a work whose very
form suggests that the author is usually present as such,
either in the act of writing or while addressing his readers
as if he were not writing at all. When he refers to himself,
the author is seen at his desk, his inkhorn well in evidence,
his documents spread out on the table before him. (So subjective is this world of his that when he quotes those documents, he rewords them in the act of appropriating them:
"Now it appears, by a memorandum in my father's pocket-
book, which now lies upon the table, 'That on *Lady-Day*,
which was on the 25th of the same month in which I date
my geniture.' " The evidence of the author's presence
takes precedence over the evidence of his documents.) But
even as he is writing, the author is also addressing identifiable interlocutors. Nor does this represent an abstract
set of conventions: the writer (not Tristram) makes

---

[7] Though even this formality will be subverted by breaches of
form (as noted by W. J. Farrell, in "Nature versus Art as Comic
Pattern in *Tristram Shandy*," *ELH*, XXX [1963]).

conscious use of his reader in elaborating his novel. When
the allusions become scabrous, the apostrophes are usually
addressed to "Madam." Structural subtleties that would
normally be hidden within the fictional weave of the novel
Sterne deliberately exposes for the purpose of turning his
book into yet another kind of parlor game which he plays
with his reader; he subordinates the interest of the story he
is telling to that of controlling and recalling all of its previous parts: [8]

———How could you, Madam, be so inattentive in reading
the last chapter? I told you in it, *That my mother was not a
papist.*——Papist! You told me no such thing, Sir. Madam, I
beg leave to repeat it over again, That I told you as plain, at
least, as words, by direct inference, could tell you such a
thing.——Then, Sir, I must have miss'd a page.——No,
Madam,——you have not miss'd a word.——Then I was
asleep, Sir.——My pride, Madam, cannot allow you that
refuge.——Then, I declare, I know nothing at all about the
matter.——That, Madam, is the very fault I lay to your
charge; and as a punishment for it, I do insist upon it, that you
immediately turn back, that is, as soon as you get to the next
full stop, and read the whole chapter over again.

I have imposed this penance upon the lady, neither out of
wantonness or cruelty, but from the best of motives; and
therefore shall make her no apology for it when she returns
back:——'Tis to rebuke a vicious taste which has crept into
thousands besides herself,——of reading straight forwards,

[8] It is in this sense that one might confirm Dorothy Van Ghent's
view that Sterne's "concern is to create a world [. . .] formally defined only by internal relationships" (*The English Novel*, p. 83).
For her thesis, according to which the novel's unity derives not
from its action but Tristram's consciousness, see also B. H. Leh-
man, "Of Time, Personality and the Author" (in B. H. Bronson
and others, *Studies in the Comic*).

more in quest of the adventures, than of [. . .] deep erudition
[I, xx].

Whereas the admonition repeats Rabelais' half-serious, half-
humorous advice to seek "the substantial marrow" hidden
within the work, and while the lady thus apostrophized
may be fictionalized through her interpellation, the apostrophe and the challenge strike the reader, who has been
made conscious of the author's devising in a way that
places Sterne before his novel.[9] In fact, it might not be too
much of an exaggeration to suggest that Sterne's fiction is
no more than what little interrupts his exchanges with the
gallery. But even in the act of writing that fiction, Sterne
remains conscious of his parafictional dialogue.

It is at this level of Sterne's cat-and-mouse game with his
reader that must be considered another form of his teasing,
the sexual innuendo, which is a frequent mode of his. The
pleasure of the *double-entendre* is in the discovery of the
concealed term. But Sterne extends the stylistic device to
structural dimensions: his relation of incident always stops
short of sexual action. Verbal equivocation, that reaches its
most sustained development in the chapters on "Noses" and
"Whiskers," has been ironically described by the narrator
himself:

[9] This is a game that Sterne wins (before the end of the chapter,
the penitent lady is confronted with the evidence she missed):
starting with a title that deliberately eschews the usual "Life and
Adventures" for the pointedly accurate *Life and Opinions of Tristram Shandy, Gentleman*, Sterne's is a skillfully controlled work.
Among those who have analyzed this control are Theodore Baird,
in "The Time-scheme of *Tristram Shandy* and a Source" (*PMLA*,
LI [Sept. 1936]), for the chronological structure; and Wayne C.
Booth, in "Did Sterne Complete *Tristram Shandy?*" (*Modern Phi-
lology*, XLVIII [Feb. 1951]), who demonstrates that Sterne fully
untangles his skein before the end of Volume IX.

Have not beds and bolsters, and night-caps and chamber-pots stood upon the brink of destruction ever since? And are not trouse, and placket-holes, and pump-handles——and spigots and faucets, in danger still, from the same association?—— Chastity, by nature the gentlest of all affections——give it but its head——'tis like a ramping and roaring lion [V, i].

Such equivocation, tempting the prurient intelligence of the reader while it preserves the author in a semblance of propriety, is emblematic of similar temptations devised by the story: the reader will never be treated to Widow Wadman's actual examination of Uncle Toby, any more than the trumpeter's wife will ever be allowed to touch the stranger's nose in "Slawkenbergius's Tale"; there will never be any evidence to confirm what it was that the ill-timed remark of Mrs. Shandy interrupted. When the author's digression turns away from the story for only a while, Sterne is operating as a structural tease; when his intrusion departs from the event for good, as a sexual tease: if the reader then supplies his own vision to complete the scene, the responsibility is his alone.[10]

The reader's responsibility is to be even more extensive: "No author, who understands the just boundaries of decorum and good breeding, would presume to think all: The truest respect which you can pay the reader's understanding, is to halve this matter amicably, and leave him some-

[10] The reader, in his phenomenal awareness, separates himself from the character, who remains in a world of words: when Widow Wadman asks Toby where he was wounded, he sends for his map—an instance of the kind of noncooperation that has already separated most of the characters from Walter. It is this (perhaps unwarranted) separation by the reader that Burkhardt sees as a necessary step toward the author's ultimate irony: "Sterne's final joke is again and again that he is not joking" (*op. cit.*, pp. 70–71).

thing to imagine in his turn, as well as yourself" (II, xi). But these gracious words are intended to leave the reader little initiative, since they have nothing much to do with the freedom of fictional contriving. For Sterne realizes that even when he is not writing a work of fiction, when he addresses his reader most directly, he is causing an object to grow between them, since his address, however direct, is effected through the medium of a book. If he is to project himself from the printed page into the *salons* of his readers, Sterne must do more than objectify an occasional character or devise games that involve the reader beyond his usual responsibilities: he must ultimately objectify the book itself. Few works prior to the surrealists' experiments with the printed word have attempted in such a variety of ways to turn the book into an object, something external to both the author and his reader, which will allow them both to view it from the same spatial perspective. The lines of type are full of oddities that convey a visual rather than an intellective understanding of the text: pointing fingers unexpectedly draw attention to a word or paragraph; Gothic script suddenly emphasizes the official prose of a contract; a line separates the present from the preceding text in order to close a door; serpentine lines of various kinds diagram the narrator's digressions; two solid black pages (both sides of a sheet) are given over to mourning in memory of Yorick; blank lines are conveniently provided for the reader to swear in, and a full blank page for the free play of his imagination to suggest how "concupiscible" was Widow Wadman ("thou wilt have one page, at least, within thy covers, which MALICE will not blacken, and which IGNORANCE cannot misrepresent" [VI, xxxviii]).

The blank page consecrated to Widow Wadman is a

fraud: it cannot provide the reader with a privileged interim for the development of his erotic fancies. It is a calculus within the fiction, a device of the author to give a
part of his telling the dimension of a tangible object. The
nine volumes of *Tristram Shandy* contain a number of
such objects in various forms. One of them is the sermon
discovered by Trim within the pages of Uncle Toby's
Stevinus—the same sermon that Sterne had preached (and
published) nine years earlier as a prebendary of York, and
that he was to publish once again six years later in *The Ser-
mons of Mr. Yorick.*[11] This sermon for which Sterne had
an obvious fondness, enjoyed not only an objective existence prior to the novel, but a serious one as well: it could
not therefore be woven invisibly into the fabric of a comic
novel. Although it is repeatedly broken up by the least
prepossessing audience ever to hear a sermon (Father
Shandy, Uncle Toby, Dr. Slop), it reaches a tragicomical
climax when the fictional Trim is unable to continue because he has become so overpoweringly aware of the In-
quisitional horror which the nonfictional sermon denounces.

The intrusion of an external or objective relevancy frequently affects the fiction. One might note, for example,
that not all of the author's footnotes are either merely
plausible or frankly apocryphal. In the brief chapter on
"Chapters" (IV, x), Tristram lists as part of his documentation Licetus, who "was born a fœtus, of no more
than five inches and a half in length, yet he grew to that
astonishing height in literature, as to write a book with a
title as long as himself." This bit of fictional erudition
is illuminated by a footnote in which Sterne gives the

[11] See Work's edition, p. xx and p. 142, n. 2.

substance of the French source (Adrien Baillet, though he ascribes it to M. De la Monnoye), thereby appropriating Tristram's show of learning and returning the tour de force—a chapter on chapters—to its legitimate author.[12]

The author who stands clear of his fictional narrator is not necessarily a prankster, a parlor wit or game maker: he is able to so detach himself from his novel that not even its comic cast need contaminate him. It is this possibility that accounts, at least in part, for the serious strain that runs through the nine volumes, confirming the desire expressed by the author in the epigraph to Volume III: "a jocis ad feria, a feriis vicissim ad jocos transire." This passing from the gay to the serious is awkward for the specialized characters of comedy, as can be gathered from the conversation between Uncle Toby and Corporal Trim on racial equality (IX, vi), whose purpose is to help the author "weave the Tale I have wrote, into [. . .] the service of the afflicted."[13] The transition is better effected when the author moves from the comic intent of the book to the seriousness of his own purpose through detachment from his fiction, as when he defines certain esthetic criteria that are beyond the power of a comic book to demonstrate: "Writers of my stamp have one principle in common with painters.——Where an exact copying makes our pictures less striking, we choose the less evil; deeming it even more

[12] This is not the sole instance of Sterne's desire to have his reader more aware of his learning than of his wit. After the digression that introduces the amusing reference to the "petite canulle" (I, 20), Sterne added a footnote in the second edition: "Vide Deventer, Paris edit., 4to, 1734. p. 366," because the authenticity of the citation had been questioned.

[13] In answer to a letter, he had received the year before from the Negro Ignatius Sancho (see Work's edition, p. 607, n. 1).

pardonable to trespass against truth, than beauty" (II, iv).[14]

The esthetic concern is an abstract reflection of the author's self-awareness. He has titled his work *Life and Opinions* because he has little use for the "adventures" that displace the author in the reader's awareness. In yet another attack on "this self-same vile pruriency for fresh adventures in all things," Sterne distinguishes once again between a useless fiction that exists for the coarser pleasure of the unenlightened reader at the expense of "subtle hints and sly communication" which, if lost on the audience, are "as if they were still left in the bottom of the ink-horn" (I, xx)—an image that clearly indicates the focus of Sterne's concern. When he apostrophizes friends and fellow-artists such as Garrick and Hogarth, it may be because he is aware that their craft affords them a less strongly mediated communication; but it is certainly also because their power and assertiveness derive from an existence beyond the novel within which Sterne felt so confined: "O *Garrick!* what a rich scene of this would thy exquisite powers make! and how gladly would I write such another to avail myself of thy immortality, and secure my own behind it" (IV, vii).

As a piece of writing born at a time when the social

[14] That the statement represents the author's esthetics is confirmed by his love of the conceptual freedom evidenced by Italian artists, "the insensible MORE or LESS [that determines] the precise line of beauty in the sentence, as well as in the statue" (II, vi). But he is also aware of its controversial nature and uses it as one more thrust at his reader (a little like that delivered through the lady who was a careless reader): "This is to be understood *cum grano salis;* but be it as it will,——as the parallel is made more for the sake of letting the apostrophe [to my Uncle Toby, in the previous chapter] cool, than any thing else,——'tis not very material whether upon any other score the reader approves of it or not."

grace of good talk was greatly valued, Sterne's novel
shows the author's efforts to free himself from the limitations and the anonymity of the printed word: he offers to
the laughter of his *salon* readers characters who are victims
of their verbal definition, and he contrasts with these, for
the sake of a more subtle enjoyment, his own self-control
as conversationalist, as craftsman, as wit.[15] In this effort,
his digressions occasionally reach sadistic heights, as when
he is moved to inquire of his reader, "Is it not a shame to
make two chapters of what passed in going down one pair
of stairs? for [. . .] there are fifteen more steps down to
the bottom" (IV, x); or when he expresses at last a fervent
wish that he might achieve henceforth in his writing the
single purposefulness of the straight line but concludes the
volume with conscious absent-mindedness, "before I write
my chapter upon straight lines" (VI, xl). Such comments
not only mask with wit the taunting which the show of his
skill requires, but also reflect the lingering distaste of
Sterne for the ways of fiction—the author-burying anonymity of "adventures."

It is this distaste that causes Sterne, after taking away
from Walter the humanity with which he has endowed
him and after usurping the learning he has vouchsafed
Tristram, to remove from his narrator the fictional impress
within which he was born—that of time. The fictional
symbolique that has been established through the episode
of the clock winding is now analyzed by Sterne—an analysis effecting a first removal from the cloak of fiction to
the openness of extrafictional discourse. Chapter viii of the
second book begins by objectifying the notion of fictional

---

[15] W. J. Farrell (*op. cit.*) has shown the manner in which Sterne
makes his characters fail when it is they who attempt to make use
of the formal modes.

time, equating it with the reader's time: "It is about an hour and a half's tolerable good reading since my uncle *Toby* rung the bell" (a comment twice extraneous to Sterne's fiction, since it measures especially the digressive excursion beyond the fictional narrative). But Sterne reverses himself immediately thereafter by taxing an imaginary critic for doing exactly the same thing—equating fictional and extrafictional duration. The author then realizes his mistake: "this plea, tho' it might save me dramatically, will damn me biographically, rendering my book, from this very moment, a profess'd ROMANCE, which, before, was a book apocryphal." The confession is interesting: Sterne demands complete freedom from any kind of structure, even to the extent of turning on his own argument, because his is not a work that develops according to the rules of dramatic devising (like the romance), but a "book apocryphal," something that is much closer to "biography"—an account of a person's life, not as literature, but as it is actualized through the evidence of that person's presence. This appropriation of time by Sterne becomes more evident as his self-assertion grows. The precise dating of his fiction becomes his too when in Book IV it is Sterne, not Tristram, who pauses to celebrate an anniversary: "I am this month one whole year older than I was this time twelve-month; and having got, as you perceive, almost into the middle of my fourth volume" (IV, xiii); [16] the painstaking chronology that had

[16] Dorothy Van Ghent (*The English Novel*) attributes this last quotation, as well as the structural unity of the entire book, to the consciousness of Tristram. Such an argument, which sees the work as Tristram's "stream of consciousness," is difficult to defend in view of the repeated intrusions of Sterne's own consciousness —his hyperawareness of his reader.

accounted for a part of the fictional weave has now become an instance of the author's self-reflection.

But Sterne cannot overcome his literary incubus. Every effort he makes to break loose from it demonstrates the strength of its hold, and none more clearly than his attempt in Volume VII, which, though it abandons nearly every fictional pretense, shows to what extent Sterne is enmeshed in his fiction. This is the curious book in which Tristram is suddenly made to run away from death, re-enacting Sterne's impulse, mood, and actual flight to France in 1762, and which now becomes Sterne's climactic effort to run away from the twin deaths with which his phthisis and his fiction threaten him. An awareness of death is present at every moment: "had I not better, *Eugenius,* fly for my life?"; "Sick! sick! sick! sick!——"; "this great catastrophe, which generally takes up and torments my thoughts as much as the catastrophe itself"; "I who must be cut short in the midst of my days"; "why could I not live and end my days thus?" There has been no apparent reason to thrust Tristram suddenly into a similar awareness, unless one realizes to what extent, every time Tristram was maimed to mock the ineffectuality of his father Walter Shandy, it was at the expense of his non-fictional father, Laurence Sterne: the author vouched with his illness for the literary disfigurement of Tristram when he substituted for the fictional narration the truth of his own presence. But as the death-hounded Tristram gallops through the post routes of Sterne's French provinces,[17] another inversion occurs: while what had been Sterne's truth is now being given over with little more than a

[17] Recorded in a somewhat different form in the *Sentimental Journey* of 1767–1768.

change of name to the fiction of Tristram, the travel journal it contrives as written evidence attempts, for the sake of accuracy, deliberately to destroy travel books and devises in the name of truth only a spurious chapter that looks identically like that which it is not. The cities and curiosities which he encounters are mostly downgraded in order to contrast the praise that these wonders are generally accorded in travel books and the disillusionment that actual presence forces upon the traveler (a vein that Proust was to exploit one day): "so this is *Paris!* [. . .] humph!"; "All you need say of *Fontainbleau* (in case you are ask'd) is, that it stands about forty miles (south *something*) from *Paris*"; "I flew from the tomb of the lovers— or rather I did not fly *from* it——(for there is no such thing existing)." Proof through the reverse operation follows with the insertion of a bit of deliberate fiction: a detailed account of Calais, about which city the author explicitly asserts, "I know no more [. . .] than I do this moment of *Grand Cairo*" (VII, iv and v).

Such reversals are not very different from those that have preceded them: whether Sterne is tearing himself away from his fiction or whether it is that fiction which imposes itself upon his private wounds, the process is the same and demonstrates the extent to which Sterne is entangled with his writing. Such entanglement is fatal: even as an alien book grows between Sterne and his reader in order for the author to point to it from the vantage of that reader, Sterne remains within the book from which he is crying out and is slowly, unavoidably fictionalized. Hereafter, Tristram grows more and more gravely ill as, following Book VII, the story is once more resumed in its old form; allusions to his impending death become more frequent: "is it but two months ago, that in a fit of laughter

[. . .] thou brakest a vessel in thy lungs, whereby, in two hours, thou lost as many quarts of blood" (VIII, vi). Books VII and VIII were published in 1765; Sterne died three years later: successive hemorrhages had weakened his lungs; a final attack of pleurisy carried him off. But the "fit of laughter" endured in the fictional character against whom Sterne had struggled for such a long time.

6

Kafka:
The Trial

In his book *Franz Kafka: Parable and Paradox*, Heinz Politzer quotes Martin Buber, who asks with reference to that novelist, "Is there any connection left at all between a sense of order in the universe and this nonsense, the disorder of the human world?" (p. 13). It is as much a human constant to fear the dark forces that lie in wait for man as to attempt to bring about their submission. Along with elation, love and an intuition of the infinite, fear is an inherence—whether of the millennium during the darkness of the Middle Ages or of flying saucers in the mid-twentieth century: agencies beyond the grasp of man keep sending him ominous but ill-decipherable messages. If the writer believes that his fictional bond with the reader is to be secured through a sense of *life*, and if he views that *life* as inherence instead of topical reaction,[1] he may turn

---

[1] As opposed to others, such as the sociological or existential writers, who believe that a *life*-truth is to be found in the unique response to stimuli particularized according to their social or historical moment (see Chapter 8). But inasmuch as all believe in the possible entrapment of the reader through a literary recreation of the phenomenal world and its phenomenological translation within the fictional character, they share a common view of literature which is, a priori, more Aristotelian than experimental.

away from exalting definitions in order to seek the human quintessence in a truth that man shares with other animals but that is no less defining—his fear, or what is specifically his, his awareness of that emotion, his anxiety.

There was occasion to note in *La Princesse de Clèves* the radical separation between the physical and metaphysical worlds. One level of behavior established the social ritual as a functional and negligible convenience; at another level, freedom was unrestricted, because of the social cover and because it was accepted that ethical questions were confined to the level of seeming. The either / or of the social mechanism that could operate without reference to animal assertions and the untamed animal which the mechanism served to conceal made it possible to avoid altogether the otherworldly voice that raises metaphysical questions. The characters of Mme de Lafayette were supposed to die in their beds with Christian exemplariness but without having ever demonstrated a concern about questions of Christian ethics, the hereafter, or their immortal souls; *La Princesse de Clèves* is a novel without anxiety.

There is a reason for the metaphysical indifference of Mme de Lafayette's characters: the torment they endure they inflict on each other. The people of Kafka are generally not much better at asking questions, yet few of them can escape becoming aware of, and ultimately haunted by, a voice that does not belong to the realm of their former experience. Though they dwell at the very navel of the bourgeois world, the world least likely to draw the attention of the supernatural, someone in their midst awakes one morning (a morning like any other) to hear that he has been condemned, without any semblance of what would have been previously and is still, for him, evidence, logic, or common sense. And henceforth, the phenomena that occur in a recognizable time and place, the objects, the faces, the gestures that have never been noticed because of their familiarity, will have a dangerously tentative look—their world, its most stable beliefs and unquestioned ritual notwithstanding, having been turned into a mere mask through which the otherworldly voice is heard. So powerful is that strange immanence that it may even transmute for a brief moment yesterday's objects and people into monsters—the thing Odradek ("The Worries of a Family Man"), the beetle that was Gregor Samsa ("The Metamorphosis"), the webbed fingers of Leni (*The Trial*)—and without symbolic intent, for the anxiety of these people is to be the reader's as well: beetles, webbed fingers, or other such instances of human monstrosity must be no more strange than the sight of a curious old woman peering from her window once the normal balance of the world has been subverted—the reader should experience a feeling of alienation derived, not from mental inferences suggested by the objects, but from the objects themselves in a world to whose functionality they can no longer contribute.

The opening pages of *The Trial* describe and detail the unexpected start of such a process of alienation.[2] It all begins "one fine morning." Joseph K. has done nothing wrong: since the reader is still in the first sentence of the book, he may well assume that the third-person reference to the hero represents a guarantee by the author of K.'s innocence. K. is in bed, expecting his landlady's cook to

[2] The German title, *Der Prozess*, refers to the fact that this is a process in more than merely the legal sense. Fears and failures are, until the final awareness, "at this stage" (e.g., pp. 101, 139). Pagination and text are from the "definitive edition" by Willa and Edwin Muir.

bring him his breakfast, as usual, at eight o'clock. The day is fine; nothing appears to have disturbed it. There is therefore no reason to believe that its routine should be any different from that of other days; and yet, the mysterious emanations are already abroad: the old lady who lives across the way is peering at K. "with a curiosity unusual even for her." The minute he moves, K. will upset irremediably the balance of his former universe. He rings his bell; the door opens at once, and the first agent of another existential mode appears—a man wearing what might have been the functional outfit of a tourist in a world where functions could still be accounted for. But his cannot: the threat of the unknown enters with the agent.

To this agent, whom K. will come to look upon as a "warder," he puts the first of the many questions which, like this one, will be turned aside: the unknown is so termed because it does not respond to questions. From now on, the world may or may not function according to previous patterns: its very unpredictability will be unpredictable. At the present moment, K.'s request that Anna bring his breakfast merely elicits an echo as the man turns to convey the message to someone beyond the door: this structure has changed from means of access to boundary, from a dismissibility to an immanence. Whatever is beyond it adds mockery to its uncooperativeness: K.'s request elicits only a "short guffaw" and the information that it cannot be granted. Joseph K. leaps to the offensive and attempts to reassert his command and dignity by "quickly pulling on his trousers" and voicing his thoughts aloud: "I must see what people these are next door, and how Frau Grubach can account to me for such behavior." But this show of self-assertion is immediately jeopardized by K. himself, who wonders whether he should have spoken aloud, since, "by so doing he had in a way admitted the stranger's right to superintend his actions."

As it will do periodically henceforth, the new world yields to his pressure only enough to show him the insignificance of his assertions. Joseph K. refuses to remain in his room and turns on another warder, who collapses instantly: " 'I meant well enough,' said the stranger, and then of his own accord threw the door open." This only leads K. from one part of the unknown to another: beyond the door he is informed by yet another agent that he is under arrest. His indignant "What for?" remains of course without answer—"We are not authorized to tell you that."

For K., the expectation of a former normalcy is still overpowering; the present must be explained as a momentary deviation from enduring regularity:

K. lived in a country with a legal constitution, there was universal peace, all the laws were in force; who dared seize him in his own dwelling? He had always been inclined to take things easily, to believe in the worst only when the worst happened, to take no care for the morrow even when the outlook was threatening. But that struck him as not being the right policy here, one could certainly regard the whole thing as a joke, a rude joke which his colleagues in the Bank had concocted for some unknown reason, perhaps because this was his thirtieth birthday, that was of course possible, perhaps he had only to laugh knowingly in these men's faces and they would laugh with him [p. 7].

Like the very morning, the legal and political worlds appear to be the same as ever, stable and unchanged. If so, the proprietary laws are still in effect, and the thought sends a flash of indignation through K. Still, the facts are there; as a rational being, he is not given to excessive imagining. Since his customary world reveals no flaw, Joseph K. concludes inaccurately about the necessary aberration of the present moment: this can only be a joke. After all, he is thirty today—things are as they have always been; is chronology not evidence of continuity? He even takes a further step in the wrong direction by affirming that if this is a comedy, he will insist on playing it to the end.

The affirmation is fleeting. In the next moment, Joseph K. attempts once again to hurl the evidence of his former being at these trespassers. He looks for the incontrovertible proof of his definition as it existed prior to their arrival—his identity papers. These should logically defeat the intruders whose trespass contemns him—since within the world that once acknowledged him (to the extent of giving him an officially documented identity), this sort of trespass was unthinkable. He finds his bicycle license, decides out of a sense of past hierarchies that this is too trivial a document, searches again until he finds his birth certificate and confronts the warders with it. Even to them, subalterns though they be, the gesture is ridiculous: "If you would only realize your position [. . .] . What are your papers to us? [. . .] You're behaving worse than a child."

It is only gradually that K. becomes aware that former criteria and present reality are incompatible. He is in another *world*—a word which, in itself, raises a number of difficulties, since that world is not a Darwinian ensemble of reasoned mechanics, but "is divined by intuition and intuitively transmitted to others" [3]—among whom primarily,

[3] E. M. Estrada, "Intuition" (reprinted in *The Kafka Problem*, ed. Angel Flores). Estrada relates this concept to the thinking of Laotse (German translations of whose writings Kafka might have read)

one assumes, is the reader. K. is under arrest; the fact is so enormous that it cannot be defined simply as detention. He is indeed free to come and go as in the past—but from now on, he is no longer innocent; and all questions attempting to fathom this extraordinary state of affairs will be evidence of his guilt. One of the warders remarks: "he admits he doesn't know the Law and yet he claims he's innocent"; until the moment of his ultimate discouragement and death, Joseph K. will be a man obsessed with the hope that there may be a resolution to this hopeless paradox.

Most analyses of Kafka's work become sooner or later analyses of Kafka himself, as if the critics found it difficult to separate the man from his fiction. Joël Jakubec (*Kafka contre l'absurde*) cites a number of sources in support of the claim that the author was "psychopathological" (the adjective is derived from the study by G.-F. Monnier on Kafka).[4] Jakubec quotes Charles Moeller (*Littérature du XX^ieme siècle et christianisme*) to record that government offices in Prague, prior to World War I, were frequently housed in the upper stories of private homes and were not unlike the nightmarish recesses of the Law described in *The Trial*. Maurice Blanchot shifts the emphasis of that novel from the curse to the cursed, in order to draw analogies between the author and his hero.[5] Michel

---

but does not mention Schopenhauer, who would seem to be a more immediate influence if Kafka read theoretical writings on the unconscious.

[4] Among others who look first to a disturbance in the author are E. B. Burgum, in "The Bankrupcy of Faith," and D. S. Savage, in "Faith and Vocation" (in *The Kafka Problem*).

[5] "The fault of Joseph, most likely similar to that with which Kafka was taxing himself at the time he was writing the book, is the desire to win his case in the world to which he still believes that he belongs" (*L'Espace littéraire*, p. 75).

Dentan (*Humour et création littéraire dans l'œuvre de Kafka*) has pointed out that parts of Kafka's *Diary*, and especially certain notes jotted down in Zurich in 1911, evidence a vision similar to that of his fiction, "strange, incomprehensible and yet unquestionably real" (p. 41). Critics may therefore tend to limit questions of intentionality and experimentation in the fiction of Kafka; indeed, one might even conceive of a structural reason for arguing the subsumption of author and hero under the initial K., but more important is the fact that this structure, whether through conscious devising or not, inverts some of the usual modes of fiction.

It has been noted already (in Chapter 1) that fiction operating as *life* can attempt to translate the effects of the phenomenal world in two ways: it can try to synthesize the effects of the phenomenal stimuli through the creation of a correlative object with similar influence; or it can seek to imitate the phenomenal world with sufficient accuracy to achieve the same effects upon the reader. It has also been noted that the more a work of fiction attempts to subordinate itself to the requirements of mimesis, the further it moves away from the concept of *pattern* and the freedom to evolve the statement of its own artistry; mimesis supposes the more naïve kind of art, that which hopes to lure its reader through simple phenomenal recall. But in Kafka, the imitation of a phenomenal world serves a different purpose, since that world exists only for the needs of the immanence that subverts it. In *The Trial*, as in most of Kafka's fiction, that immanence is seldom sensed through the fictional creation of a *pattern* (e.g., the use of symbolic correlatives) and is not necessarily demonstrated through other devices of fiction such as plot and character analysis. As a matter of fact, the

most powerful assertion of immanence is in its bare statement: "Someone must have traduced Joseph K., for without having done anything wrong he was arrested one fine
morning." The *someone* can never be identified, and the
traducing is merely an ironic euphemism of the author:
the guilt of K., once he is "arrested," is the fact of his existence. In one of his grimmer "Reflexions," Kafka analyzed
this burden of the human inheritance:

Expulsion from Paradise is in its main aspect eternal: that is to
say, although expulsion from Paradise is final, and life in the
world unavoidable, the eternity of the process (or, expressed
in temporal terms, the eternal repetition of the process)
nevertheless makes it possible not only that we might remain
in Paradise permanently, but that we may in fact be there
permanently, no matter whether we know it here or not
[*Dearest Father*, p. 41].

Paradise, the realm of utmost perfection for the soul of utmost perfection, becomes in this view the moment of a
sentence ("expulsion from Paradise is final"), and the
awareness of Eden is preserved only in the repeated statement of its loss, which is the very process of our "unavoidable" life.[6] No demonstration is required, since this
sense of condemnation is acknowledged by the same human awareness which, in the nonfictional world, formulates certain of its existential intuitions as original sin,

---

[6] The "unavoidable" sense of that life has been variously reported
by some critics through the analogue of an incurable disease (A.
Spaini, "The Trial") or of cabalism viewed as a cosmic free-
masonry (C. Neider, "The Cabalists"). For others, Kafka's is a
view of the world akin to that of Kierkegaard, whose writings
Kafka knew and commented on (see e.g., J. Kelly, "*The Trial* and
the Theology of Crisis"; R. O. C. Winkler, "The Three Novels").
(These articles are reprinted in *The Kafka Problem*.)

death, or a sense of the infinite that derides man. If the reader can apprehend his own liability in the arbitrary condemnation of K., he will find himself committed retrospectively to the fictional imitation of the phenomenal world as, with his sense of jeopardy impairing his phenomenal security, he enacts the fiction's mistrust of its own imitations and establishes through rejection an equivalency between his phenomenal world and its fictional record.

The condemnation of K. may have implications that are metaphysical—and it is most likely impossible to envisage that condemnation without awakening a metaphysical sense; but what triggers this metaphysical assertion will be insignificant indeed: a human gesture that ought to be of no consequence is attempted, and an utterly unrelated response far beyond human understanding ensues. Joseph K. rings for service; the custodians of another order of experience appear. He asks for his breakfast; his question disappears as an echo down an unknown hall and elicits a brief burst of laughter. Similarly, Karl Rossmann is seduced by a subsequently pregnant servant girl and packed off to the United States before the initial sentence of *Amerika* is half stated; a snowstorm and the need to find a horse bring strange horses and a bestial horselike groom, etc., into "A Country Doctor"; the start of nearly any Kafka tale is likely to produce yet another example. The most commonly held assumptions are contradicted: the country has laws; they are the permanence upon which sanity and the social order rest; there is no national emergency to rescind them. Why then is K. apprehended in the privacy of his own dwelling? A sense of the distance between anticipation and effect informs even the most trivial of actions: Joseph K. looks for legal evidence of his identity and finds his bicycle license.

After an appeal to the enduring stability of law, mental and social constructs are instinctively thrown up against a rising sense of disarray. "A few words with a man on my own level of intelligence would make everything far clearer than hours of talk with those two," thinks K. (p. 10). But this thought refers to an order that no longer exists—as does K.'s subsequent appeal to bygone hierarchies: "He felt fit and confident, he would miss his work in the Bank that morning, it was true, but that would be easily overlooked, considering the comparatively high post he held there" (p. 12). Such self-justifications make of K. an increasingly comic figure when their inadequacy is considered with respect to the absolute nature of his jeopardy —whose magnitude they also serve to measure through contrast. The extent of that jeopardy is gauged in other ways as well. As opposed to the characters in the worlds of Ionesco and Beckett, for example, in which every human endeavor is frustrated almost automatically, K. is able to exert his will in a limited way. He requests the right to telephone a lawyer and is granted that request; when he notes that the prying old lady has been joined at her window by an old man and a younger one, K. can shout at them with sufficient effectiveness to cause them to move back. But these are attempts upon a surface and their very success emphasizes their lack of scope: it is K. himself who will next decide that it is futile to telephone; and after their retreat, the trio "seemed to be waiting for the chance to return to the window again unobserved." These scenes are symptomatic: later on, K. will achieve only a sufficient number of steps within the world of the Law to get lost in its meanders. The hero of *The Castle* will find himself frustrated by a similar labyrinth; and the industrial complex in *Amerika* serves the same purpose, starting with the maze of stairs and gangways on the ship. Beyond the present effort there is always a more powerful assertion that mocks the human will and dwarfs its gesture.

It is K. who decides that he will not make the phone call, not his prosecutors: acquiescence comes from the condemned in this strange game which is played at two different levels and which assumes two different moments of an identical process. Condemnation requires neither prior evidence nor witnesses of any kind; the voice that condemns speaks as an ultimate assertion, whereas in his attempt to prove his innocence, the one who is condemned refers to an anteriority (to questions of accusation and evidence) that is irrelevant to the apriority of the condemnation. He begins the acknowledgment of his guilt by incorrectly assuming antecedent steps: he seeks a defense against accusations, though there has never been any mention of an accusation; his final acquiescence is secured when, in the moment of his eventual discouragement, he gives up the vain argument of his defense and remains with only a tired sense of his guilt—i.e., tacit acknowledgment that it is right for a hostile and ironic providence to have chosen him as its victim.

It is clear from the preceding that this curious antidialogue assumes two different levels of understanding as well: the condemnation is spiritual and abstract; it is spoken without reference to facts, circumstances, or relationships. But in his search for evidence and justification, the man condemned remains largely in the physical world and the realm of tangible objects. When the painter Titorelli explains the workings of the Law to K., he specifies that the Judges, though they can remove the burden of the charge (material), cannot absolve the accused from guilt (spiritual). And in his quest for alleviation, the earth-bound victim runs up against the same frustrations that plague most of his actions in the physical world. There are three types of legal alleviation: definite acquittal, ostensible acquittal, and indefinite postponement; but of the three, the first has never been heard of and the two others are equally unsatisfactory.

The fictional method of Kafka follows this metaphysical process. The matter-of-fact condemnation seeks little of its awsome effect in fictional documentation: for the reader, as for the victim, acquiescence depends on intimate fears and a sense of guilt. Unexpected warders do appear one morning in Joseph K.'s room as hostile invaders, eating his breakfast and attempting to talk him out of his clothes, and their presence does generate mysterious effluvia: curious spectators appear at a neighboring window; Frau Grubach shows a surprising understanding of her tenant ("above all, you mustn't take it too much to heart. Lots of things happen in this world!" [pp. 25–26]). And later, while disguising his search for the Court of Inquiry by asking for an imaginary joiner called Lanz, Joseph K. comes upon a woman washing a child who directs him through her tenement flat to the courtroom for which he is looking. But what is shocking about these occurrences is that, though they respond to intuitions which their normalcy denies, the manner of response remains such as not to alter the familiar texture which their being contrived heretofore and which the implications of their response now subvert. Frau Grubach should not be able to show a sense of what her lodger will not be able to define for himself until the end of his adventure—even though solicitude is a not unnatural part of her personality. The curiosity of the people at the window should not be greater than usual on the particular morning, though at least one of them has

always been defined as curious. The warder's appearance is
an affront to the very laws that preserve normalcy, but
even these K. will be able to dominate to the extent of first
questioning, and ultimately dismissing, their supernatural
nature. The washerwoman will later give a perfectly simple reason for having been able to direct K. through her
room into another world: the court allows her and her
husband to live on the premises which it maintains. But
should she have guessed that K. was using the name Lanz
as a euphemism?

More generally, however, such unwonted occurrences
project an inner sense in K. In the somber Cathedral of the
ninth chapter, a voice calls out his name; this has happened
intermittently since the moment of his condemnation.
That voice is the echo of K.'s self-incrimination. He walks
amidst the sounds and the visions of his own guilt, as
when, going down the Bank corridor, he hears through
the closed door of a lumber room the sound of human
pain. He opens the door and discovers his two warders
about to be tortured because he has allegedly complained
about them to an Examining Magistrate. When on the following day he cannot resist opening the same door, the
first part of the scene is about to be re-enacted before he
hastily closes it again. This is an instance of how thor-
oughly this particular agency of the unknown has been
defeated: the familiar surface that masked the unknown
has become simply an instance of human jeopardy replacing that unknown.

Even so, these instances are rare. Kafka prefers to keep
his novel attentive to the physical world, the level at
which the victim seeks his justification and is beset by
frustrations that are both mundane, in that they result
from his inaccurate reasoning, and symbolic, in that they

refer to the impossibility of the dialogue which he is attempting.

The world of Joseph K. is one of entrapment and largely an entrapment of his own making. From the moment when he tries to answer the intruding warders, K. finds himself questioning his responses and discovering their unsatisfactoriness—whatever the terms of their formulation. That which is analyzed is abnormal *because* of analysis: scrutiny applied to a whole that has been formerly assumed and functional removes it from its operative mode and disjoins it through questioning; analysis alters the proportions and function of its previous relation to the analyzer. But K. cannot realize this, impelled as he is by a need to submit to his understanding the utterly incomprehensible. Therefore, his words begin to catch him up: "Certainly, I am surprised, but I am by no means very much surprised" (p. 15). The day the warders appear, the very door to his room, the obvious and functional means of egress, turns into an enigma and a barrier. The Court which is at the center of the ostensible threat against him becomes for that reason the place where he might argue the logic of his viewpoint; although he never receives a second summons, he assumes a cyclical obligation and returns to the Court of his own volition.

This is a world in which the familiar gesture fails in its hoped-for effect. Frau Grubach's living room is usually a badly cluttered place; on the day of his arrest, K. notices that it has a little more free space than usual; but when he tries to sit down, the reason becomes apparent: there is not a seat in the entire room. Winter brings a chilling dampness out of doors, but inside the heat is intolerable; attempts to open a window are frustrated: in Titorelli's studio, the window is hermetically sealed into the roof; in the offices of the Court, the opening of the skylight draws in so much soot that it must be closed again. Words are unavailing and cause the dialogue to move away from its purpose. K. and the usher who conducts him through the offices have a number of interests in common—the usher's wife and the workings of the Court—but the usher's concern over his wife's infidelity contends with K.'s desire to discover something about the Court processes that will be reassuring, or at least informative; meanwhile, his own ambivalence about the usher's wife prevents him from being a sympathetic respondent, just as the fear and fatalism of the usher with regard to the Court prevent the latter from giving K. any kind of satisfaction. Words can only reflect a mind foundering in its multiple and cross-purposive attempts to impose upon the immanent wantonness an order or a pattern which it will be able to understand. There is a meaningful aftermath to the priest's parable in the Cathedral chapter (a man awaits entry before the guarded door leading into the Law—his own individual door—but dies there without having ever been able to gain admittance); critics have devoted much attention to the significance of the parable but have paid scant attention to its aftermath. The parable is complicated; after it is told, the priest and K. argue possible interpretations; at the end, K. is "too tired to survey all the conclusions arising from the story, and the trains of thought into which it was leading him were unfamiliar, dealing with impalpabilities better suited to a theme for discussion among Court officials than for him. The simple story had lost its clear outline" (p. 277).

The frustrating dialogue between the usher and Joseph K. indicates yet another failure—that of human contact. Not only is the individual's desire to understand his per-

sonal circumstances obsessive; it is an exclusive concern as
well, one that takes hold of him completely and leaves him
no sympathy for others who, since they are human beings
too, might well be suffering a similar predicament. When
K., guided by the usher, encounters fellow defendants, he
finds that his questions confuse the one to whom he addresses them. K. is in a position of momentary dominance;
after he has resumed his role as victim, Block will tell him
(ch. viii) that the reason the man could not bring out an
answer was the shock of looking at K.'s lips, upon which
he could see his condemnation—because of a superstition
that the outcome of a case could be read from a defen-
dant's lips, and because K.'s bear the unmistakable sign of
his own impending doom. A man notices another only
when his own jeopardy is involved; the warders are K.'s
tormentors in one vision, his victims in another—an appeal
goes out from one to the other in turn, but the preoccupation of each with his own dilemma cuts short the human
memory and inhibits response.

The more intense the gesture, the more absurd it appears performed upon this human wasteland; sexual relations are no more than a mechanical, sometimes vexatious
continuation of a habit acquired earlier, in another existence. The characters never seem to be able to respond as
they should to the consequences of their sexuality. The
hero of *The Castle* goes through desultory *passades* but is
suddenly bored in an erotic moment. With even more perverse futility, Gregor Samsa uses the glass-covered print of
a woman to cool his hot belly. Joseph K., for whom sexuality has never been more than a question of hygiene, experiences once a reversal of the usual mode: after the har-
rowing experience with the warders, he feels a need for
human contact greater than that supplied by his weekly

visits to a girl called Elsa, who "during the day received her visitors in bed." His next-room neighbor, Fräulein Bürstner, becomes an object of sexual need—perhaps in part because Frau Grubach has described her as something of an abandoned woman. The moment of their talk together is desultory and inconclusive, in the manner of dialogues previously described. When at last Fräulein Bürstner tells K. to leave, he seizes her and kisses her "like some thirsty animal lapping greedily at a spring of long-sought fresh water" (p. 38). But this attempt at intimacy is subverted: all the while, there is a strong suspicion that someone is listening at the door; and when K. wants to call Fräulein Bürstner by her first name, he realizes that he does not know it. Among the other women that K. encounters, Leni, Dr. Huld's nurse, is a lascivious creature whose peculiarity "consists in her finding nearly all accused men attractive. She makes up to all of them, loves them all, and is evidently also loved in return" (p. 229). But in her embrace, K. never ceases asking questions that have reference to his case and the Court and is nonetheless annoyed when he discovers that she can give him only her body and her lust. The sexual urge, as a force persisting in spite of human needs that have become more assertive, is suggested also by the wife of the Court usher and by the young girls who surround the studio of Titorelli, peering, reaching, and calling out at every crevice, while K. is trying to discover through the painter something about the threat that is now his single passion.

Joseph K. meets Leni the first time his uncle takes him to consult Huld; she leads K. to the lawyer's unoccupied office, where they remain for the duration of the visit. After the interview, the uncle is indignant: "how could you do it! You have damaged your case badly, which was beginning to go quite well" (p. 138). This sort of reverse optimism corresponds to hope within the inexorable process described here: the present evil looks hopeful only when it is seen in retrospect. In fact, there is no future—that very concept is no more than an old habit not yet broken. The obsession is constant; the threat is everywhere: in a populous street filled with the business and clamor of a Sunday morning, a laugh already heard irrupts briefly at a window over K.'s head; a pushcart nearly knocks him down. The image of defeat is always present: "The lawyers' room was in the very top attic, so that if you stumbled through the hole your leg hung down into the lower attic, into the very corridor where the clients had to wait" (p. 145). The urge to live, the ruthless need for self-justification—those obsolete instincts subside; awareness comes gradually—defense is "not actually countenanced by the Law" (p. 144). The last human contact fails: "I have more trust in you than in any of the others, though I know many of them. With you I can speak openly," says K. to the priest in the cathedral. "Don't be deluded," answers the priest (p. 267). Ultimate wisdom is at hand—beyond running, human logic, obsessive effort, argumentation.[7] When the two men in the frock coats and top hats come for K., he is ready.

K. takes one last look through his window into the

---

[7] " 'Alas,' said the mouse, 'the world is getting narrower with every passing day. At first it was so broad that I was afraid; I ran on, and was happy when I finally saw, right and left, walls in the distance, but these walls are running toward each other so quickly that I'm already in the last room, and there in the corner stands the trap into which I'm running.'

'You just have to run in a different direction,' said the cat, and ate her" (F. Kafka, "Small Fable," in *Die Erzählungen;* this translation is by Burton Pike).

darkened street: "At one lighted tenement window some babies were playing behind bars, reaching with their little hands toward each other although not able to move themselves from the spot"; the vision is like so many of the others in a world whose physical moments stand out in a sudden vividness that endures without signifying, though here it may well suggest to the reader an image of man born into his fate and imprisoned behind bars, whose reach will not avail him. This is anyway a day for symbolic lessons. On the way to the execution grounds, a figure appears which might be that of Fräulein Bürstner. Since it is K. who is determining his itinerary to the end (it is *he* who first rang so that the warders might appear; it is *he* who set himself a time for his first summons in court; it is *he* who contrived his subsequent appointment, etc.), his guards allow him to go to his doom in his own way, and for awhile he follows her—"not that he wanted to overtake her or to keep her in sight as long as possible, but only that he might not forget the lesson that she had brought into his mind" (p. 282). It is a simple lesson: he had wanted to "snatch at the world with twenty hands"; the children behind the tenement bars and indeed Fräulein Bürstner herself long ago have already shown him the vanity of attempting salvation by reaching out to another human being. When diversion in the form of a policeman impends, K. is the one to lead his guards away quickly: there must be no interruption; this existence has endured too long already, now that awareness has been achieved. A similar fatigue, or knowledge, overcomes those characters who take their own lives at the end, in "The Judgment" or "In the Penal Colony," through what R. M. Adams terms an act of "self-lacerating submission" (*Strains of Discord*, p. 177). In his private "Reflexions," Kafka notes,

"One of the first signs of the beginnings of understanding is the wish to die" (*Dearest Father*, p. 35).

As he is gotten ready for the execution, a light goes on and a casement window flies open:

a human figure, faint and insubstantial at that distance and that height, leaned abruptly far forward and stretched both arms still farther. Who was it? A friend? A good man? Someone who sympathized? Someone who wanted to help? Was it one person only? Or was it mankind? Was help at hand? Were there arguments in his favor that had been overlooked? Of course there must be. Logic is doubtless unshakable, but it cannot withstand a man who wants to go on living [p. 286].

But this, at last, is the logic of the other world, and K.'s last animal reflex notwithstanding, that logic defeats him once again and for the last time: a hand will not reach out to him; there is no friend, no good man, no sympathizer; no one wants to help—no man singly nor humanity collectively. Nothing has been overlooked: the victim has been posited beyond such redemptory gestures. K. must die, "Like a dog!"—and in the echo of those, his last words, the shame of the human condition outlives him.

Fiction may consider its characters synthetically, as a mode of being within the world, or analytically, as a mode of being within the self. The character viewed synthetically will usually be placed in an external, third-person perspective by an omniscient author who may extend his mediation from description to commentary. The analytical character generally restricts the omniscience of the author to his own being and acts as his own commentator—a process that may involve a change from a third- to a first-person narrative. Joseph K. is seen by a commenting author whose purpose is, somewhat like Cervantes', to establish a distance between himself and his creation. Kafka measures his character by situating him without paying much attention to his instinctive reflexes—or, if he does, without allowing that attention to be sympathetic. And yet, it is the confrontation of such a derelict character with the utter intransigence of his fate that is supposed to return the reader to a sense of his own human finitude.

Dentan quotes J. Starobinski as writing that, with Kafka, "we are in a materialization of the psychic world" ("le psychique matérialisé" [*Humour et création littéraire dans l'œuvre de Kafka*, p. 17]). The psychical concern leads back, once again, to the author; but a sense of *materialization* is central to the work itself and to the author's fictional method, which anticipates the surrealists through its awareness (and the devising of characters equally conscious) of objects—of the tactile and resistant nature of the physical world. When Gregor Samsa ("The Metamorphosis") is turned into a beetle, the constriction imposed upon the mobility that once defined a human being is not of the kind it would be if he had been changed into a caterpillar or a fly: he is imprisoned within a hard carapace which is *inhuman* because it defeats *physically* the human expectations of Gregor; the cumbersomeness and the resistance of matter are the nonmetaphorical part of his curse. K. is similarly condemned: it is not only that prior assumptions, conveniences, words turn into obstacles; the living organism itself becomes sclerotic and object-like in a world where human gestures are divorced from significance because the aprioristic condemnation has been formulated in order to defeat human significance. A prying old woman at a window becomes, in her immobility, the disembodied and dehumanized expression of curiosity; the crowd in the courtroom of the second chapter changes from a divided and partisan multitude into faces with dart-ing black eyes and stiff and brittle beards (that are like in-animate but dangerous claws), and finally into a single and hostile mass as K. discovers that each wears a badge like that on the coat collar of the examining magistrate. And after all, it is only a matter of time until K. himself and his executioners leave, linked together in "a unity such as can hardly be formed except by lifeless matter" (p. 281). The worlds of Kafka tend toward immobility, since they are no more than the lingering unawareness of a sentence that has already been passed. It is not only motion that dis-appears as one of the dimensions that distinguish the living organism from the object: time disappears as well. The in-exorability of the process subsequent to condemnation has already been indicated (n. 2); it is akin to stagnation. Ironically, in this timeless world, time serves only to mea-sure the distance between the human gesture and its effect:

At the doors which were shut K. knocked and asked if a joiner called Lanz lived there. Generally a woman opened, listened to his question, and then turned to someone in the room, who thereupon rose from the bed. "The gentleman's asking if a joiner called Lanz lives here." "A joiner called Lanz?" asked the man from the bed. "Yes," said K., though it was beyond question that the Court of Inquiry did not sit here and his inquiry was therefore superfluous [p. 46].

When one considers that the tediousness of this process disguises the true purpose of that process and that an achievement, even if it were contemplated, would still be illusory, time becomes, within such timelessness, a way of gauging frustration. Dentan has termed as "oneiric" what he believes to be the projection in fiction of Kafka's inner world; it would appear, at any rate, that Kafka is describing the dreamlike impotence of the human being conceived as victim.

There remains at last that curious object, the book itself. Claude-Edmonde Magny (*Les Sandales d'Empédocle*), another of the critics for whom the author and his fiction are closely related, believes that Kafka has turned his creation into the objective correlative of his own anxieties—into an objectifying object that changes his anguish to myth. But from the point of view of the reader that object has a reverse function: the book is not only the translation into fiction of the existential quandary, but becomes through its own refusal to answer questions a phenomenal instance of that same quandary.

These assumptions are valid only if Kafka is successful, if he has been able to make the reader accept the premise that the social ritual has been subverted by an immanence that is more powerful than the human need to structure and endure—a need more likely to cause a reader to dismiss in a work of fiction an overly assertive immanence than to accept the subversion of more conventional appearances. To counter this threat to the purpose of his fiction, the author's humor comes into play—that of an author who, when reading to his friends the first chapter of *The Trial*, was unable to proceed because of his laughter and theirs, according to the recollection of Max Brod.[8] It has been noted previously that the author has intentionally and ostensibly detached himself from his victim; he has had good cause to do so, since that victim is comical. The Kafka hero is caught up in the petty arguments and pos-

[8] *Franz Kafka: A Biography*. Though the temptation to view Kafka as a Democritus should be resisted, especially as Brod, in the words of L. Bergel, "is anxious to stress the 'healthy' side of his friend's life and writings" ("Max Brod and Herbert Tauber," in *The Kafka Problem*).

turings of a mode which is rendered obsolete from the first "morning" the reader encounters him—whether it be Joseph K., Gregor Samsa, or the others who approach their doom in the offhand way of the narrator—believing, as their author suggests, that this "morning" is going to be like any other. The reader determines that the character is comical, able as he is to detect the bad faith of the author before the character can detect the mischievous nature of his fate. Condemned by a perverse metaphysics, the victim argues all the aspects of the question except the metaphysical; there is no appeal from his sentence, but he is too busy examining the petty aspects of his predicament to become aware, for a long time, of its tragic nature—his level of response is incommensurate with the exemplariness of his selection.

In this respect, the eighth chapter of *The Trial* is of some interest. The book is composed less as a unit than as a series of episodic visions.[9] In this particular one, Kafka intended to show an ultimately greater failure on the part of Joseph K. through an initial assertion of greater force: this is the chapter in which K. rejects Leni more roughly than usual, manhandles that other victim Block (who fascinates him, nevertheless), and dismisses his lawyer Huld. But this assertion could never achieve its fictional intent, since it conferred too much volition on the victim, and Kafka was never able to complete the episode.

Within his fiction, the author remains most generally on the side of malevolent fate (part of his humor is his con-

[9] The work was begun some time in 1914 and was still in progress the following year; there is still no complete agreement between Kafka scholars on the order of the ten complete (or relatively complete) parts of this manuscript which was published posthumously (1925) and without the prior consent or knowledge of the author.

stant creation of circumstances intended to frustrate his hero), but the world in which, and against which, that hero moves is the character's own; what the reader sees of it, he will see through the eyes of that character. It is a painstakingly detailed and petty vision—as concrete as his plight is abstract. When Raban ("Wedding Preparations in the Country") imagines that he is a beetle, he *sees* himself as clearly as does Gregor Samsa, in whom the metamorphosis has actually taken place; he has an acute awareness of his shrunken legs operating ineffectually against the great mass of his belly. This kind of circumstantial imagination is derived from a minute and nonmetaphorical view of the world as something massy and tactile; retrospectively, it affords the reader a metaphor for human finitude and frustration through a physical sense of material resistance. (It is interesting to note that those who, like J. Urzidil, see "nothing but dream scenery" will tend to view the entire writing as symbolic.) [10]

K. does not have the imagination of Raban, but he does have an equally concrete and nonspeculative eye. His circumstances are for him either incident or conditioned response, for whose causal links he either assumes or seeks (if he must) the patterning norms of his bourgeois society. The author notes parenthetically about K. that "it was not usual for him to learn from experience" (p. 8); it is beyond his powers of imagination to believe that any force might be such as to subvert the unquestioned norms that he has always accepted. Out of a sense of relief, and because he believes that he has learned a lesson, K. resolves after the invasion of the warders that he will correct this defect (discovered in one of his rare moments of self-awareness). But driving away from them in a taxi, "he im-

[10] "The Oak and the Rock," reprinted in *The Kafka Problem*.

mediately turned away again and leaned back comfortably
in the corner without even having attempted to distinguish
one of them" (p. 23). The limits of his horizon are those
of Heideggerian inauthenticity; he is metaphysically deaf,
and the disease is chronic (Raban provides at least a theoretical contrast when he distinguishes between "one" and
"I"). It is at this level of spiritual slackness that his vision is
able to maintain a factual precision unclouded by doubt or
speculation; but it is also the level at which, following the
author, the reader separates himself from the character.

The reader is in fact alone. The author's bad faith consists in pretending to understand as little as the character
he is leading to perdition; and that character records only
his phenomenal world. It is in his own surprise that the
reader becomes aware of his isolation, as he notes the disparity between the imperturbable eye through which he
views the phenomenal world of K. and the magnitude of
its metaphysical subversion. What Politzer calls "the absence of any metaphysical frame of reference" (*Franz
Kafka: Parable and Paradox*, p. 212) is not a concern of
the character but a need felt by the reader because of an
intuition that is superior to the character's. Dentan quotes
J.-P. Sartre's definition, in the first volume of *Situations*, of
comic description as the accurate notation of phenomena
without any concern for their meaning: an account of
adults in short pants fighting each other and rolling on the
ground in order to make a round leather object pass between two wooden stakes would describe a game of rugby
if the sense of the game were omitted. Sartre is attempting
to demonstrate how, divorced from man-imposed categories, the object becomes free and man-resisting.[11] Since

[11] And Sartre cheats in so doing since his example depends for its
humorous effect on the acceptance of other categories: adults, by
definition, do not wear short pants, do not roll on the ground,
etc.

the world of Kafka prevents its objects from secreting themselves within their justifying function, they become for the reader catalectic moments of an inhuman vision (as, in the opening scene of the first version of "Wedding Preparations in the Country"), while providing the substance of a metaphysical joke played on the victim, who sees accurately but cannot derive from his vision or the indifferent author the metaphysical significance of what he sees. For Joseph K., as for Roquentin in *Nausea*, objects are a genuine menace, but K. is a comic character for as long as he remains unaware of that menace. However, the reader cannot laugh at K. without acknowledging his own awareness which states K.'s comic deficiencies. His recognition of K.'s metaphysical shortcomings thus brings to the fictional world an extrafictional dimension: that of the reader's sense of his own human limitations—his anxieties, his guilt, his sense of ineffectualness. The reader's triumph through laughter over a character of Kafka is his acceptance of a tragic sense still lacking in that character.

Such are the reasons for the author's aloofness and his identification with the capricious destiny of the character. He dismisses even before his obtuse victim the improbable machinations of what Politzer calls "a whimsically unfathomable fate" (*Franz Kafka*, p. 73). That aloofness prevents reading between the lines of a text which records no more than the perception of a naïve character and the pranks of a malicious author: the moment an attempt is made to read *into* the text, the reader brings from his own experience an otherworldly presence to the fiction that is the experiential equivalent of the fiction's "unfathomable fate."

It is only when the victim has at last understood what the reader has known for some time and gives up his comically ineffectual gestures that Kafka the author joins his defeated victim, allowing the initial "K" to subsume them both in the reader's awareness of a common condemnation. "Like a dog!" is spoken for all mankind—for Joseph K., the author, and the reader.

The Trial reveals none of the self-consciousness that is found, for example, in *Tristram Shandy* or in *Don Quixote* —the trap which Kafka sets for his reader does not operate through disclaimer; he does not talk directly to his reader about the nature of books in order to have him accept, through the entrapment of speculative argument, the one he is writing. But neither does Kafka suggest what would be the normal alternative—that the book be absorbed into the credulity of the reader, that its topography, incident, and fauna be accepted as given. Instead, the book is meant to remain as a hard, irreducible moment of the reader's experience, a segment of phenomenal *pattern*. It must represent within the existence of the reader what the intrusion of the warders represents in the existence of K. In so operating, *The Trial* does not seek its overt purpose (to relate the story of a trial, or that of Joseph K.); it becomes instead a book concerned with its own modalities in spite of its precise weave of incident and scrupulous analysis of surfaces. Incident and surfaces are there to create an object, the book, that endures as a metaphysical question thrust at the reader, like those apples hurled at Gregor Samsa by his father—those apples that unexpectedly cause the festering wounds of which Gregor Samsa dies.

7

Proust:

Remembrance

of Things Past

The Trial represents an extreme among books whose purpose is the creation of a book. Its attempt to become phenomenal evidence (instead of a "fiction" whose acceptance by the reader depends on an act of faith) demonstrates the mode of *pattern;* but it goes beyond the intention of other works by transforming the literary lesson into an object, becoming truly an object lesson, something that resists the blandishments of human recognition or the claims of reason in order to materialize a moment of its own fictional world—a world whose characters are alienated through an identical process. Description of that alien world in *The Trial* constructs a book that is a part of its refractory *otherness*. Still, *The Trial* is not unique in weaving a tale out of a concern for the weave. *Troilus and Criseyde* ridicules an obsolescent convention, courtly love, by turning into a perversion of that convention; its architect, Pandarus, is comical through the very scope and rhythm of his contriving, before he goes out, in the author's wink, as a mere figment of courtly romance. As part of Cervantes' effort to force from the reader an acceptance which he feels that his skill and artistry require, he engages that reader directly in a dialogue through, and about, the book which becomes the object-link between them. Mme de Lafayette constructs a literary object whose conventional form and ritual concerns are those of her class and times, but as part of the object mold she also reconstructs its inner matrix in the exact form of the animal that first devised the concealment which made of his social life a formal object; the reading of her book thus becomes for her reader a self-redefinition as he masks himself once again but becomes, in the doing, aware of what he is masking. Each of these authors sought, in his own way, to objectify his book as book. If that statement can be accepted, it will come as no surprise to readers of Proustian criticism that Proust intended to objectify his as metaphor.[1]

Metaphor is to Proust what parafictional discourse is to Sterne or the phenomenal object to Kafka—an attempt to cast off from art and into the existential reality of his reader. Like Kafka, he must devise a mode that will extend beyond the written word. But in order to do so, Proust starts with the conventional metaphor as a conditioning exercise, consciously enlarging his awareness that all speech tends to metaphor. He knows that reference to metaphor is a reference primarily to the extent or con-

[1] To mention only a few of the critics who have been concerned with the metaphoric nature of Proust's writing: R. Brasillach (*Portraits*), G. Poulet (*Etudes sur le temps humain* and *L'Espace proustien*), S. Ullmann (*Style in the French Novel* and *The Image in the Modern French Novel*), R. Shattuck (*Proust's Binoculars*), L. Bersani (*Marcel Proust: The Fictions of Life and Art*), and the one to whom Ullmann is so indebted, L. Spitzer (*Stilstudien*).

sciousness of its trope: any attempt to progress from declaration to specification presumably involves a change from unconscious to conscious metaphor. Every statement of equivalency is the start of a metaphor; the very auxiliary "is," if it introduces more than itself, stands as a metaphorical link. The attempt to avoid a metaphorical construction will merely involve very similar processes at a different level, even if one supposes a declarative sentence whose specifications are nominal—that is to say, whose denotations of quality (shape, dimension, number, and so forth), are so fundamental as to be in reality part of the symbols which they describe, for in the realm of words, even the term "description" is misleading: what is being "described" is only a creation of those words; there is no actual object to which can be attached the verbal symbols that suggest it. "Fiction" is an unreality, not merely because its circumstances have been imagined, but because those very circumstances and their objects exist only as a symbol-induced suggestion; their nonsymbolic moment of being is in the mind of the writer. But though there is no phenomenal object to provide the term of reference for a writer, there is a reader in whose consciousness parallel though unrelated memories may endure. Therefore even the declarative sentence (the subject, its action, the object of its action) represented simply by its verbal equivalents must reach the reader as metaphor, as a reality supposing two distinct interpretations, because no matter how essential the symbols, their reinterpretation by the reader can only be *similar* to the writer's perception that first evoked and ordered them; words are a common coin for values that merely approximate each other.

Being dependent on metaphor, on an equivalency for his terms within the existential reality of his reader, Proust first seeks that equivalency through his own use of metaphor. He thus expands a necessary process by appealing to a greater complexity in the reader while offering him more possibilities of recognition than would the single statement of the fictional experience. As strategy, provided he uses metaphor in a conventional way, it enables him to mask from the uncooperative reader the term which he intends with a term of the reader's making, if he is able to reach the latter's senses before his critical faculties are alerted. Synesthesia assumes the possibility of such circumventing, relying as it does on a correlative sense, rather than on a correlative experience, common to both the author and his reader. Should the author be able to awaken this sense in his reader without reference to his object, he might then construct his object out of that sense—*within* the reader, as it were.

There appear to be only three general ways in which writing can identify sense impressions: they can be analyzed technically; they can be evoked through sound and rhythm; they can be *described* in a manner that does not correspond to technical identification. Technical description would involve the barest of all possible notations, subject to the same limitations as the declarative sentence: it would be a form attempting to appeal exclusively to the mind. Evocation through the senses and rhythm, like all processes that operate through a re-enactment by the reader, will appeal to the author who wants to influence his reader by a form of mesmerism rather than dialogue, since it removes his words from the analytical, objectifying, and distancing propensities of the reader. However, extended prose forms manipulate sound and rhythm inadequately: only within the formal control of relatively economic structures such as poetry do sound and rhythm become fundamental determiners of meaning.

The third mode of conveying sense impressions, non-technical description, is nearly wholly dependent on comparison with the impressions of another sense or other forms of the same sense; any description of sense perception is therefore likely to involve, sooner or later, some aspect of the synesthetic process. In his discussion of this problem with reference to the work of Proust, Ullmann counts "over three hundred transpositions" in the imagery of *Swann's Way, Within a Budding Grove,* and the first volume of *The Guermantes Way,* leaving out of his count what he terms "clichés" such as "piercing voice." [2] That so-called cliché is an adequate starting point for an analysis of sense description and is not radically different in its formulation from other and more elaborate examples of synesthesia. "Piercing" describes sound through reference to another sense (touch) in order to render the experience of the hearer who feels as if his body were being penetrated by the acuity of such a sound. In a single experience of this kind that entails no more than the substitution of one sense for another, it is hardly less of a cliché to describe the same sound technically as "high-pitched": words denoting a single and fundamental quality come close to being nominal adjectives (and there are therefore synonyms for "piercing" such as "shrill" or "sharp"—even though the latter once again draws its meaning from several sense worlds). The process of synesthesia is generally thought of in connection with more complex transferences. The example that readily comes to mind is that of Baudelaire, who, in his poem on "Correspondences" (1857), refers to three of the senses through "perfumes,

[2] *Style in the French Novel.* English versions of Proust's work are, wherever possible, from the Moncrieff-Blossom translation in two volumes. The first of the double paginations refers to volume and page numbers of this edition, the second to volume and page numbers of the Pléiade edition of Clarac and Ferré.

colors and sounds"; he modulates the sense perceptions stimulated by two kinds of perfume, one of which might be termed light, the other heavy. Light perfumes are evoked synesthetically—they have the freshness of a child's flesh (touch, sight, scent), are as sweet or agreeable or soft ("doux") as the sound of oboes, as green as meadows. Those that are heady he describes metaphorically as corrupt, rich, and triumphant, referring the reader to states of being rather than to sensory equivalents (the former are more generalized and require for their apprehension a more elaborate mental process).

The more complex the transfer, the less direct will be the sense references: any one sense may be described through any other or through any combination of the others. Of the five, taste seems to be the most specialized and the one least likely to describe the rest, while in a mode that is largely descriptive, the sense of sight will be called on most frequently as illustration. In his chapter on Proust's imagery, Ullmann breaks down "the types of experience which tend to invite such associations" into four major groups: "Sound-impressions," "Visual impressions," "Taste and smell," "Touch, mass, heat." He believes that in "Proust as in other writers, the majority of synaesthetic images centre on impressions of sound and, to a lesser extent, those of sight"—an assertion that does not allow a clear distinction between the sense that is being commented upon and the commenting sense or senses; whereas the sense commented upon is wholly dependent upon its context, Ullmann's own examples make it clear that the illustrative senses are most frequently visual.

Under sound-impressions, Ullmann lists first the recording of musical experiences, in particular the "little phrase by Vinteuil." He notes analogies with other sense impressions in describing the effect of music—"the wandering current of its fragrance"; analogies with sound (and other sensations) in describing a state of consciousness—"the shrill points of the fifes which caressed it with a vague, cool, matutinal warbling."[3] He concludes however that "most of the images are drawn from the visual sphere," referring to the arabesques and to the breadth, tenuousness, stability, and so on, of the visual patterns into which Proust transforms the auditory stimulus. From there, Ullmann moves to more complex images, such as "the [last full-blown spray] of the [bursting and] clangorous [bouquet]" (I, 774 / II, 85). He then quotes the following passage:

a sustained *tremolo* from the violin part, which, for several bars, was unaccompanied, and filled all the foreground; until suddenly it seemed to be drawn aside, and—just as in those interiors by Pieter de Hooch [whose depth is intensified] through the narrow framework of a half-opened door—infinitely remote, in colour quite different, velvety with the radiance of some intervening light, the little phrase appeared [I, 167 / I, 218].

Ullmann analyzes this passage as referring to the pictorial quality of music, which, in his next example, "is even more personified" (when the musical motives in the Rivebelle restaurant are pictured as women seducing the guest). There appears, however, to be a difference in kind between images of a sound which the reader must draw from his own experience (a bouquet or a seducing woman) and those that refer to the fixed and incontrovertible evidence of an object in the phenomenal world (such as the door in

[3] I, 162 / I, 212; I, 774 / II, 85. A number of minor errors in Ullmann's quotations have been corrected.

a genre painting by Pieter de Hoogh). In the first case, the
experience is diffused within the subjectivity of the reader
who rearranges parts of it to conform with the author's
suggestion; in the second, the defining term of the metaphor is prescribed by a phenomenal entity and the analysis
of the reader specifically coerced.

Ullmann goes on to speak about the acoustic themes
that result from the synesthetic associations of proper
names, especially with reference to the third chapter of
Swann's Way, "Place Names: The Name." He sees them
as "an important factor in the fundamental discrepancy
between imagination and reality": "Names are, no doubt,
but whimsical draughtsmen, giving us of people as well as
of places sketches so little like the reality that we often experience a kind of stupor when we have before our eyes,
in place of the imagined, the visible world." (I, 418 / I,
548). But what is it exactly that leads the Proustian character astray? And can Proust similarly mislead his own
reader? Ullmann describes the way in which Proust establishes color associations with names: Guermantes suggests
an orange color (by analogy with "amarante," denoting
yellowish hues); since the color amaranth is in fact deep
purple or purplish pink, the association is a private one—
the syllable "antes" evoking for Proust a tawny lumines-
cence. But this kind of analogue is of a completely different quality from the example which Ullmann quotes later,
of the "lady in white" speaking ("in a piercing tone") the
name of Gilberte, heard by Marcel in Tansonville, "ut-
tered across the heads of the stocks and jasmines, [tart]
and cool as the drops which fell from the green watering-
pipe" (I, 109 / I, 142). Here, the description of sound as
tart ("aigre"), cool ("frais"), and green analyzes correctly
the "piercing tone." It is similar to Baudelaire's analysis of

"light" perfume as modulations of freshness: the sound has the quality of the child's as yet uncorrupted flesh (as against the "corruption" of heavy perfume) and of its youth, suggesting qualities of physical and moral purity that indicate the "slenderness" of the sound.[4] The sound of the oboe, a reed instrument, is likewise "thin"; it is also shrill or "tart" (one regrets Baudelaire's use of the adjective "doux"). These attributes correspond to the color green (suggested by the subsequent image of the meadows) in their coolness, newness, and purity. Thus when Proust uses the association of a piercing voice with what is fresh, tart, and green, he is hoping to awaken in the reader psychological connections that remain below the threshold of intellective comparisons rather than imposing upon him the orange arbitrariness of the sound "antes" (which would be indeed an argument for the deceptiveness of nouns). Using the modes of synesthesia in this way, Proust is attempting, like Baudelaire, to entrap his reader through the intimacy and the immediacy of poetic devices. When he speaks of colors, he generally associates them with objects that add to the density of his metaphor. Ullmann refers to the passage in which Proust speaks of the cooing of pigeons as being "[iridescent], unexpected, like a first hyacinth, gently tearing open its fostering heart that there might shoot forth, purple and satin-soft, its flower of sound" (I, 816 / II, 142). Ullmann does not elaborate, perhaps because the associations are fairly obvious, starting with the pigeon's breast taken as the origin of its sound: that sound is like the breast feathers, iridescent ("irisé"),

---

[4] Thinness and purity (opposed to fatness, an immoral state connoting sloth, lack of control, carnality) are a common association—e.g., the heroines of Anouilh (*vide* Grossvogel, *The Self-conscious Stage in Modern French Drama*).

and later, purple and satiny. The "unexpected" quality, one of visual surprise, introduces the image of the emergent hyacinth ("a first hyacinth") both growing out of its sheathlike leaves and unfolding its clusters of flowers; its satiny and bluish-red emergence is like that of the sound from the "fostering heart" of the pigeon (a pelican-like or maternal image—the breast that feeds the young?).

It is thus probable that when Proust is associating colors with proper names for the benefit of his reader, he is similarly attempting to avail himself of psychological tropisms rather than attempting to lead his reader astray. In defining the importance of imagination, he may picture the disappointment of a character whose experience falls short of that which a fabled name had conjured for him. But such disappointments cannot be imposed on the reader for whom the fabled name must embody the suggestions intended by the author if it is to have any fabulous qualities at all. Ullmann states that "the 'couleur vive, *empourprée* et charmante' of the name *Champi*, in George Sand's novel" is doubtless suggested by the red color of the book she has previously referred to. One might wonder whether it is not the name of the book that first suggested a color to the author, since *Champi* is no more than a sound in this context (no reference is made to a "red" level of meaning beyond the title, and the unusual word drawn from the Berry dialect—meaning "foundling"—has only a phonemic resonance to most French ears; Proust himself calls the word "unknown"). The phonemic stimulus acting on linguistic homonymy in French would evoke immediately a *field* ("champ"); it is therefore not unlikely that the stressed syllable "pi," connected with "champ," might recall the common association "champ de pivoines" ("poppy fields"). One feels the more secure in hazarding such a

guess because of the endless etymologies, fanciful and accurate, through which Proust analyzes his proper names.
When the Cambremer family is known to the reader only
through an upstart daughter-in-law and a somewhat farcical old lady, Proust examines their family name with
amusement through the wit of the Duchesse de Guermantes and of Swann: the first remarks that "It ends just
in time, but it ends badly!"—to which Swann retorts that
"It begins no better" (I, 262 / I, 341). But as the family
comes to be associated with its estates around Balbec (La
Raspelière and Fréterne), the syllable "mer" acquires a
different meaning. And when the Verdurins show
greater appreciation for the beauty of La Raspelière than
do its rightful owners, the dialectic of Proust's portrayal
reveals through that beauty and its paradoxical appreciation by the Verdurins the inborn aristocracy of the Cam-
bremers; they remain by and large ridiculous, but the
syllable "cambre" is redeemed to the extent of moving
away from the euphemistic "Cambronne" and closer to
"cambré" ("cambered"), with its intimation of noble
bearing (in Harraps's *Standard French and English Dictionary: "Personne à la taille cambrée,* well set-up person").

In a more serious vein, place names suggest their own
mythology, though Ullmann's listings can be analyzed to
show a far wider variety in the manner of their suggestion.
Parma is "[mauve and] soft" through an analogy with the
color of the violet to which it gives its name; but Bayeux,
"so lofty in its noble coronet of [reddish] lace, whose highest point caught the light of the old gold of its second syllable" (I, 297 / I, 388–389) is singularly more complex.
Its nobility is suggested by its age, the loftiness of its
twelfth- and thirteenth-century cathedral (it is a bishop-

ric), the lace (and the Gothic tracery) for which the
town is famous. The "second syllable" ("yeux"—"eyes")
connotes a source of light—a light caught by the full
eminence of its steeples; but that light is the red-tinted
glow of the nearing sunset—the patina, "the old gold" of
its temporal, material, and chromatic splendor. "Vitré,
whose acute accent barred its ancient glass with [black]
wooden lozenges" (I, 297 / I, 389) is first an ancient window ("vitrail"—stained or leaded glass), whose acute accent indicates the diagonal shape of the lozenge (that of
old leaded panes such as can be found in the church in
Combray) and its sharp angles. Even when Proust imposes
arbitrary colors for certain sounds, other analogies seek to
justify them: "Coutances, a Norman Cathedral, which its
final [diphthong], rich and yellowing, crowned with a
tower of butter" may pick up, in addition to the obvious
analogies, the reminiscence of the Rouen tower that was
built with butter-tax money.

Since the synesthetic process is concerned with the in-
fra-perceptions of the reader, one might suppose that
Proust is attempting to awaken a sensuous response
through which would be transmitted at least the *mood* of
his book. Whereas this is obviously enough a part of his
technique, his use of the other forms of metaphor makes it
clear that Proust has ultimately a completely different purpose in mind. In its other forms, the metaphor as used by
Proust evidences a stylistic structure that is more extended,
as is the grasp of its imagery and the modes of response
which it anticipates. Interestingly, the extended forms are
congenial to the lavishness of Proust's style; at one level of
his writing, he appeals through one term of the synesthetic
metaphor to the reader's subliminal store of experience so
as to illuminate its other term by surprise, before the

reader has had the opportunity for sufficient reflection to raise his critical guard. But at another level, Proust, ever a prodigal host, offers a profusion of analogues: of the some hundred and fifty extended tropes that illustrate Ullmann's chapter on Proust in *The Image in the Modern French Novel,* nearly two-thirds are similes of the most explicit sort—the greatest number being introduced by the word "comme"; and of the remaining third, many elaborate this link instead of eliminating it through the ellipsis of metaphor.[5]

In *Time Recaptured,* close to the moment of the hero's final epiphany, Proust defines his concept and his use of metaphor:

An hour is not merely an hour. It is a vase filled with perfumes, sounds, plans and climates. What we call reality is a certain relationship between these sensations and the memories which surround us at the same time (a relationship that is destroyed by a bare cinematographic presentation, which gets further away from the truth the more closely it claims to adhere to it) the only true relationship, which the writer must recapture so that he may forever link together in his phrase its two distinct elements. One may list in an interminable description the objects that figured in the place described, but truth will begin only when the writer takes two different objects, establishes their relationship—analogous in the world of

---

[5] The section called "Imagery as a Means of Portrayal" has not been included in this count: interestingly, Proust's characters seem to favor similes less than does their author. This is especially true of the characters whose comic definition is through their speech; these tend to use metaphors in the narrowest and strictest sense of the word, their comic automatism deriving from a linguistic inconsiderateness which assumes that their expression will be understood, no matter how outlandish, without the benefit of the term that denotes likeness (see, e.g., Bloch).

art to the sole relationship in the world of science, the law of cause and effect—and encloses them in the necessary rings of a beautiful style [II, 1008 / III, 889].

Style is a necessary concommitant of metaphor, but metaphor is more than a matter of style: the Proustian metaphor reaches beyond words into the phenomenal world. References to paintings, already noted in the discussion of the synesthetic process, are attempts to insert a referable, nonimaginative object within the metaphorical construction. This is an elementary form of transposition in which, for example, characters are given referable traits: Bloch looks like the portrait of Mohammed II by Bellini; Swann is the Magus in a Luini fresco and appears as Charles Haas in the "Cercle de la rue royale" by Tissot; Charlus is El Greco's Grand Inquisitor. Sometimes the actual references are multiple and / or analytical: Odette is Botticelli's Zipporah; she is also the Virgin in his "Magnificat"; her smiles are like the smile sketches by Watteau. Albertine is detailed in a variety of ways also: she is Giotto's Idolatry and nonidentified faces by Michelangelo; but her hooked nose can be found in caricatures by Leonardo. Occasionally, a footman or a secondary character is suddenly cast in a similar light. The kitchen maid in Combray has become famous beyond her role because Swann associated her with Giotto's "Charity." The otherwise obscure M. de Palancy is recalled for a nose derived from Ghirlandaio; Mme Blatin is the spitting image of Bartolommeo's Savonarola; and Marcel's own father, in his nightclothes, is like an etching in imitation of Gozzoli's "Abraham." At other times, it is horses in the Bois that are like those painted by Constantin Guys, or soldiers at Doncières who suddenly call to mind the peasants of Breughel. Occasionally, the phenom-

enal objects construct a dialectical vision that is wholly external to their fiction: the roof of the Gare Saint-Lazare is
like a sky by Mantegna or by Veronese. And, more
subtly, gestures and moods derive from paintings, textures
from brush technique.[6]

Taken as the mere juxtaposition of surfaces (though of
real and fictional worlds), such metaphors amount to little
more than comparisons and are more like the "bare cinematographic presentation" that Proust rejects. The unnaturalness of artifice and the violence done to the human
mode that are implicit in the painting by El Greco evoke
too readily parallel implications in the aging and "painted"
Charlus, even though Proust refrains from pointing them
out. As Shattuck has noted, Proust's truth is predicated on
prior error. Through the stereoscopic effect of the narration as metaphor, the one-eyed and inaccurate vision must
be complemented suddenly to attain its epiphany: only the
unexpected contribution of the second eye can dispel the
former vision and reveal the new, as when a servant is
found to have, all at once and without justification, the
traits of an old master (or when, for the sake of comic
effect operating in the same way, the innocent Mme Blatin
imposes herself unwarrantedly as Bartolommeo's Savonarola). Art is the evidence of clear sight discerning the
world and its objects in their pristine truth; as such, it can
serve to elucidate even phenomenal realities—to reveal, for
example, what functionality had obscured in the glass roof
of Saint-Lazare: the sense of a brooding threat that the
visions of Mantegna and Veronese imposed upon their
skies. It is this aptitude of the work of art as metaphor to
awaken more than a reminiscence of surfaces, its psycho-

[6] See especially J. Monnin-Hornung, *Proust et la peinture;* also
M. E. Chernowitz, *Proust and Painting.*

logical prehensility, that Proust explores through the paintings of Elstir.

It is Proust who uses the word metaphor to explain how Elstir's vision must be understood as it is transferred to his canvases. His painting forces a dissociation from former habits of the mind and eye because he is gifted with the essential vision of a great artist:

> is it not logical, not by any artifice of symbolism but by a sincere return to the very root of the impression, to represent one thing by that other for which, in the flash of a first illusion, we mistook it? Surfaces and volumes are in reality independent of the names of objects which our memory imposes on them after we have recognized them. Elstir attempted to wrest from what he had just felt what he already knew, his effort had often been to break up that aggregate of impressions which we call vision [I, 1018 / II, 419].

Elstir rejects symbolism because symbolism would suppose an understanding of the artist's vision through what would amount to parallel reasoning. But the artist is before all else an eye; the viewer's epiphany must result from his response to the metaphor of which Elstir's canvas represents one of the terms—that metaphor being composed of the equivalence which the viewer can recognize in a different world from the one in which the painter is seeking his truth, a truth originally apprehended by Elstir to which he can now refer his viewer. The artist's eye remains in the realm of immediacy and feeling, while the removal through habit derives from functional naming (a distinction between existential perception and essential classification which Sartre will pick up)—"as we give the names of Mars, Venus, Saturn to planets which have no place in classical mythology. We feel in one world, we think, we

give names in another" (I, 748 / II, 50). Proust concludes
that this innate attunement of the artist to his object is more
important than imagination, even in a work of imagination: "It is quite possible that, to produce a literary work,
imagination and sensibility are interchangeable qualities and
that the latter can, without much disadvantage, be substituted for the former." [7] This need to apprehend phenomenal truth directly, beyond its seeming, and the belief that
the artist is its special medium are shown in Marcel's grandmother's wishing her grandson to have in his room reminders of esthetic worlds, but "for all the subject of the
picture had an aesthetic value of its own, she would find
that vulgarity and utility had too prominent a part in
them, through the mechanical nature of their reproduction
by photography." She would therefore attempt

to introduce, as it might be, several "thicknesses" of art; instead of photographs of Chartres Cathedral [. . .], she would
inquire of Swann whether some great painter had not made
pictures of [it], and preferred to give me photographs of
'Chartres Cathedral' after Corot [. . .]. But although the pho-
tographer had been prevented from reproducing directly the
masterpieces or the beauties of nature, and had there been replaced by a great artist, he resumed his odious position when
it came to reproducing the artist's interpretation. Accord-
ingly, having to reckon again with vulgarity, my grandmother would endeavour to postpone the moment of contact
still further. She would ask Swann if the picture had not been
engraved [I, 31 / I, 40].

This illogical sequence demonstrates a need to come as
close to the truth of the object as possession through its

---

[7] II, 1017 / III, 900–901. A systematic distrust of the mind was
part of Proust's first analytic method. See A. Feuillerat, *Comment
Marcel Proust a composé son roman.*

seer will allow. The mechanical camera is ineffectual before the "beauties of nature" (the same passage refers to
Vesuvius); it cannot account, either, for a "masterpiece"
(such as Chartres Cathedral) that represents a first translation of that natural beauty. But if the dialectic of that
translation has been interpreted by a Corot, the dialectical
"thickness" of the work of art is such that even the camera
may account for some of it. However, even at this level,
Marcel's grandmother still feels a sense of remoteness; it
will be the etching of Corot's commentary by yet another
artist that affords at least direct contact with a comment
upon the commentator.[8]

It is perhaps not incorrect to equate apprehension of
such phenomenal truth, and its translation, with the modes
of esthetic experience. But Proust is concerned with more
than esthetic analysis: he has in mind the very definition of
the artist as the one who can decipher and convey. Elstir
sees as others cannot and *creates* the common denominator
through which will become visible what was too familiar
to be known by those unable "to break up that aggregate
of impressions which we call vision." Elstir does so by iso-
lating a "root-impression" conveyed prior to the intellective associations that accrue about, and ultimately obscure,
the object. Phenomenological vision of this kind is evidenced by his painting of Carquethuit:

One of his metaphors that occurred most commonly in the
seascapes which he had round him was precisely that which,
comparing land with sea, suppressed every line of demarca-

[8] Possession through the eye as something that is nearly tactile and
exceeds the power of the mind is described by Proust with reference to himself; in the Preface to his translation of Ruskin's *Bible
of Amiens,* he notes how he journeyed to Venice in order to be
able to "touch" the ideas of Ruskin on medieval architecture.

tion between them. It was this comparison, tacitly and untir-
ingly repeated on a single canvas, which gave it that multiform and powerful unity.[9]

Carquethuit is a harbor, a hybrid of land and water. Not
only is the sea evident in its every detail, but its people are
sea creatures that extend the existence of Carquethuit beyond the land. Each part of this reciprocal metaphor defines the other: "Elstir has prepared the mind of the spectator by employing, for the little town, only marine terms,
and urban terms for the sea" (I, 629 / I, 836); the steeples
of the distant Criquebec are like sunlit foam rising from
the waves, while the masts in the harbor are so densely
clustered that they cancel the water through their man-
imposed stability.

Marcel has hitherto sought Balbec in the Cimmerian
fogs of an inadequate vision suggested by Legrandin a long
time ago, in Combray: "I had taken care when I stood by
the sea to expel from my field of vision, as well as the
bathers in the foreground, the yachts with their too daz-
zling sails" (I, 676 / I, 902). The painting and the explana-
tions of Elstir now enable him to see Balbec in its successive and simultaneous forms—a city that is both medieval
and Oriental, as well as a modern and elegant resort; that
"multiform unity" is the density and actuality of Balbec.
There remains for Marcel to experience one last aspect of
the city once he has overstayed the season and discovers
the town returned to its Cimmerian mists and gloom; but

[9] I, 629 / I, 835–836. M. Butor notes, with reference to this passage, the similarity between "cette multiforme et puissante unité"
and Baudelaire's "Dans une ténébreuse et profonde unité" in the
already quoted "Correspondances" (*Les Œuvres d'art imaginaires
chez Proust*—a monograph that analyzes in detail the relevancy of
the Carquethuit painting to the rest of the book).

his mind's eye is now able to preserve the more complex truth that Balbec represented in the golden dress of its sunlight.

The achievement of Elstir is that which Proust will attain with the completion of his own writing—"that invisible vocation of which these volumes are the history" (I, 1002 / II, 397). He has always been alert to elusive intimations of the phenomenal world, and a number of incidents describe his progress in coping with them. He recalls a verse of Racine, to which Bloch had called his attention, whose "absolutely meaningless beauty" made him a "more unwell" and tired child than he should have been. His love of hawthorns would leave him with the same sense of a hidden yet hinting truth:

> But it was in vain that I lingered before the hawthorns [in order] to breathe in, to marshall before my mind (which knew not what to make of it), to lose[,] to rediscover their invisible and unchanging odour, to absorb myself in the rhythm which disposed their flowers here and there with the lightheartedness of youth, and at intervals as unexpected as certain intervals of music; they offered me an indefinite continuation of the same charm, in an inexhaustible profusion, but without letting me delve into it any more deeply, like those melodies which one can play over a hundred times in succession without coming any nearer to their secret [I, 106 / I, 138].

He experiences incompletely what the mechanism of control might be one day in autumn, at the edge of the Montjouvain pond, near a hut in which Vinteuil's gardener keeps his tools. The sun comes out unexpectedly, the tiled roof of the hut casts a shadow on the pond that has suddenly become clear in the sunlight, and a wave of exultation sweeps through Marcel: "seeing upon the water, where it reflected the wall, a pallid smile responding to the smiling sky, I cried out in my enthusiasm, brandishing my furled umbrella: 'Damn, damn, damn, damn!' " (I, 119 / I, 155). For the first time, the experience has found the semblance of a translation into words—though they express mostly frustration (and the brandishing of the furled umbrella shows the wasted expenditure of energy that should have gone into an elucidating analysis). A little while later, Marcel will go through the analytical process to seize the joy of a special relationship between the steeples of Martinville and Vieuxvicq; he transcribes his impression immediately:

[When] I had finished writing it, I found such a sense of happiness, felt that it had so entirely relieved my mind of the obsession of the steeples, and of the mystery which they concealed, that, as though I myself were a hen and had just laid an egg, I began to sing at the top of my voice [I, 140 / I, 182].

The moment and its symbols are especially significant, for Combray, the cradle of these memories, was at first and at a distance "no more than a church epitomising the town" (I, 37 / I, 48).

What is involved in such an analysis is the careful transcription of the multiple perceptions that account for the total response to a specific phenomenon. The fame of the *madeleine* whose savor recalls a world gone by has eclipsed that of the tea into which it was dipped and whose preparation for Aunt Léonie is an extended metaphor detailing precisely the manner in which the work of art operates:

it would be my duty to shake out of the chemist's little package on to a plate the amount of lime-blossom required for infusion in boiling water. The drying of the stems had twisted them into a [whimsical] trellis, in whose intervals the pale flowers opened, as though a painter had arranged them there, grouping them in the most decorative poses. The leaves, which had lost or altered their own appearance, assumed those instead of the most incongruous things imaginable, as though the transparent wings of flies or the blank sides of labels or the petals of roses had been collected and pounded, or interwoven as birds weave the material for their nests. A thousand trifling little details—the charming prodigality of the chemist—details which would have been eliminated from an artificial preparation, gave me, like a book in which one is astonished to read the name of a person one knows, the pleasure of finding that these were indeed real lime-blossoms, like those I had seen, when coming from the train, in the Avenue de la Gare, altered, but only because they were not imitations but the very same blossoms, which had grown old [I, 39 / I, 51].

The ultimate object of this operation is to achieve again the original lime blossoms as they once were. As a matter of fact, that which will produce them is a precipitate of the former reality, a part of it (though only a part), and not in the same form. Still, that part in its new form offers an esthetic truth of its own that recalls many things which the lime blossoms are not, but in a "most decorative way." These lime blossoms correspond, in their present state, to "the necessary rings of a beautiful style" enclosing one term of the truth-revealing metaphor (see p. 202); they are "the charming prodigality of the chemist" who deals in honest dehydrations. If the metaphor is to be fully and successfully stated, its disguised truth must reach the reader unawares: as the boiling water is added to make the infusion, the lime blossoms will undergo a transformation that will be recorded by several senses. The moment the lime blossoms are affected by the water, they lose the "whimsical" shapes that drying had given them: their fanciful randomness disappears as they assume the single shape of their natural state. As the vapor then distills their essence, they also change into themselves through the pungency of their former scent and flavor. The boiling water turns the lime blossoms, through the senses of sight, smell, and taste, into what they were in the past, the reality of the Avenue de la Gare, when Marcel first saw, smelled, and savored them.

As Elstir is explaining the principles of his art to Marcel, the possibilities of another kind of awareness are being suggested, whose pictorial metaphor is another painting that interests Marcel greatly—the one called "Miss Sacripant." It is an old, seemingly discarded watercolor whose subject matter Marcel finds especially fascinating—the curious portrait of a plain but oddly compelling young girl. She is wearing a headband that suggests a bowler hat. Her hands are gloved; one holds a cigarette (at a time—the picture is dated 1872—when a young lady smoking was not a common sight), the other a large-brimmed straw hat against her knee. Her hair is puffed under the bowler-like headpiece but short. A vest of black velvet without lapels over a white shirt front makes Marcel unsure of her sex and the year in which such fashions might have been worn. Moreover, the lines of the face describe alternately a rather boyish girl or an effeminate youth in a perverse and pensive attitude. Elstir is surprised that Marcel does not know the model but does not reveal her identity. It is only in a sudden and fortuitous apprehension of the truth that Marcel recognizes Odette de Crécy:

The portrait dated from before the point at which Odette, disciplining her features, had made of her face and figure that creation the broad outlines of which her hairdressers, her dressmakers, she herself—in her way of standing, of speaking, of smiling, of moving her hands, her eyes, of thinking—were to respect throughout the years to come [I, 646–647 / I, 861].

The portrait is an early one, but Proust points out that one more recent would see, retrospectively if need be, through such metamorphoses. The portrait is not only a moral commentary on Odette ("the most damaging of birth certificates" [I, (648 / I, 863]), but a truth composed of several moments in her past, none as true as their aggregate statement. Marcel, like Swann himself, has already known Odette in a variety of persons (the lady in pink at his Uncle Adolphe's, the lady in white at Tansonville, the worldly mother of Gilberte, the elegant walking companion near the Etoile), and there will be still others; but until reflection blends them, these moments are analytical and without special reference to each other. The painting by Elstir is able to achieve a depth of characterization by uniting in a temporal simultaneity several former moments of being.

But the painting is old: it belongs to the first manner of Elstir. Seen as a moment of the painter's progress, Odette's portrait is an archaism that casts her out, her own temporal complexity notwithstanding, into the anonymous past of "other models who already belonged to the oblivion of history." The temporal depth sensed by Marcel in the portrait of Odette is suddenly absorbed into the continuing stream of time represented by Elstir. The artist becomes more than a way of understanding beauty or sententious statements about human nature that reciprocally illuminate the man and his work; "this man of genius, this sage, this eremite, this philosopher," whom Marcel is learning to know and Proust is creating, leaps into the consciousness of Marcel out of the density of his past by unexpectedly standing clear of himself as a perverse and ridiculous painter who had been taken up, many years ago, by the Verdurins. The temporal depth of "Miss Sacripant" has revealed to Marcel that Elstir was the hitherto unrelated Biche, an intuition spanning two distant moments in time and closing its circle.

Filtered light affords Proust one of his images for time as the metaphor through which can be shown the stratification of being. Marcel's lamp is converted into a magic lantern that alters his room. Projected through the lantern screens, the light does not cancel out his room but superimposes on it, through "an impalpable iridescence" (I, 7 / I, 9) the story of Geneviève de Brabant. In the church of Combray are two high-warp tapestries representing the coronation of Esther, whose features are supposed to be those of a Guermantes lady beloved of the king who appears as Ahasuerus. The fabulous name of the Guermantes, especially of the Duchesse de Guermantes, becomes in the mind of Marcel, because of these scenes and memories, a figure out of "a tapestry or a painted window" (I, 134 / I, 174–175). The first time Marcel sees the actual duchess is at a wedding in the chapel of the Combray church whose stained glass represents Gilbert the Bad and where, "beneath its flat tombstones [. . .] rested the bones of the old counts of Brabant." As usual, Marcel is disappointed by the reality that contradicts his imagination—a woman not unlike others he has seen in Combray, whose prominent nose is an intimation of temporality confirmed by a small pimple. But this time he is able to replace the living person within his emblematic vision: a benevolent glance of the duchess falls on him, "blue as a ray of sunlight that might [have entered through the stained glass] window of Gilbert the Bad" (I, 136 / I, 177). Alive, Madame de Guermantes has become for him the projection of a ray of light filtered through the many emblematic meanings of its long journey out of the past.[10] Time thus sensed as the density of being enables him to say of the church which has contained all of these moments that it is "a building which occupied, so to speak, four dimensions of space—the name of the fourth being Time—which had sailed the centuries with that old nave, where bay after bay, chapel after chapel, seemed to stretch across and hold down and conquer not merely a few yards of soil, but each successive epoch from which the whole building had emerged triumphant" (I, 46 / I, 61).

This equation of time and space has been suggested by Poulet (*L'Espace proustien*), who notes similar references as early as *Jean Santeuil* (III, 126), for whom Proust records that time resembles space. This equation accounts for a part of *Remembrance*'s architecture to which both Poulet and Moss have called attention: its people and incidents are seen in peep-show fashion, through windows, doors, hallways, as static, figured moments of being, the graphic analysis of which is provided by Marcel as he looks out into neighboring courtyards while awaiting the return of the Duc and Duchesse de Guermantes and has a vision that combines reminiscences of Venice, Delft, and Haarlem:

the extreme proximity of the houses, with their windows looking opposite one another on to a common courtyard,

[10] For the significance of the filter itself, as a static point of reference and as an objective frame for the work of art, see H. Moss, *The Magic Lantern of Marcel Proust*.

makes of each casement the frame in which a cook sits dreamily gazing down at the ground below, in which farther off a girl is having her hair combed by an old woman with the face, barely distinguishable in the shadow, of a witch: thus each courtyard provides for the adjoining house, by suppressing all sound in its interval, by leaving visible a series of silent gestures in a series of rectangular frames, glazed by the closing of the windows, an exhibition of a hundred Dutch paintings hung in rows [I, 1124 / II, 572].

Here Proust multiplies the dumb show of static images through which a spatial journey would provide the other dimensions of existence, such as time, sound, and the density of sequential experience. It is through a journey of this kind that Marcel becomes acquainted with the people of his world and they with each other, each experiencing through his motion the motion of others as a temporal metaphor that documents their substance.

Swann's failure with Odette is a negative but striking instance of this process. Proust has deliberately created her as the kind of woman to whom Swann should pay no attention: he is lettered, she ignorant; he is a creature of subtly refined tastes, while hers (at least now) are crude; there is a sickly quality to her, and he likes women whose fleshiness is a sign of health; the carnal appeal he desires is associated with a somewhat vulgar beauty, and hers is, at this stage, her only subtlety. Upon first meeting Odette, Swann judges her through a descrescendo that states his detachment; she is not devoid of beauty, but it is of a kind that leaves him unmoved, arouses in him no desire, gives him "indeed, a sort of physical repulsion" (I, 150 / I, 195). It is Odette who pursues him. Her subsequently revealed nature and his preliminary indifference should have made of their encounter a short-lived and lighthearted affair; the esthete in Swann turns their liaison into something much more gruelling. As Monnin-Hornung has shown, Swann is a man whose culture acts as a screen between him and the everyday realities of the world about him. For Swann to transcend his physical indifference toward Odette, he must first place her in a frame of reference:

The kiss, the bodily surrender which would have seemed natural and but moderately attractive, had they been granted him by a creature of somewhat withered flesh [. . .], coming, as now they came, to crown his adoration of a masterpiece in a gallery, must, it seemed, prove as exquisite as they would be supernatural [I, 172 / I, 224].

For the esthete the frame of reference is art: Swann endows Odette with a temporal depth which is not hers, choosing to see her as the incarnation of esthetic moments that belong only to his own past. On his second visit to her, he finds that she looks like Zipporah, the daughter of Jethro, in the Sistine fresco by Botticelli. From that moment on, the idea that she is a Florentine work of art will make Odette herself largely incidental to his love affair, whose perversion consists in heightening his enjoyment of certain paintings through the assumption that he is possessing them sexually. Every part of the mental world in which he displays this illusory Odette represents a simple redistribution of his esthetic notion: "the little phrase by Vinteuil" becomes the "national anthem" of his romance; he rejects an old rumor about Odette's having been a kept woman by visualizing *the* Kept Woman as a Gustave Moreau figure decked out in poisonous flowers and precious jewels—an image which cannot possibly correspond to the one into which he has cast Odette; etc.

But alongside this false metaphor which Swann has created for Odette out of two moments of his own being,

Odette is enacting the inevitable metaphor of her trajectory through time: her depravity becomes daily more
obvious. Her whereabouts, her letters, her very attitudes
are more and more difficult to account for; she deceives
Swann with Forcheville; Swann eventually receives an
anonymous letter that refers to her affairs not only with
other men but with women as well. She is much more than
unfaithful; she turns into a monster of perversion. However, Swann is a negative object lesson counterposed to
Marcel; he cannot enter into a complexity that is external
to him: "He knew quite well as a general truth, that
human life is full of contrasts, but in the case of any one
human being he imagined all that part of his or her life
with which he was not familiar as being identical with the
part with which he was" (I, 275 / I, 359). The loss of
Odette's love makes him suffer curious jealousy which is
as much a fear of figments created by his imagination as
a regret of others he can no longer conjure forth. And
throughout it all, the same works of art continue to be the
mediators of his reality. In the beginning, Odette's attitudes as she lies to Swann still remind him of women by
Botticelli; now, they simply remind him of different ones.
Vinteuil's phrase brings to him in his pain the Swann who
had first endowed the music with special significance, and
he is "jealous, now, of that other self whom she had loved"
(I, 266 / I, 347). He is able to grow completely detached
from the woman who has left him, but his pain is fostered
by the injury to his vision: he feels Odette's loss in her betrayal of his imaginary figurations.

Gradually, the flesh-and-blood Odette dissipates the
possibility of further illusions on the part of Swann: she
has become too much a specific denial of his needs. He
rehearses his pain one last time in a nightmare that trans-

poses, without altering them, the circumstances of his loss, and on awaking, is returned at last to reality. He is now able to dismiss from his mind the false metaphor of Odette; this is a form of killing, since he knows her only as figment and as the single dimension of her pre-metaphoric being that did not appeal to him. Swann returns through time to that first moment and formulates once again his first impression: she "was not in my style!" (I, 292 / I, 382). Unable to live in the reality of Odette, Swann has been deceived by time as well, conjuring up a figment between two moments of indifference. Viewed alongside the dimension that Marcel must attain, Swann's failure was one of psychological rhetoric: he did not proceed beyond the static and one-dimensional image (like the ones suggested to Marcel by courtyards which he sees through the Guermantes's window) into the genuine metaphor whose two terms measure the flux of time.

The perverse dialectic of Proust contrives that henceforth Odette will be the fashionable arbiter of style: it is Swann, her husband in years to come, who will dress to match her good taste and elegance. Nor is this the last Odette: she must still go through the miracle of youth in old age, the tragedy of senility that suddenly ensues, the redemption of the name "de Crécy" legitimated in retrospect, and the subsequent title of Forcheville that establishes her as the mistress of the Duc de Guermantes. Nor is there to be an ultimate Odette; her final image will be composed of all the others viewed through the transparency of time past. None of the characters can be only his own final incarnation: such is the truth that Marcel must experience through duration. His "vocation" depends on his ability to record and analyze the phenomenal world in its flux more accurately than Swann. (It is interesting to

note the candor of both the narrator and Proust. Marcel,
in his questions, is impelled by only a single concern—to
know. Throughout a trajectory that takes him out of his
bourgeois family and from the most glittering heights of
the *faubourg* Saint-Germain to the depths of depravity,
Marcel remains an utterly candid recorder, all of whose
questions are equivalent, without the hint of either an
afterthought or a moral sense: to each, he brings the good
will and open-mindedness of genuine interest and complete
naïveté, and never does Proust betray him through comment, detachment, or another point of view. Prince and
pervert, sinner and saint interest Marcel only to the extent
that they offer him entry into new worlds; his questions
never put the worlds themselves in question.) [11]

Nevertheless, the density of that trajectory, its human
and temporal weight, is dependent on the mistakes that
Marcel will make. Like Swann, he will fall in love with
creatures of his own contriving, like the wholly literary
construct Gilberte, endowed by him with the prestige of
his admiration for Bergotte—simply because Bergotte is
supposed to be a good friend of hers. He will try to entrap
Albertine within the single visage that his well-being requires of their love, before realizing that Albertine is a
creature very much like Odette.[12] These necessary errors
are ways of distinguishing between desire and time—
desire, with its need for a self-defining permanency, being
powerless to arrest the character in any moment of his

[11] At least until the embittered rewritings and expansions after
1918 (the date suggested by A. Feuillerat, in *Comment Marcel
Proust a composé son roman*).
[12] One of the changes that records the passing of time is the sexual alternation of the characters; it is significant not only in
Odette and Charlus, but in many other major figures such as Albertine, Gilberte, Saint-Loup, the Prince de Guermantes, etc.

continuous change. Each character, when he first appears, is already in the fullness of a motion that never ceases and that causes his body, his manner, and his world to go through continual transformations, no matter how paradoxical they might appear when judged retrospectively.[13] Swann himself, the fashionable esthete, the darling of high society, too worldly to have been more than a fraction of a Jew through the remoteness of forgotten genitors, ends, in sickness and at the height of the Dreyfus Affair, mistrustful of the very Guermantes, embittered by their complacent anti-Semitism, and is seen finally "returning to the spiritual fold of his fathers" (I, 1130 / II, 580) in the physical guise of a monstrous old Jew.

The last image of Swann demonstrates the cyclical way in which some of the characters relive an antecedent state to show graphically how, if they are to be designated accurately at the end of their lives, they must be seen as all the lives that have been encompassed within the circle of their days. In its graphic form, the illustration shows no more than the superficiality of aging: it is the putting on of a mask, an experience to which Marcel refers fre-

---

[13] This is parallel to the paradoxical vision that suddenly illuminates minor types as incarnations of epic paintings: every surface is deceptive. The tyrannical servant of Marcel's family, Françoise, has the mien and the features of an aristocrat—she has everything of nobility but nobility itself, and that she lacks to the point of crudeness and cruelty: whereas the most quintessentially elegant of these women, Oriane de Guermantes, was born on old French soil, and the peasant in her is visible now and then. The increasingly frequent footnotes toward the end of *The Past Recaptured* which show that the work was incomplete at the time of Proust's death show also how intent he was on demonstrating the complete relativity of any truth: time and again, the notes are no more than mechanical inversions of what the reader has been told previously.

quently, as when he speaks of the charming and slender Mme X... who had seemingly lost track of time; her mother had always looked to Marcel like an old Turkish woman, humped-over and squat; then, one day, "in a hurry, almost overnight, she had become shrunken and had faithfully reproduced her mother's resemblance to a little old Turkish woman" (II, 1048 / III, 941). It is in this way that Gilberte becomes so like her mother that at the end Marcel mistakes her for Odette. A more moving version of the circularity instanced by Mme X... and her daughter is provided by the two characters who represented nearly an absolute ideal for Proust and who could only, like some inalterable flow, turn into themselves: Marcel's grandmother ages and dies "almost overnight" and is reincarnated through her daughter, Marcel's mother, who has aged "overnight" to perpetuate her.

The structural design of the book, in its detail and its synthesis, is an attempt to achieve equivalences of time. When Proust makes use of even poetic devices such as synesthesia, he demonstrates a deliberate refusal of economy that is nonpoetic. Synesthesia is the trick through which the author avoids the conscious process that description requires of the reader (the bringing together of two or more relatively distant terms) by inducing that comparison through an automatic response; yet Proust returns even synesthesia to the realm of argument which it was meant to circumvent. When he comments synesthetically on a list of proper nouns, he seems less concerned with showing the reader actual towns or fictional people than with demonstrating the poetic derivations which the names allow. His use of a less intimate form, the metaphor, is generally formalized (as previously noted) by the leisurely use of the conjunction that makes of its terms a simile. Moreover, Proust does not use metaphors, any more than he does the synesthetic process, merely for their intended purpose; they become instead the pretext for digressions on metaphor: he notes the ways in which metaphor records experience in the world of art, within the depth of time, within his own experience as it refers to his "vocation"—both through the progress of that vocation and within the world which that progression describes. There seem to be two main reasons why Proust objectifies, in such a leisurely and peripheral way, processes generally meant to eliminate discourse between the writer and his reader: the first is that Proust needs time; the second is that he is deliberately preparing the reader to assimilate his work in the same way as metaphor synthesizes experience.

Poulet (*L'Espace proustien*) has called attention to the defect of intelligence pointed out by Bergson: intelligence is fallible in that it cannot grasp separate moments of consciousness simultaneously and therefore does not respond to the intuitive sense that states being as a continuity. Proust answers that the vision of art is retrospective and that it can effect its synthesis through the control of time and the interrelations that define it: art, not desire, is able to arrest time by fixing within a metaphor the single terms with which intelligence provides it. The work of art exists as a controlled period traversed by its recorder and the reader. The image of something static through which the informing, analytical intelligence proceeds is frequent in Proust's novel. It appears at the very start in the dual worlds of Swann and the Guermantes—worlds into which one can walk, but which exist also at the consecrated level of the symbol:

I had invested each of them, by conceiving them in this way as two distinct entities, with that cohesion, that unity which belongs only to the figments of the mind; the smallest detail of either of them appeared to me as a precious thing, which exhibited the special excellence of the whole [. . .]. But, above all, I set between them, far more distinctly than the mere distance in miles and yards and inches which separated one from the other, the distance that there was between the two parts of my brain in which I used to think of them, one of those distances of the mind which time serves only to lengthen, which separates things irremediably from one another, keeping them for ever upon different planes [I, 103–104 / I, 134–135].

The mental view that keeps these worlds apart must be dissipated eventually by the synthesis of the work of art; but prior to that, it is Marcel, as he walks down those paths, who must bring them to life. Similarly, there is outlined against the Balbec sea a frieze of young girls, motionless in their flight. Their movement waits for the time when Marcel will enter their world and move alongside them, his trajectory becoming the motion of their flight. Walks, bicycles, trains (and, a little surprisingly for a novel written around the time of the first World War, even private cars and planes) provide the means of a journey, either actual or symbolic, the analytic moments of which compose a fragmented landscape until the completed journey turns the fragments into a coherent synthesis through the retrospect of its informing motion.

These are of course the modes of fiction. The experiential journey of Marcel may in fact describe that of Marcel Proust, but the manner of its relation suggests its ultimate dependency upon another reality.[14] "Control" within the novel defines in part the attempt to place its reader within the rule of the limited experience which it proposes. The

[14] The extent to which both worlds may be contrasted can be judged through G. D. Painter's painstaking biography (*Proust: Vol. I, The Early Years; Vol. II, The Later Years*).

worlds of Tansonville and the Vivonne, the frieze of the
young girls at Balbec will be experienced by Marcel, but
the fictional time created by his analysis becomes for the
reader the reality of phenomenal time. According to Shattuck, it is Proust's purpose "to make us *see* time" (*Proust's
Binoculars*, p. 46). Shattuck is defending his thesis, according to which Proust's world becomes dimensional for the
reader through the means of what he terms a "binocular"
vision—the possibility of seeing two different images of a
truth separated by a distance of error. Such an analysis
offers a valid explanation of the Proustian metaphor, and
the verb *see* presumably subtends both moments of perception, since no more than the faulty imagination defined
by Bergson can human vision grasp simultaneously two
images that are sequential in time. But the distance between the two terms does constitute for the reader the experience of a temporal reality. While Marcel journeys
through fictional time, something happens (as it does in
nearly every great work, a part of whose greatness is
size): [15] the magnitude of his journey develops within the
period of physical time required for reading about it.
When Marcel realizes at last that "all the materials of the
literary work were my life past" (II, 1015–1016 / III,
899), the truth of that "life past" is situated within a span
of time that is now the past of the reader: he is the one
who holds together in his experience the various moments
whose memory provides the synthesis of Marcel's awareness. The frieze of young girls unfolds within the reader's
recollection; the paths along the Vivonne and toward
Tansonville become at last the two terms of a single meta-

---

[15] An identical phenomenon occurs, for example, in Cervantes: all
of *Don Quixote*, Part II, is played against the temporal awareness
of the reader informed by the reality of Part I.

phor that rings the world of time as it is closed at the end of his journey through the book.

There is truly little else for the reader to experience, since every part of Marcel's experience has been ordinary. He has learned about the cities a young boy wanted to visit, the people he wanted to know; he recalls moments of elation and, as a recurring period, the awareness that elation was unjustified or that it must lead to the *ascesis* of creation; he remains with a vision of loves that failed and of the two that endured (a mother's and a grandmother's), of beautiful women like marine divinities in their gala splendor at the opera, of the yellow splash on a wall in a painting by Vermeer recalled by a dying author,[16] of a sick and aging father who wanted his daughter to be received into the world that had been his—a few humble gestures performed within a luxurious expanse of time. It is that expanse of time alone that makes them significant —that time which has become the reader's.

[16] The author is Bergotte, but the reader's awareness is intensified by the knowledge that the experience was Proust's, who amended that passage on his deathbed.

8

Sartre:

Nausea

Sartre's *Nausea* provides a postscript to *Remembrance of Things Past,* since it is so clearly a restatement of a number of Proust's themes. References to the novel appear in Sartre's critical writings from the start. Before the war, in 1939, he published in the *Nouvelle Revue Française* a brief note on Husserl's concept of intentionality in which he subscribed to a psychophilosophical view similar to that which Ruskin termed in criticism the "pathetic fallacy"—a belief that the subject's psychological response to the object describes a quality that is inherent in that object. This argument allowed Sartre to conclude that here at last was deliverance from Proust—a statement which may have been the more heartfelt for coming so close upon the writing of *Nausea* (1938). However, one must suppose that Sartre's declaration was somewhat premature: his lead editorial in the first issue of *Les Temps Modernes* (1945) was devoted to considerations of the writer's responsibility and contained an indictment of Proust based largely on an analysis of Swann's love affair. There had been previously some passing swipes at the ill-laid ghost, in *Being and Nothingness* (1943); there were to be still others.

For Sartre, literature is primarily a human manifestation. He is more concerned with Proust, the author who created Marcel, Swann, and Odette, than he is with investigating as final terms the behavior of Marcel, Swann, and Odette within the novel; the subject of every reference must be, in the last assertion, a person—not a fiction or an idea. But Sartre also rejects the possibility that Proust's characters might provide meaningful insights as far as human behavior is concerned. Nevertheless, his criticism has something to say about Proust's novel and considerably more about novels in general, the relation of author to reader, the purpose of literature. And when Sartre writes his own novel, he contrives a number of devices that are interesting as commentary and as instances of technique in the continuing dialogue between the writer and his reader.

Some mention has already been made of Elstir's phenomenological apperception, the model through whose imitation Marcel will avoid the failure of a Swann and acquire the ultimate dimension of Marcel Proust, the author who turns his hero's idle days and failures into a book. Elstir's way of looking at the world was compatible with Sartre's philosophical method at the time he was writing *Nausea*, his epistemology deriving from an apprehension of the world through its impression on him (a point of view that requires him to base his ontology and his ethics on an attempted description of the world, that is to say its statement through his single perception). Sartre and Elstir resist reference to criteria that are external to them as percipients. They acknowledge no external authority, intending to preserve the rectitude of their vision from the distortion it might suffer within a frame of reference that extends beyond it. The world exists for them as impress, not as a set of relations between itself and their apprehen-

sion of it or the truths of others. The security of their
analysis rests on the intensity and the acuity of their sight:
it does not require a concern with the causes of their perception. This concentration on their single experience
places them alone before a world which is unremittingly
theirs to interpret for the very first time.

The world of Sartre is a continual becoming whose recorder is caught up in its flux: there is no constant landscape; there are no fixed vantage points; there is no inher-
ited wisdom. His human being knows only the object
within the beam of its consciousness, but that consciousness is in its entirety an "exploding towards" that object:
his apperception is not the sensitizing of an inner image;
it is a tension, a striving *outward*.[1] Sartre therefore
taxes Proust with a certain rigidity, arguing that his characters conform to patterns of behavior that determine
them and for which their author finds physical causes. The
character's psychological fatality inhibits the freedom of
his becoming and makes of his acts the causal result of his
categorical definition. Sartre has harsh words for a psychology of characters that intellectualizes them, turning
them into the molecular fragments of their analysis. This
kind of analysis implies first, and incorrectly, that there are
categories of behavior, that the passion which Swann feels
for Odette is a constitutive part of man; secondly, it assumes that the molecular bits and pieces of that affection
can be revealed by the author's analysis as existing in juxtaposition to each other, preserved from the constancy of
mutual interaction. In the view of Sartre, love cannot be
analyzed, because, like all feelings, it is dialectical: the
mechanistic analysis of Proust does not allow the organic
development of his characters, since it makes them exem-

[1] As the article on Husserl makes clear. (The development of this
argument within its context appears in *L'Imaginaire*, 1939.)

plars of a condition that exists, according to Sartre, outside them.

Since emotion is for Sartre a way of relating to an object, a tropism that inclines the subject toward its quality-informed object, the author can only describe that object and the form of the subject's tension. That tension, however, is not a human inherence: it is the result of a complex conditioning. The synthesis represented by an individual at any given moment is the result of forces acting on him; a character must be shown reacting in a way that is representative of his social class, his moment in time, and so on. Just as Proust assumed that there are enduring states within the human psyche, he erred as a bourgeois by supposing that the bourgeois response to love (Swann's, for example) is the only kind. It was as much a mistake for Proust the homosexual to think that he could extend his experience to heterosexual love as it was for him to infer through omission that a worker would have responded to Odette in the same way as Swann.

This criticism of Proust does not suggest the possibility of a better novel but of a more purposeful one. As conceived by Sartre, the object of literature is to "reveal" the world, a project that is different from the aims of esthetic enjoyment contemplated by the bourgeois novel: that revelation is not immediately pleasurable; it is certainly not its own ultimate object; it is achieved, to a degree, at the expense of the writer. Quite aside from the social struggle that determines a part of it, the Sartrean world is ambiguous and ultimately negative—"this hostile and friendly, terrible and derisive world." [2] A moral responsibility is thus placed on the writer to change such a world by turn-

[2] *What Is Literature?*, p. 239. The esthetic views of Sartre that follow are largely a summary of that book, which represented his literary creed in 1947.

ing his writing to a social purpose. In contrast to the bourgeois writer who seeks to institutionalize and perpetuate an unsatisfactory situation, the socially conscious writer must keep his reader mindful of that unsatisfactoriness in order to elicit a reaction that will lead to change. All literature presumably effects some sort of change, but whereas bourgeois writing seeks no more than an intimate change within the reader,[3] the change envisaged by Sartre is to be effected ultimately on society. The moral choice of the socially responsible writer forces an *ascesis* on him: even though he is the mediator between the world and his reader, he must disappear for the good of his mediating object; the literary object is expected to transmit only that world, not the author.

Sartrean man is polymorphous, at least potentially. He is thrust out among men, shapes and is shaped by social forces, continues in motion through time and upon a restless land: such is his "situation." The means through which the author is expected to demonstrate that "situation" and the manner of the reader's understanding show that Sartre depends on a wholly intellective link between author and reader. The novel cannot be thought of as an isolated object: its correct definition states its mediating position between world and reader. It supposes automatically a reader, just as surely as it supposes "disclosure." If the book is successful, the reader reacts to its description of incident as he does, in the nonfictional world, to the

[3] Unless the bourgeois writer is attempting for the bourgeois world what the socially conscious writer attempts for the havenots: to generate some form of social action. (The bourgeois writer would of course represent the point of view of the haves; his social action would seek to preserve rather than to change the class structure, a self-evident evil.)

solicitation of the quality-informed object. But such response through emotion must not be, as in the bourgeois novel, an end in itself.

To effect the reader's response, the writer uses words—what Sartre calls "signs," intenders of a meaning beyond themselves. They are the quasi-automatic reach of the writer into the world and should not become his special concern, an intrusion between the world and its description: the writer must point with them, unconsciously, as he would with a part of his own body. His words must not become for him what they are for poets, objects used for their own sake, conveyors of a sound rather than of an immediate sense—things without a reference. It is this difference in usage that helps Sartre to distinguish between poetry (presumably lyric poetry) and literature; the former is not literature but an art of incantation ("on the side of" painting, sculpture, music). Literature refuses such magic; it does not rely on persuasion at levels other than that of the conscious mind. Literature tells a story that describes the phenomenal world; it must remain such and guard against the "obscure harmonies" that exist beyond that description.

The transcription effected by literature must be so direct that the manner of removal of the author from his writing is spelled out by Sartre: there is to be no third-person narrator through whose eyes the reader is forced to see. For similar reasons, the omniscient author is not allowed through overt manipulation or comment to influence the reader's view:[4] the author's description must be sufficiently accurate and impersonal to construct a substi-

[4] As will be shown later, Robbe-Grillet believes that Sartre failed when he attempted to carry out this element of his literary doctrine.

tute for its phenomenal object to which the reader will be able to react in identical fashion. Within this fictional world that is so faithful a copy, there must be a character as perilously free as is man, one who is not constructed or bounded by his fiction—a character whose beginnings antecede the beginning of his story, the end of which does not foreordain him to that particular end.

And withal, Sartre still expects esthetic concern and control from his writer, who has a duty to himself as a writer as well as to the man he is within the world of men. He may not be able to mirror himself within his writings, but still he must assert himself as a user of words. His novel must be cast in a specific form, related to his assumptions and the requirements of the characters. He must not reach his reader through the insidious osmosis of poetic means, but his style is nonetheless the instrument through which the reader must be influenced—even though it is only the free cooperation of that reader which is sought. Sartre does not make clear how this influence short of influence is to be achieved, but he does note that style cannot procure esthetic pleasure for its own sake; the pleasure it is to procure consists in allowing its reader an accurate appreciation of the world as "a task proposed to human freedom."

It is possible to read *Nausea* as simply a realistic novel describing the bourgeois doldrums of a French provincial town. It is the diary of Antoine Roquentin, an intellectual, who, after a life spent in many parts of the world, has come to Bouville, a dreary seaport (actually a combination of Le Havre, where Sartre taught between 1931 and 1933, and his childhood memories of La Rochelle). Roquentin is in Bouville in order to pursue research on a biography of the Marquis de Rollebon, a minor figure of intrigue in boudoirs and courts of the late eighteenth century. What prompts him to start his diary is a curious sensation described in the "undated pages" that precede it. A few days before, some children were playing at skimming stones. Roquentin wanted to do the same. He picked up a stone: "I saw something which disgusted me, but I no longer know whether it was the sea or the stone." [5] He dropped the stone and left.

After this anecdote follows the diary, a chronicle of what Roquentin will come to identify as his nausea, the preliminary symptom of which is the self-assertion of objects. They have inverted roles with him: they are no longer the unnoticed extension of a human function; it is as if *they* were touching him. Feeling them, he now feels himself feeling them. What starts as a "nausea in the hands" (p. 20) becomes an all-pervading sense, Roquentin's subjective reaction to his awareness of being; in asserting themselves, the objects assert Roquentin's difference. He has become a density of self-awareness, a massy consciousness, and the feeling is one of sweetish sickness. It is not altogether new; once before, in Indochina, he had felt, all of a sudden and unaccountably, out of things: "What was I doing there? Why was I talking to these people? Why was I dressed so oddly?" (p. 13). But now, the sense of nausea has become endemic; he realizes through its stubborn persistence, not only that his life is unsatisfactory and largely unpleasant, but that there is no coherence or necessary sequence to it. His past is the recall of desultory scenes; since he can give no structure to it, his attempt to

[5] P. 8. The translation used is that by Lloyd Alexander. Bracketed material represents changes made to bring the text into closer conformity with the original.

resurrect an alien figure out of a different world will soon
prove unfeasible. He eventually gives up the biography of
Rollebon; a subsequent entry reads, "Nothing. Existed"
(p. 140).

Bouville provides a fitting decor for the nausea of Roquentin; his diary records the petty dreariness and the
closed horizon of bourgeois life in a provincial town: the
deadness and the false front of its Sundays; its museum
with the glazed likenesses of generations of its sclerotic
notables; the public park with its perverts and chestnut
trees; the ugliness of its public monuments; the cafés with
their perennial card players; the restaurants behind card-
board chefs holding a menu; the public library where
Roquentin meets a self-taught man reading his way
through the shelves, methodically—"Today he has
reached 'L'–'K' after 'J,' 'L' after 'K' " (p. 45)—until one
day he is thrown out for attempting a homosexual pass.
And throughout it all, Roquentin's nausea persists, with
but a single alleviation; that occurs whenever he hears a
scratchy old jazz record—"Some of These Days." In the
brief silence that follows its playing he realizes, *"Something has happened"* (p. 34): his sense of nausea has been
dispelled for a while.

In days past, Roquentin had a girl friend, Anny; he
thinks of her occasionally, imagining at times that her
presence might dissipate his present sickness. He recalls
that she had a "love of perfection" (pp. 86 ff.), a need for
what she called "perfect moments." She was an actress and
would attempt to stage such perfect moments in their private life with some elaborateness. There being nothing to
keep him in Bouville any more, Roquentin decides to leave
for Paris in answer to a summons from Anny, only to find
out nearly immediately that his Bouville reminiscences

about Anny belong to a time and world that are irremediably beyond their grasp. Anny has changed: there are no more perfect moments; things disgust her too. Roquentin wonders whether she is not suffering from the same sickness. She tells him how the privileged moments began: they came from an illustration in a history book, the large edition of Michelet's *History of France*, which she had when she was a child: "I had an extraordinary love for those pictures; I knew them all by heart, and whenever I read one of Michelet's books, I'd wait for them fifty pages in advance" (p. 196). These pictures—there were few of them—represented the perfect moments of the book; they were the definitive form into which history had been moving. Later, Anny attempted to order her life that way:

First you had to be plunged into something exceptional and feel as though you were putting it in order. If all those conditions had been realized, the moment would have been perfect. [. . .] You *had* to transform privileged situations into perfect moments. It was a moral question [p. 199].

But now it is over, Anny has given up such attempts. Like Roquentin, she has been evicted from a world in which objects and moments can be controlled, and forced into an awareness of her own displacement within the world. The near-identity of their states will thus prevent Anny and Roquentin from being able to reach one another: each has become aware of existential isolation. Antoine and his nausea return to Bouville.

The damp and morose embrace of Bouville is unchanged. But the record can still be heard—"Some of these days . . ." There is still release in it for Roquentin, who perceives through the song the glimmer of a kind of salvation: might it not be possible for him to be in a sense his own record of himself, for him to write a book, not about Rollebon but about himself, that would make of his nausea something like the song into which its creators once turned their misery?

The experiment that Roquentin is about to undertake is not unlike the project of Marcel: both will try to recapture the past—their past—by writing a book about it; both works end at the moment when they are about to start writing it. Each will use as his vehicle the society through which he moved, and the eye of both is equally destructive. A number of critics have noted how Proust repeatedly tears down a world whose mental re-creation is to be such a source of satisfaction.[6] At first glance, it would seem as if Sartre is pursuing the same illogical purpose when he suggests that the salvation of Roquentin might come through the chronicle that documents his unhappiness; for Sartre, however, that chronicle will be a conscious way of dealing with his unhappiness.

Each author is concerned with the process of time and memory, and as the writer of a novel, with the need to involve the reader is something more essential than merely the reading of a novel; each is attempting to give his fictional statement the experiential dimension of his reader; for both, that reader must be a participant in the re-creation of time. But time and memory mean different things to each author. Sartre objects to Proust's dissolution of the past. For Proust, the past as past is little more than an unawareness of its present presence: time and again,

[6] See, e.g., R. Kuhn, "Proust and Sartre: The Heritage of Romanticism," *Symposium*, XVIII (Winter 1964); R. Champigny, "Temps et reconnaissance chez Proust et quelques philosophes," *PMLA*, LXXIII (March 1958).

Marcel stumbles over it physically, for example on the uneven flagstones in the Combray church or the cobbles in the Guermantes' courtyard. Sartre cannot accept that, after tasting the *madeleine*, Marcel should no longer feel contingent and mortal, a change which presupposes that he carries the past in him and can be delivered of it by turning it into a form of the present.[7] For Sartre, the self cannot exist in such a relation to the past: the past is a deadness within a being whose becoming carries with it a constant sense of futurity. The tension of the human consciousness toward its object is also a tension toward an unachieved moment in time.

Memory, the belief that the present self was involved in a former moment, is fallacious. The self was involved, but it was another self, not the present one; that other self is the "facticity," the object-like part (since it cannot be affected) of *being* defined as a drive to the future. Marcel recalling Marcel-that-was can be only Marcel recalling: the difference between the two Marcels is the difference between the part of him that is object (the past, his "facticity," the "en-soi") and the part that is project (the one drawn ahead toward the object of its consciousness, the self as "pour-soi"). The present "I" has only awareness, not duration; the present Marcel can never be his past self through an act of present will, even though that past is forever an unmovable part of him.

The flight ahead dispossesses even the present—that springboard receding from the leap into the future. The present can be conceived only as part of an ontological span of nothingness, tensed between a present canceled by

[7] For a full account of Sartre's views on time as here summarized, see *Being and Nothingness*, especially the chapters on temporality and transcendence.

the onward surge and a future that remains forever unstated. It follows from these differing concepts of temporality and memory that Marcel and Roquentin will try
to relate themselves to their past experience in different
ways.

Nausea describes several attempts on the past, starting
with Roquentin's biography of Rollebon. Any such act,
in Sartrean fiction, is given as a clue to the ontological development of the character. At this point, Roquentin is not
conscious of his reasons for writing about Rollebon, but it
is noteworthy that in the past the task has given him occasional pleasure (a startling note in a diary that is the
record of his present gloom):

How I loved M. de Rollebon that year! I remember one evening—a Tuesday evening: I had worked all day in the Maza-
rine; I had just gathered, from his correspondence, of 1789–
90, in what a magisterial way he duped Nerciat. It was dark, I
was going down the Avenue du Maine and I bought some
chestnuts at the corner of the Rue de la Gaité. Was I happy!
I laughed all by myself thinking of the face Nerciat must
have made when he came back from Germany [p. 22].

Roquentin does not yet realize that he will not be able to
continue writing the biography. Though he is conscious of
neither, there are two immediate reasons for his joy: he
has brought an ordering to Rollebon's past (his discovery
of the true nature of the relation between Rollebon and
Nerciat); he has achieved what Sartre describes in *What Is
Literature?* as the reason for artistic motivation—the need
to feel essential with reference to the world. In discovering
the true relation between Rollebon and Nerciat, Roquentin has turned a former contingency into a necessary link;
he has given an essential ordering to an existential random-

ness, for even through his misguided attempts on Rollebon, he is seeking to establish a viable relation with a part
of time. Roquentin is at fault primarily because of his object; Rollebon is as dead as any past, but his deadness is not
a necessary part of Roquentin.

Roquentin's visit to the Bouville museum illustrates the
inexcusable reverse of such a process, an intent to make
the past the truth of the present, out of a conviction
which Sartre calls "l'esprit de sérieux"—the belief that
there are ultimate and absolute values, that the moment of
an act can be isolated and arrested in order to serve as the
exemplar of exemplary imitations to come. At one level,
the portraits hanging in the museum extend the caricature
of the bourgeoisie in the dim, provincial town. But the
paintings also demonstrate an ontological mode. The past
dignitaries of Bouville are caught in the single dimension
of pigment on canvas, a suggestion of life that is in fact a
lie but an accurate representation of their moral endeavors,
their desire to arrest the existential flow for the sake of social or economic considerations benefiting their class.
They are like the dead in *No Exit* (1944), for whom the
line has been drawn and who are nothing more than the
sum of acts which they can no longer contradict through
the realization of themselves as "project." But the living
are constant "projects" (the *projection* of their consciousness towards its object): they cannot will themselves into
static objects, hence cannot impose that will on others.
The will of the Bouville grandees attempts to go against an
ontological assertion: it is philosophically unsound and socially pernicious; their paintings in the Bouville museum
are emblematic of the reasons for which Roquentin calls
them "bastards" (p. 129).

A more congenial instance of a similar error is the Self-taught man. He is a humanist, a believer in a system of thinking that makes a man and his interests dominant. The Autodidact is first guilty of thinking systematically— humanism represents an "esprit de sérieux" that is not fundamentally different from any other attempt to inhibit the dialectic of becoming by superimposing upon it pre- conceived ideas. The Autodidact sees the world, including Roquentin, through conventions which contradict existen- tial truth, especially as it applies to the domains of experi- ence and literature, because he derives these conventions from books. He has spent seven years in the Bouville li- brary reading its books without any plan other than their alphabetical sequence. He is the victim of a tautology: be- cause they are instances of human creation, he has a boundless faith in books and their power to show him definitive man in all his forms. He does not know that what is in books (even if he were able to "acquire" it) must be as unmanageable and unrepresentative as any other "facticity": a book can be no more than a moment receding, arrested and removed by its own death. The fact that life has nothing to do with books will be proven to him when it invades and collapses the sanctuary of the false world he has provided for himself. His homosexual gesture ("hardly sensuality—rather a form of humanism" [p. 214]) will lead to his explusion from the library, forcing him to start "his apprenticeship in solitude" (p. 215); this means that henceforth, he must be his own book—a statement not necessarily as pessimistic as it might seem.

Dwelling exclusively in a world of books, the Self- taught man makes other mistakes of an ontological and lit- erary nature. One of the first times he meets Requentin he decides, from having seen the latter at work in the library, that he must be repeating passages from his manuscript to himself, in order to spot and remove Alexandrines that might have slipped in—"Should we not, Monsieur, carefully avoid Alexandrines in prose?" (p. 43). It so happens that words are among the few things that Roquentin does not have trouble with—they at least, inasmuch as he is a writer, do not turn into alienating objects. Roquentin is suspicious of "literature" that allows the autonomy of words; even through Rollebon, he is attempting to elucidate a *life*—his words are prehensile and outward bound; they do not become those self-reflecting objects that keep out the world for the pure artist. But to the Self-taught man, Roquentin is a writer, that is to say, someone concerned with form—form which, after all, reflects a man creating.

As a matter of fact, when the Autodidact addressed him, Roquentin was confronting the malevolent statue of Impétraz, a nineteenth-century academic now fittingly returned to the rigidity of bronze; but the Self-taught man is doomed to make incorrect assumptions about Roquentin. A creature of books, he believes in their world but still senses a need for actualization: paradoxically, he wants the world of his literary categories to become existential. Roquentin seems to him like an incarnation, the near-reality of adventure:

He leans towards me, his eyes half-closed, and asks:
"Have you had many adventures, Monsieur?"
"A few," I answer mechanically, throwing myself back to avoid his tainted breath. Yes. I said that mechanically, without thinking. In fact, I am generally proud of having had so many adventures [p. 52].

Like many other parts of this world which he previously took for granted, this one also is becoming prob-

lematical for Roquentin; an adventure too is a function of
time:

Something is beginning in order to end: adventure does not
let itself be drawn out; it only makes sense when dead. [. . .]
Each instant appears only as part of a sequence. I cling to
each instant with all my [might]. I know that it is unique, irre-
placeable—and yet I would not raise a finger to stop it from
being annihilated. [. . .] All of a sudden something breaks off
sharply. The adventure is over, time resumes its daily [indo-
lence. . . .] I think I would accept—even if I had [once
risked death, lost a fortune], a friend—to live it all over again,
in the same circumstances, from end to end. But an adventure
never returns nor is prolonged [pp. 54–55].

Roquentin then hears his favorite record and thinks that if
his own life were the texture of that melody, the adventure of his existence would seem less unsatisfactory. This
incomplete formulation represents a tentative start along
one of the paths he must walk. But he leaves it in order to
consider another which he must explore as well; adventures are also a mode of telling:

a man is always a teller of tales, he lives surrounded by his
stories and the stories of others, he sees everything that happens to him through them; and he tries to live his own life as
if he were telling a story.
    But you have to choose: live or tell [p. 56].

Once in San Pauli, while he was waiting for a woman, he
began to tell himself what had happened since he landed:
"Then I felt violently that I was having an adventure."
But when the woman came back and put her arms around
his neck, he began to live once again and the adventure
faded—for nothing happens while one lives.

But everything changes when you tell about life; it's a change no one notices: the proof is that people talk about true stories. As if there could possibly be true stories; things happen one way and we tell about them in the opposite sense. You seem to start at the beginning [but] in reality you have started at the end. [. . .] the end is there, transforming everything. For us, the [storyteller] is already the hero of the story. His moroseness, his money troubles are much more precious than ours, they are all gilded by the light of future passions. And the story goes on in the reverse: instants have stopped piling themselves in a [random] way one on top of the other, they are snapped up by the end of the story which draws them and each one of them in turn draws out the preceding instant [pp. 57–58].

And Roquentin gets a first glimpse of the truth: "I wanted the moments of my life to follow and order themselves like those of a life remembered. You might as well try and catch time by the tail."

Fiction has a quality lacking in existence: the consciousness of experience appears to be more satisfactory than its enactment. And yet, that fiction relates an enactment—it is just that enactment and consciousness are generally separate. The experience of Anny is exactly parallel to his. She senses that the pictures in Michelet's history tomes are the *end* of a now predictable sequence of events: history seen from the moment of the picture is no longer the accumulation of "random" ("au petit bonheur") moments. So in her own life, when the moment was sufficiently exceptional for her to be able to remove herself from it in order to *sense it*, when she felt that the moment was privileged, she thought that if she could arrest and orchestrate its context, turn it into a static picture like that in the Michelet, she would be able to transform the privileged situation into

a perfect moment. And that is precisely what Roquentin
describes as trying to "catch time by the tail." The mistake
of Anny is that she is guilty of estheticism; she is trying
through art to give life a form—life, which by the definition of its flow forward, is *formless*—like the good men of
Bouville who protected the interests of their class because
they assumed (in Proustian fashion) a bourgeois universe
and a bourgeois inevitability. Like the Autodidact who believed that life must be necessarily shaped by and like man,
Anny is guilty of attempting to place within the flow of
existence the dam of a preconceived notion; she is guilty
of believing that she can bring the present into being.

The works of nonfiction which the Self-taught man
reads along the shelves of the Bouville library are dams of
this kind—like the bronze Impétraz or the glazed paintings of the notables—ossifications which an "esprit de
sérieux" had envisaged as truths for all time, without
realizing that truth, at its most accurate, is caught up in
time and that the onward flow is forever canceling the
present and its truth. Bad as his nonfiction may be, the
Self-taught man's fiction must be even worse. First and
foremost, the mode of fiction is to arrest, but it arrests that
which is arrested already: it renders conspicuous and places
in a sequence the moment that would otherwise be lost in
the death of so many others. But literature generally claims
an immanence for itself, and none with less justification
than bourgeois naturalism—a genre that must be plentifully
represented in Bouville, to judge from its other tastes. Perhaps because his own fiction looks so much like a product
of French naturalism, Sartre has particularly decried that
mode in *What Is Literature?* [8] He accepts the principle, as

[8] In *Nausea* he shows the noncongruence of *Eugénie Grandet* by
juxtaposing it against the background conversations of the cus-

did Zola when he applied to his writing the methods of nineteenth-century experimental physiology, that the naturalistic novel treats its subject matter as the scientist studies a human organism within his laboratory, supposing predictable reactions to specific conditions. Since, moreover, the human organism presents a pattern of irreversible decay, it is easy to see why Sartre cannot accept naturalism, so-conceived, as either an ontologically accurate description of man's freedom or an adequate framework for his ethical action.[9]

Naturalism of either sort would suppose a reader of abundant good will, willing to accept as his own and without transitions *life* as described by the author. And in fact this kind of acceptance is not what Sartre wishes; on the contrary, he believes that everyday vision is shaped, not so much by its object, as by the categories that define that object. The ability to see things as they are, without reference to causes or predetermining categories, the phenomenological vision, is what will make Sartre's naturalism look different. The most famous instance of such a vision is that of Roquentin before the roots of the horse-chestnut tree in the Bouville park:

> Then I had this [revelation].
> It left me breathless. Never, until these last few days, had I understood the meaning of ["existing"]. I was like the others,

tomers in the *brasserie* where Roquentin is trying to read it. This trick makes Balzac's talk seem too purposelessly purposeful.

[9] In *What Is Literature?* he refers to the determinism of the naturalistic novel as crushing life, in that it has only a single subject, the slow disintegration of a man, an endeavor, a family, or a society. If the novelist assumes that his subject has only such potentiality as is evidenced by the organic tissue upon which the physiologist experiments, then he must of course assume an inexorable movement toward decay.

like the ones walking along the seashore, all dressed in their spring finery. I said, like them, "The ocean *is* green; that white speck up there *is* a seagull," but I didn't feel that it existed or that the seagull was an "existing seagull"; usually existence hides itself. It is there, around us, in us, it is *us*, you can't say two words without mentioning it, but you can never touch it. When I believed I was thinking about it [. . .] I was thinking of *belonging*, I was telling myself that the sea belonged to the class of green objects, or that the green was a part of the quality of the sea. [. . .] And then all of a sudden, there it was, clear as day: existence had suddenly unveiled itself. It had lost the harmless look of an abstract category: it was the very paste of things, this root was kneaded [out of] existence [p. 171].

The word [Absurdity] is coming to life under my pen; a little while ago, in the garden, I couldn't find it, but neither was I looking for it, I didn't need it: I thought without words, *on* things, *with* things. Absurdity was not an idea in my head, or the sound of a voice, only this long serpent dead at my feet, this wooden serpent. Serpent or claw or root or vulture's talon, [it makes no difference]. And without formulating anything clearly, I understood that I had found the key to Existence, the key to my Nauseas, to my own life. In fact, all that I could grasp [thereafter] returns to this fundamental absurdity [p. 173].

This sudden dereliction by object of their classifications, their very names, estranges the reader as it does Roquentin.[10] Both are cut off from denotative categories: they share an identical surprise born of a similar loss of familiarity.

This state is the "absence of any metaphysical frame of

[10] As F. Jameson puts it, "The object suddenly comes loose from its name" (*Sartre: The Origins of a Style*, p. 104).

reference" already noted in Kafka's world (see p. 186); it is also the vision of Elstir, who knew that "surfaces and volumes are in reality independent of the names of objects which our memory imposes on them" and who therefore attempted "to break up that aggregate of impressions which we call vision" (see p. 204). Kafka forces the reader to see his world through the eyes of Joseph K. (whereas Proust is content to describe and comment upon the world of Elstir as if that world were merely *possible*); but Kafka also turns Joseph K. into an object of his own amusement, in order to allow the grimness of his vision to settle upon the reader through understatement. What amusement Sartre feels (and Bouville provides him with considerable amusement) never jeopardizes Roquentin: it is through him that the reader is projected directly into the phenomenological vision of the author.

The paintings of the notables are a lie that can never be more than the symbolic truth of an ontological aberration. But "Some of These Days," sung for the sake of Sartre's political consciousness by a Negro woman and composed by a Jew, *is* truth. In his anlysis of the paintings, Sartre is not seriously concerned with the vision of the painters (as Proust is concerned with the vision of Elstir), presumably because they had no vision. The passage mocks a way of thinking through its use of the allegory of academic paintings, but it does not analyze them as instances of painting.[11] In "Some of These Days," however, Sartre is concerned with only the Negro and the Jew who brought the song into being. The paintings are mere tokens, while

[11] Even when he is interested in the painter, Sartre has relatively little to say about the nonliterary elements of his painting; see *Situations*, Vol. IV, which contains a number of articles on the fine arts (especially the one on Giacometti and "Le Séquestré de Venise," on Tintoretto).

the music endures, beyond analysis, as being. Whereas the
"little phrase" by Vinteuil echoes the former moment of a
personal landscape associated with it by chance, "Some of
These Days" is the awareness of its authors, the self-
achieved ordering of two lives. The Negro and the Jew
are Morality figures of suffering; but what might otherwise have been a useless and random misery has been regulated, orchestrated by their song. For them, in retrospect,
their misery is no longer the automatic response to fortuitous incidents: it is the sharp and modulated outcry into
which they have turned it. For others, it is by contrast the
shame of the listener's existential drift.

The record is old, but the melody remains "young and
firm, like a pitiless witness" (p. 235), *beyond* the scratching and the wear. Roquentin cannot appropriate that music, as Swann appropriated Vinteuil's or as Roquentin's
Aunt Bigeois appropriated Chopin's—"Chopin's Preludes
were such a help to me when your poor uncle died" (p.
232). Even if Roquentin were to break the record, it
would still be there, since it does not exist: its people are
pure essence; the record is no more than the "en-soi" of
someone else's existence, alongside which, in the *now* of
the record's scratching and wear, Roquentin is superfluous, as he was superfluous in the presence of objects—the
roots of the chestnut tree or the pebble—that first day
along the sea.

Roquentin realizes that he wanted to *be*, like that melody: he wanted to drive existence out of himself so that it
might be ordered, predictable, static. It is possible to see in
the distance "the other side of existence" (p. 234), even
though that other side can never be approached, and what
Roquentin sees in that distance is "an exemplary suffering.
Four notes on the saxophone" (p. 233); the melody is say-

ing, "you must be like me; you must suffer in rhythm" (p. 234). The only part of Roquentin that can be object, that can be "en-soi," is the moment of his being as it drops out of the present. Forever tensed between an unknown future and the part of him that freezes suddenly as it hurtles away, into the past, Roquentin can take on the task of ordering that passing; this would amount to working on the future in the only manner in which it can be apprehended: as it passes out of existence. This would also give the writer in him a purpose ("I don't know how to do anything else"):

My error [was trying] to resuscitate [M.] de Rollebon. Another type of book. I don't quite know which kind—but you would have to guess, behind the printed words, behind the pages, at something which would not exist, which would be above existence. A story, for example, [of the kind that] never happen, an adventure. It would have to be beautiful and hard as steel and make people ashamed of their existence [p. 237].

A possibility for Roquentin would be to do with his life what the Negro and the Jew have done with theirs; he is thinking of the kind of story that corresponds exactly to "Some of These Days": one that "would not exist," that would consequently represent the now permanent and forever ordered part of his being; one that would "make people ashamed of their existence" because its ordering would stand in such contrast to the reader's headlong and continuous flight *into* being; one that would be, in its ordering, beautiful, permanent, and hard as steel. (The jazz tune has already been described as "young and firm"; each saxophone note is "sharp, precise" [p. 234]; and it cuts "like a scythe" [p. 233] through the lukewarm intimacy, the soft and shapeless present of Roquentin's existence).

"Some of These Days" is a prolonged cry modulated as the sharp, clear notes of jazz. The misery of Roquentin is "Nausea," an oppressive, metaphysical sense of existence reflected in the ugliness of a humdrum and narrow-minded city, existence alone amid indifference—his and that of the people around him. His adventure is the discovery of his alienation from objects and his consequent submersion into indissoluble awareness. He anticipates a resolution of his dilemma in the hope that this sense of drowning can be overcome by turning its moments into the structured object of his consciousness. Roquentin attempts such a structuring twice. The "Undated Pages" at the beginning are random notes, first short-lived attempts to explain exactly the way in which objects have changed; there is a mention of the previous incident with the stone (the first of these weird, privileged moments) and shortly thereafter, the end of the episode: "What is there to fear in such a regular world? [. . .] I'm going to bed. I'm cured. I'll give up writing my daily impressions" (p. 9). The "Editor's Note" preceding the jottings indicates that "there is good reason to believe" that the undated pages were written some weeks before the diary itself. There is good reason indeed: those few weeks follow Roquentin's discovery that he was not cured (the diary starts with "Something has happened to me, I can't doubt it any more. It came as an illness does"), a period of self-exploration during which he tried to escape through such activity as his work on Rollebon and his visit to Anny—a period that ended the day the jazz record allowed him his final revelation.

That final revelation requires Roquentin to write a story, though he still does not know of what kind, that will turn his life into "something precious and almost legendary" (p. 238), as the jazz record has done for a Jewish composer and a Negro singer: the silent outcry of Roquentin must find a mythical form. That form cannot incarnate Roquentin if it does not give a sense of him as he was, a man caught up in the viscidity of being, desperately trying to arrest the unarrestable. It is clear that his novel will be rather similar to the ideal model proposed by Sartre: its story will situate a recognizably representative man within the present form of the class structure. The statement of that story will be direct, without the mediating presence of a belletristic author, a manipulating god, or an all-knowing narrator—the plain record of moments, people, and objects noted with sufficient accuracy and impersonality to prevent their making more complicated demands on the reader's way of perceiving them than would their phenomenal models. The hero will not be especially fashioned to suit his adventure; instead, he will shape a story that leaves him free of any impress: his trajectory must be unpredictable, the constant projection into a "problematic" destiny. And lastly, to convey his sense of the world, Roquentin must devise a fictional mode that can *actualize* the vision of an Elstir: the reader must see through the eyes of the hero a world that is strange in its familiarity, fresh in the most intimate recesses of its nastiness, and withal, accurate in its every particular.

Roquentin will not be long in doubt as to the form of his novel or the identity of its hero: if it is to be the same integument for him that "Some of These Days" was for its makers, his novel can only be about him, a chronicle relating his self-examination during the period of his Nausea, so that when he reaches the moment of his resolution, when he sees that he can order his life in retrospect by turning it into a structured object, the reader will be holding that object in his hands, having followed Roquentin through the full experience of Nausea.

That self-examination takes the form of a diary; this means observation by only one set of eyes, the loss of omniscience for the author, the immediacy of contact with the hero. The pathological quality of Roquentin's vision has already been noted, with the phenomenological advantages that it confers upon a work of fiction. His effortlessness with the written word has been mentioned also: his style is racy and spare. Whereas every extended sentence of Proust contains his book in brief, with its ending coming at the conclusion of a circular movement that reveals its meaning as does the book itself through a similar circularity, Roquentin is terse and tentative; his words never construct the event, never run ahead of his momentary insight. They make even the simple prose of *Eugénie Grandet* seem like the obvious contriving of a coercive author. The book about Roquentin will never be more definitive than he is, since it is not to be a novel about time past but about the sense of time as it passes from the unknown pages yet unread into the awareness of pages past.

Because a "diary" is devoid of mediators, it can be no more than its informing vision. That vision may open onto the world, but the world will merely confirm a subjective state of mind. However, that subjectivity will be immediately apprehensible to the reader, through what is said, through what fails to be said, through the very rhythm of the saying. Roquentin can render the most fleeting of his apperceptions, guiding himself (and the reader) through a veritable re-enactment of their moments: he notes one Sunday morning that the public park is beckoning to him —hardly an impression that can be described, since it is no more than a sensation, but Roquentin is able to decompose the feeling into its physiological articulation:

The park was bare and deserted. But . . . how can I explain?

It didn't have its usual look, it smiled at me. I leaned against the railing for a moment then suddenly realized it was Sunday. It was there—on the trees, on the grass, like a faint smile. It couldn't be described, you would have had to repeat very quickly: "This is a public park, this is winter, this is Sunday morning." [12]

Only the self-rehearsing diary can tell its reader how to read.

And lastly, to make the subjective blend even more fully with the actual, Roquentin will place his diary-like novel within a framework that includes an "Editor's Preface," "Undated Pages," footnotes, and so on. Everything must contrive to show that at the core of this devising there is a reality—Roquentin. There must be as little difference as possible between Roquentin the hero of *Nausea* and Roquentin the author, so that one day others will "read this book and say: 'Antoine Roquentin wrote it, a red-headed man who hung around cafés'" (p. 238). As little difference, perhaps, as there is between Roquentin the author and the never present Jean-Paul Sartre?

Sartre placed upon the novel such a heavy burden of theory that in the end he himself had to give up writing novels: after the publication of *Troubled Sleep* in 1949 (the third volume of his projected *Roads to Freedom*), he abandoned the attempt and turned to other forms. The novel as simple entrapment develops as the result of an interaction whose evolving form is determined by the requirements of the author and the resistance of the reader. If the author requires in addition that his writing support

[12] P. 58. This is also an instance in which Sartre follows Husserl in returning to the object an emotion-determining quality (see p. 226).

the orthodoxy of an external purpose (such as the formulation of philosophical problems according to a specific mode), he will jeopardize the necessary freedom which he requires for the evolving form of his own response to the response of the reader. And the author's response will be further impeded if it attempts to conform to any predetermined theory meant to render it more effective, since its only effective mode is that of its dialectical freedom. Sartre as a theorist is guilty of imposing essential restrictions on a form of writing that was meant to evidence all the consequences of existential freedom.

Nausea survives its antecedent theory, but it survives as an occasional paradox with reference to that theory. The Negro and Jew who are to impose upon Roquentin his final awareness, the "shame" of his existence, "exist" only as pure essences—a spiritualization which Sartre had not intended philosophically. Their suffering as symbolic representatives of oppressed minorities, is a *sine qua non* which the essential category "minority" can only state preexistentially without documentation, even though their racial symbolism provides one of the few instances of the author's social concern: as both character and object lesson, Roquentin undergoes an experience that is largely confined to intimate changes which he observes and effects within himself only; his ultimate resolution does not contemplate the social order as an object of his action or the reader's. And in its form, the story hardly ever moves beyond the subjective world wherein time and memory are significant; this particular *time* does not become historical, nor is awareness of it conditioned by any particular imperative of society. The temporal limitation that Sartre desired for responsible fiction becomes, in *Nausea,* a timelessness akin to that sought by the universality of essential writing.

Similar dilemmas can be found, and with less happy resolutions, in most of Sartre's fiction. The short stories in *The Wall* (1939) explore almost exclusively intersubjective states (with the possible exception of "The Childhood of a Leader"), paying no closer attention to the socio-political order or its historical moment than does the casual glance noted as satire in *Nausea*—satire certainly no more insistent than that which can be found in the apolitical writings of a Flaubert. Conversely, when Sartre turned to what was to have been his major work of fiction, *The Roads to Freedom,* his characters became subordinate to the workings of history (especially in *The Reprieve,* of 1945, where they move alongside historical figures), and his form was soon outdistanced by the changing form of the times. Sartre, who had always found so readily a human shape to give flesh and meaning to his speculative thought, remained without viable characters to provide a continuum within the historical flux which, according to the author's own definition, can neither stand still nor be called back in an identical relation to the ever evolving recaller.

However, *Nausea* is not affected as a novel by its failure to implement a number of the social and critical concerns of the author. It remains as an important link halfway between the experiments of the surrealists and those of the *nouveau roman*, attempting to remove from the narrative the ontologically perceptive "I" in order to make of the novel an absolute phenomenological statement providing the reader with a pure phenomenal object.

9

Joyce and
Robbe-Grillet

The devising which is the novel starts after the loss of faith, once successful imitation has become problematical because of a reader who refuses the subterfuge of the word and shows his sophistication through his interest in the mode of the author's fiction rather than in the fiction's simple statement. The writer who finds the intent of his fiction so jeopardized may try as an initial tactic to frustrate the alienating drift of critical speculation by making a propitiatory offering of his fiction to a reader who is likely to dismiss it anyway and thereby engage that reader at the level of dialogue. In so doing, the author hopes to effect entrapment by disclaiming a fiction that can no longer insure that entrapment, assuming that the only indisputability he can henceforth assert is that of his own being. And so, Cervantes joins in the mockery of Don Quixote, Sterne betrays Walter Shandy, Kafka plays tricks on Joseph K. In the distinction here proposed between *life* and *pattern*, this amounts to stating the sole but unequivocal life of the novel within the person of its parafictional author, who admits in advance of the reader that his fiction is mere *pattern*—a recognizably fraudulent object. As stated, this is generally but the author's preliminary guile: if he can engage his reader in a dialogue about the literary circumstances of his characters and their actions, the extrafictional nature of that dialogue will give a first measure of reality to those characters; to talk even disparagingly about someone is to acknowledge his existence; and, as the example of Cervantes shows, such preliminary acknowledgment can lead far.

Another kind of entrapment is calisthenic: the author's purpose is to induce in the reader certain *life*-rhythms, but not through description, once mimesis has lost its spell. The ritual postures of *La Princesse de Clèves* and the process of error and recognition in Proust are states of being which the reader *experiences* before he objectifies them as literature. For Mme de Lafayette's seventeenth-century audience, reading her book *is* a social exercise scarcely different from others performed within the courtly world of Louis XIV; the novel is but dimly perceived if its ritual style and structure are not understood. Recognition and rejection throughout the fifteen volumes of Proust's work occur not only within the fictional time of Marcel: as part of the reader's temporality, at least one dimension of the hero becomes the experience of the reader. The reader's subjectivity is thus unable to dissolve a fiction which removes itself from him in the form of an object whose reality is its unmistakable existence within the reader's phenomenal world.

In order for the book to become an object, it must be *pattern* (the structural instance of a ritual mode, a sequence of static images in time) rather than mimesis (the description of that ritual; the suggestion that those images construct a fictional motion or action). Chaucer achieves this kind of objectification by turning Pandarus into an element of the fiction which his scheming has parodied: as a climactic instance of his wizardry, the book's hitherto principal character is metamorphosed into a mere book. In Kafka, the strangeness of an alien world becomes, through the eyes of Joseph K., the subject matter of a book; and that strangeness spills over into a phenomenal world, the reader's, where such a book is written and read.

So it is apparent that after self-consciousness, the word which was once made flesh through ritual narration or simple mimesis has required the elaborate deception of the novel, based either on a narration that starts with a disclaimer of its own narrative content or with a mimesis that seeks its ends through preliminary alienation. There is a third mode, that which Ortega y Gasset subsumed under the label of modernism (*The Dehumanization of Art*): it is the refusal to treat art as more than *pattern*, avoiding the human appeal and the human quandary for an impersonal aesthetic (art for art's sake). According to such a view, the writer would be someone concerned primarily with not being a dupe, a purposeless Cervantes standing off from his creation by means of irony and refusing to consider it more than a game. Such pattern without purpose has not been considered here, since it represents little more than dereliction on the part of the author—an acceptance of new elements, however they may impoverish his writing, rather than an effort to overcome them. Ortega sees "dehumanization" once art no longer strives to be man's means of transcendence; until man can effect that transcendence in other ways, the former imperatives of literature remain, and the forms that neglect them are mere fads—novelty imposed through acquiescence and reduction, not because of the requirements of a particular perception.

Kafka represents an extreme; the author may be content simply to restrict the scope of his reader's sight to that of his alienated hero. The phenomenological vision of an Elstir or a Roquentin catches the reader off guard; his surprise is the first expression of his entrapment (since he cannot reject before he is able to recognize). As the reader rights his psychological balance through recognition, he acknowledges at least momentarily the evidence of the author's world. Sartre accepts that if the alienated eye of his protagonist is going to be the eye through which the reader is forced to *see*, he must eliminate the mediating presence of the author that tends to render speculative what must never be more than the immediacy of a visual awareness. While the world perceived by the phenomenological eye owes much to Kafka and the surrealists, it is possible that in his efforts to find the way to a nonmediated fiction, Sartre had in mind the experience of Joyce's *Ulysses.*

It is beyond the present purpose to review once again the paternity of interior monologue, whether it belongs as Joyce himself claimed, to Edouard Dujardin, or to Dostoevski, as Gide would have it.[1] It may be more relevant to note another climate of interest developing in the years immediately prior to 1919–1921, a period which A. W. Litz (*The Art of James Joyce*) has convincingly shown

[1] Dujardin himself reviewed the debate in *Le Monologue intérieur: Son apparition, ses origines, sa place dans l'œuvre de James Joyce.* Gleb Struve asserted that "this very formula (vnutrenniy monolog 'inner monologue')" was used in 1856 by the Russian critic Nikolay Gavrilovich Chernyshevsky ("*Monologue intérieur:* The Origins of the Formula and The First Statement of Its Possibilities," *PMLA*, LXIX [Dec. 1954]). Prior to this, C. D. King had found a predecessor to Dujardin in Vsevolod Garshin, whose *Four Days* (1877) appeared ten years before Dujardin's *Les Lauriers sont coupés* ("Edouard Dujardin, Inner Monologue and the Stream of Consciousness," *French Studies*, VII [April 1953]).

to be a "turning-point" in the development of Joyce's craft and the writing of *Ulysses*. H. Levin (*James Joyce: A Critical Introduction*) recalls that Jung and the international psychoanalytic movement had headquarters in Zurich during World War I, at the same time as did Joyce. The paths of exile were many, and a number of those who converged adventitiously in Zurich had interests that were curiously similar. There was a widespread curiosity about the back alleys of the mind, which appeared as a new and enticing domain in the light of intuitions and analytical attempts that broke radically with previous experience. Psychoanalysis was suspicious of the conclusions which intellectual syntheses assumed about categories of human behavior; it believed that the pristine animal is hard to discern in his acquired postures, since the unfettered impulse at whose level his truth exists is warped and reshaped at the moment of utterance. Free association allowed identification of the primitive impulse before its disguise as a structured response. H. Levin (*James Joyce*, pp. 82–83) believes that the principle of free association identified not only psychoanalysis but other forms of art and experimentation that were developing at the time. Professor Levin's point is well taken if one accepts free association as, in fact, a dissociative process whereby fragmented moments of the human psyche are released without reference to the superstructure that usually integrates them. The cinematic technique known as *montage* amounts, for all practical purposes, to an imitation of free association in the motion picture; shots that are unrelated insofar as the narrative of the film is concerned are presented in quick succession in order to establish a mood or an idea. In painting, the aim of the impressionists was to affect the beholder's senses without the mediation of mind, since they considered the image-as-copy and, a fortiori, the symbol to be indirections. In philosophy, the vitalism of Bergson defined man as an entelechy that could be comprehended only teleologically, by discounting external and mechanistic norms.

These endeavors may well have represented many aspects of a common desire to reach the unknown in man —that ultraman sensed beyond the shortcomings of normative definitions. But yet another movement deserves mention, one closer to Joyce himself in space, in time—and not infrequently in its manner. In the fall of 1915, a number of angry iconoclasts began to gather in Zurich around Hans Arp, Tristan Tzara, and Hugo Ball, the founders of the short-lived Dada. At the end of the war, when many of these exiles moved back to Paris (as did Joyce), the movement became broader in its scope through contact with the cubists who had followed the leadership of such literary figures as Apollinaire and Reverdy. After a brief course of subtle mutations and sharp schisms, Dada gave way to the surrealism of the early twenties. Dada was first of all an outraged rejection of all the respected modes, an onslaught against the custodians of wisdom, of morality, of art— against those who claimed transcendence but who acknowledged their fundamental bankruptcy by allowing periodic holocausts, subsequently condoned in the name of patriotism, of which World War I appeared to be a particularly grim instance at the time. Dada was sufficiently aware of the mind's infinite capacity to analyze and recompose every truth to understand that if it opposed one form of reason with another, its own would be in equal jeopardy. It therefore rejected discourse along with reason. But it bought the security of its intransigence at the cost of every possible assertion but that of thoroughgoing nihilism—any program or construct which it might have formulated being a priori a betrayal of its single premise. As a matter of fact, it died because pure negation is difficult to sustain: its very acts of rejection began eventually to shape the lineaments of a form and a set of values. In time, its derision evolved from physical assault to reduction through word play—a dangerous drift that evidenced an interest in language and humor. And instead of attempting the destruction of existing forms, Dada was drawn into arguing their nonrelevancy as statements of truth.[2] By the time of its death, Dada had shifted gradually from pure iconoclasm to an unmistakable interest in art; the stage was set for the essentially literary accession of surrealism.

It is against this background that must be examined Joyce's attempt to contrive a novel that would record the minute scrutiny of a private awareness—an epic in microcosm, the events of a single day reduced to their impact upon a single consciousness. In *A Portrait of the Artist*, an earlier version of Stephen had been seen rehearsing the sound and significance of names, in particular that of his patronymic, Dedalus:

—I Stephen Dedalus. I am walking beside my father whose name is Simon Dedalus. We are in Cork, in Ireland. Cork is a city. Our room is in the Victoria Hotel. Victoria and Stephen

[2] When Duchamp exhibited a marble urinal in 1917, his defiant gesture acknowledged, through its dependency on them, the worlds of mental and artistic creation (a urinal belongs to a category of mentally discredited objects; a marble urinal must be wrought in the shape of its original model): it is not easy to reject creation through creation. It was not long thereafter that, in arguing against the fraudulence of bourgeois superficiality, Arp found himself echoing Apollinaire, who, in coining the word *surrealism*, had defined art as creation rather than surface imitation.

and Simon. Simon and Stephen and Victoria. Names.
The memory of his childhood suddenly grew dim. He tried
to call forth some of its vivid moments but could not. He recalled only names. Dante, Parnell, Clane, Clongowes [ch. ii].

—Stephanos Dedalos! Bous Stephanoumenos! Bous Stephaneforos!
Their banter was not new to him and now it flattered his
mild proud sovereignty. Now, as never before, his strange
name seemed to him a prophecy. So timeless seemed the grey
warm air, so fluid and impersonal his own mood, that all ages
were as one to him. A moment before the ghost of the ancient kingdom of the Danes had looked forth through the vesture of the hazewrapped city. Now, at the name of the fabulous artificer, he seemed to hear the noise of dim waves and
to see a winged form flying above the waves and slowly
climbing the air. What did it mean? Was it a quaint device
opening a page of some medieval book of prophecies and
symbols, a hawklike man flying sunward above the sea, a
prophecy of the end he had been born to serve and had been
following through the mists of childhood and boyhood, a
symbol of the artist forging anew in his workshop out of the
sluggish matter of the earth a new soaring impalpable imperishable being? [ch. iv].

These passages enlarge the reader's view of Stephen's inner world. They also demonstrate the way in which the
event is altered as it becomes the character's reminiscence.
The event pales for Stephen; he does not retain its factual
content—only the name, the bare designation of the fact
which is then modified as a free evolution of his fancy. His
own name is deliberately suggestive: for schoolboys, the
memory of Greek paradigms and literature contrives a
bookish jibe. But the echo in Stephen is that of the Athe-
nian legend. The ox becomes the white bull of Minos and

Stephaneforos the princely title of Hippolytus (so named by Euripides). It is these sacred symbols that situate Dedalus, the architect whose fame and fate are linked to the Minotaur and whose own symbolism is sacred. Like the rest of *A Portrait*, this inner view of Stephen is described in the third person. The narrator, however omniscient, is outside his character: however intimate the disclosure to the reader, there are two sources of information—the character about whom the disclosure is made and the one making it. Stephen's reaction, however immediate, cannot be the reader's—since, if he is to perceive it, the reader must be first informed of that immediacy. The third-person narrative *proposes* to the reader; it never assumes him to be a participant. Along with the description of the action, an optimal reaction is suggested; the reader remains as close to, or as distant from, the one as the other. If he accepts the character as described, he will also accept the character's reaction. If he is suspicious of the author, he will question the behavior of the character.

To a degree, language always "creates reality." A story may be about language (about words as a primary truth for Stephen, about the words that construct the fraudulence of salvation and Jesuitry in "Grace" or others of the *Dubliners* stories); in such stories, the author comments on the worlds that words can construct beyond the world of the book. But even though the words become the very exemplars of the author's description, his presence is still a felt reality, and his words intend a collusion between him and his reader that is more important than the words themselves. Still it cannot be denied that even a simpler statement will carry a certain conviction: the author and his printed word are a persuasive force. The manner and mode of his inserts in *Nausea* show that Sartre does not take *Eugénie Grandet* seriously; on the other hand, Jean-Louis Curtis disagrees with Sartre: he is willing to accept what Balzac has to say about his characters, even without proof—"by agreement". In fact, he is prepared to grant the author "almost unlimited credit." The word "almost" is subversive: since Curtis must reserve the right to suspend credit, whatever his initial show of good will, he enters into a circular argument that returns the author's work to the hazards of critical examination. W. C. Booth (*The Rhetoric of Fiction*), who quotes the French critic to this effect, believes that the assertions of Curtis constitute a "brilliant reply to Sartre." But even thus rebutted, Sartre raises the question of persuasion in his refusal to grant Balzac the courtesies tendered by Curtis; a novel remains a mere contingency as long as its author cannot find other ways of committing the reader who will not accept his word unquestioningly.

The obstreperous reader of the Sartrean kind presents further difficulties for the third-person narrative because of his rejection of Aristotelian universals: he will not recognize certain pre-established laws and categories that make human behavior predictable and that make possible the assumption of a common response by character and reader to a given situation. In agreement with this view Booth cites a number of literary murderers with whom the reader sympathizes, in order to show that even the most threatening of human actions cannot necessarily anticipate, in literature, similar human reactions in the face of what he terms a judgment rendered by the author. Since acceptance of the author's judgment is at least as problematic as the acceptance of his character's action, the author's judgment must refer in fact to an intricate strategy. A murder committed within the nonliterary world of the reader threatens him; his reaction to a murderer is therefore relatively predictable. Within the fiction, no matter how well it imitates the category "murder," a similar threat is not necessarily concomitant. It is not enough to note that the spectator pities Macbeth rather than his victim; it is important to know what has been done to Duncan to lessen his importance to that spectator. (Conversely, as has been previously stated, the author may of course approximate the threat implicit in murder through means that have nothing to do with either imitation or an abstract moral rejection by his reader—Kafka is able to make the reader share Joseph K.'s fear of his messengers from the beyond, even though it is unlikely that these will ever appear as such in the reader's life. Even the third-person narrative that hopes to commit the reader through recognition must be tensed between the need to represent its world by using the straightforward description and statement which that recognition demands, and the more devious means that will be necessary to entrap the reader if he will not accept recognition.)

At the level of ingenuousness, no part of the third-person narrative can escape from the insulating presence of the narrator; the character's action, his reaction, the object of his action or reaction exist for the reader only to the extent that the reader is told about them: they are wrapped in a veil of telling, each a figment or a mode of the narrator's persuasiveness. The reader is informed that this day, the banter of Stephen's friends flattered him; a false indecision causes the narrator to suggest either the quality of air or the hero's mood as the reason for his reaction; the reader is then given a list of the further associations awakened in Stephen by his name. Whatever echo that name may awaken in the reader will have to be placed alongside, or subordinated to, the list of associations with which the reader has been presented.

The ingenuous narrator trusts to a reflex *life*-assumption by his reader. But the author may feel unsure of the reader's spontaneous commitment to a straightforward narrative and yet be unwilling to explore more complex forms of entrapment. If he so desires, he can attenuate his presence, giving up some of his omniscience by remaining within the vantage point of a single character. This contrives the garden variety of first-person narrative, affording the reader a sense of immediacy in his perception of the character's world through the disguise, though by no means the elimination, of the author's narrative presence. There remains the danger that having so curtailed his mobility, the author will be forced to impose upon the inner world of the vantage character a rigidity and purpose that are in fact the structure of the narrative. Variations that justify such necessary structuring are the first-person diary (*Nausea*, for example) or the epistolary novel; since these correspond to extra-literary modes of the individual's self-formalization, there is less awkwardness in presenting them as instances of the character's self-revelation and less constraint placed upon the intimacy of his portrayal.

It is the awareness that the inner landscape is something far less tidy that may have moved Joyce to seek yet another form through which to chart the further progress of Stephen Dedalus. A novel restricted to the raw datum of consciousness would limit the author's role and its own structure to an ordering of objective stimuli; that ordering would provide the essential difference between the book and other forms of the reader's phenomenal world, artistic control becoming a functional devising concerned exclusively with the modes and effectiveness of those stimuli. If

Stephen Dedalus should respond to the symbolic suggestion of his own name and his train of thought is presented
without comment, the reader remains with only such directions as are provided by the individual responses of
Stephen (such as musical sound or symbolic cognition)
and the pattern which they construct. Even as symbolic
cognition, suggestion of this kind reaches the reader
largely below the threshold of intellection and would allow him to construct an intimate parallel to the unstated
novel which he is reading. Joyce believed that the reader's
construct could rest on such fragmented awareness, provided that the fragments were of a special kind; if they
were, the reader would enjoy a more immediate and com-
prehensive sense of the character and his action than
would be afforded him by the sequential description that
required his sustained cooperation at the speculative level.
This process of achieving insight through fragmentation is
what Joyce termed "epiphany," a revelation of character
through a privileged moment of phenomenological perception without further cognitive assistance from the author:
intuition beyond telling.

The title *Ulysses* (not to speak of the book's bulk) suggests the epic; its story (for Joyce does not give up the
narrative thread) is that of a wandering, a journey whose
significance is in its trajectory rather than in its end. Litz
notes that "the 'epic' proportions of *Ulysses* are absolutely
dependent on the major Homeric analogues" (*The Art of
James Joyce*, p. 37)—to which might be contrasted a
notation by Levin: "*Ulysses* is totally lacking in the epic
virtues of love, friendship and magnanimity" (*James
Joyce*, p. 114). The two statements do not necessarily signify contradiction. Mainly through the intimate consciousness of Bloom and Stephen, *Ulysses* proposes to be no less

than the song of the city and the artist, the sometimes ribald and farcical, but always huge, threnody of the exile in Dublin. But this intimate consciousness represents the inward projection and analysis, the ingestion, of trivial events—a young boy scuffling in the street, the earthy, drink-induced fantasies of an advertising man who is also an outcast, the meeting of the boy and the outcast and their failure to touch, the life of the city in its streets, its pubs, its brothels; a burial in the morning, a birth at midnight, and at the end, through Molly, the rehearsal of the female principle, the heaving of the earth in its embrace and warmth, the blind assertion of its fertility and continuation. The actual moments of this trajectory are anything but epic; but hugely enlarged as personal echo, magnified through proximity and analysis, they convey the overpowering sense of a human consciousness whose experience of that trajectory is Odyssean, though inward.

To say, however, that Joyce remained wholly within his characters would be to misrepresent even his initial intent in *Ulysses:* their trajectories through Dublin are too cleally marked not to require at least the equivalent of an external and collaborative eye. Their inner world is self-conscious, being fully as anxious to model the external world as it is to express its reactions to that world. Stephen's thoughts about his mother as he converses with Buck Mulligan, Bloom's as he prepares kidneys and tea in the kitchen, are as much a part of their action as their spoken words or the other gestures of their performance. The principals are seldom mere monologuists. The reader's first sight of them is generally from the outside, and the progression inward is gradual. Only after their action has been sufficiently advanced to provide a clear direction are their inner soliloquies allowed greater freedom.

The musing character in *Ulysses* seldom fails the reader; his own inner world is so closely a reflection of his overt action that even the external eye, the third-person narrative, is able to convey the inwardness of the character's world through the drastic narrowing of its focus, as when Bloom is seen turning a kidney or coming up against the chamber pot under Molly's bed. At such times, the trivial, the external object is so magnified that it looms as an expression of the character's consciousness. Even when cut adrift within the privacy of his own mind, the character's associative processes are not so free as to cause him to lose sight of the event that has already been set in motion. In spite of such freedom and their own propensities, these characters resist becoming the abstractions of a wholly lyric mode. The form of their thought is closer to inner monologue than to pure stream of consciousness, seldom departing from cognitive or symbolic logic for the sake of mere sound patterns or wholly private concatenations— even though, for these magnificent creatures of language, words remain a constant temptation. ("Your postprandial, do you know that word? Postprandial. There was a fellow I knew once in Barcelona, queer fellow, used to call it his postprandial." This digression emerges, unheralded, in the midst of a recollection by Stephen of Paris faces and incidents: he has been re-enacting inwardly an attempted explanation by Kevin Egan in French; but the girl to whom it was addressed had understood that Dutch cheese was being requested. Since the adjective "postprandial" denotes what follows a meal, as cheese logically would in France, the digression represents a more restrictive process of thought than might be construed by the hasty reader. Nor does it long deter Stephen.)

These huge characters are hugely verbal. Beyond the

pain of their circumstances, the contingencies of their moments, their inner comment bespeaks the pleasure of turning their condition to words; they are above all else the reflection of Joyce's own fascination with the possibilities of language, a fascination that ultimately gives his characters and his story still another dimension. Few critics have neglected to mention that Joyce wrote like a poet, especially in his later prose fiction, and among the earliest of these was Frank Budgen, a painter and friend of the author. He believed, on the evidence of conversations with Joyce and his own perceptual mode, that Joyce's words are the objects of a poet; they are determined by a prior commitment that is more important to Joyce than their ultimate value as signs within his fiction: the word-object is like a first and self-contained epiphany (Joyce to Budgen: "I have the words already. What I am seeking is the perfect order of words in the sentence" [*James Joyce and the Making of Ulysses*, p. 20]). Beyond the general truth that the word as object has "visual" properties, it is nearly a commonplace to note that the two major novels of Joyce evidence a static and pictorial quality which synthesizes the event rather than expanding it through description or analysis; Litz is of the opinion that Joyce worked according to an aesthetic that paralleled the conclusions of Pound's imagists.[3] Examining the *Ulysses* note sheets, Litz determines that the inserts through which Joyce expanded his novel are essentially lyrical, additions meant to enrich the verbal texture of the narrative. The consequence of this sort of expansion by the author is more significant

[3] "An 'Image' is that which presents an intellectual and emotional complex in an instant of time" ("A Few Don'ts," *Poetry* [March 1913]; reprinted in *Literary Essays of Ezra Pound*, ed. T. S. Eliot). Litz also believes that the entire concept of *Ulysses* originated as a single image in the mind of Joyce.

than is the similar temptation in his characters; these are justified by their enactment of a parallel story, but no such bounds are placed on the author, whose lyrical surge, though it may open new worlds to him, may outdistance the reader. Kevin's confusion in his conversation with the waitress is intended to conjure up the utter denudation of the exile—loveless, landless, wifeless, and in the end languageless; "*Il est irlandais. Hollandais? Non fromage. Deux irlandais, nous, Irlande, vous savez?*" certainly suggests poor communication in French. But if this failure of language recalls "postprandial," then the demonstration is achieved through linguistic means that beggar the reader's control of language, since the word is scarcely to be recommended for use by anyone who is linguistically accident prone. Joyce informs the responses of the "Ithaca" catechism with a freedom which Bloom's circumstances seldom allowed the character before:

He rests. He has travelled.

With?
Sinbad the Sailor and Tinbad the Tailor and Jinbad the Jailer and Whinbad the Whaler and Ninbad the Nailer and Finbad the Failer and Binbad the Bailer and Pinbad the Pailer and Minbad the Mailer and Hinbad the Hailer and Rinbad the Railer and Dinbad the Kailer and Vinbad the Quailer and Linbad the Yailer and Xinbad the Phthailer.

The familiar alliteration that triggers the rest hews to sense for awhile but is then gradually disintegrated as meaningless sound. Since the passage is close to the very end of Bloom's soliloquy, that is to say the end of Bloom himself, the passage may well suggest the rational mind's losing control and slipping toward the void of unconsciousness.

But more immediately, it is also a purely musical digression that makes Bloom appear different from former incarnations and points up another conclusion of Litz, already alluded to: the associative process of the author represents more than the character's interior monologue; it is an elaborate construct through which Joyce is able to order the still unwrought elements of his art. If Molly's invocation to the rocks binds together for Joyce the worlds of Calypso, Circe, and Penelope, the reader will appreciate this depth of characterization only if he senses through it the recurrence of being and the metempsychosis that Molly suggests as the earth soul. But such subtlety of characterization is more likely to lead the reader to the author than to Molly. This is structuring, but of a special kind, one in which the word is revealed as world.[4] When such insights illuminate the character, the reader is an equal beneficiary; when they are the author's, it is not so easy for the reader to return them to the character or event which they are supposed to reveal. The numerous equivalents used by Joyce for "Moly" (absinthe, mercury, chastity, chance, indifference, beauty, laughter, satire, conscience, escape from poison, "Met[amorphosis?]-salt") and for the Isle of Man (mankind, isolation, and sterility, the "Three Legs of Man" in the "Nighttown" episode),[5] may serve to establish reference points for Joyce; but for the reader to avail himself of them, he would indeed have to be that unique

---

[4] A considerable step has been taken by Joyce beyond the early worlds of Stephen, the boy in "Araby," or the characters in "Grace," whose words were puppet strings manipulated by the author: in *Ulysses'* many parodies of literary styles, the words are an objectification of that very manipulation—the author himself is on display.

[5] From the heraldic device of the Isle of Man: three flexed legs joined at the thighs. (See Litz, *op. cit.*, pp. 26–27.)

devotee envisaged by Joyce, suffering from an exemplary insomnia and devoting a lifetime to such elucidations.

Words, which preserve for the characters their logical cohesion, become for Joyce an increasingly attractive means of escape. The progress described by the note sheets as well as the evolution that leads him from *Ulysses* to *Finnegans Wake* indicates a change in the author's concerns, from the inner representation of character through analysis of consciousness to a freer enjoyment of words and their revelatory possibilities. Joyce ends close to the unstructured fun of the Dadaists and relatively free of the formal concerns that normally limit the author through an awareness of his audience. This is the freedom that Litz sees as the ultimate "egoism" of *Finnegans Wake* and that Levin terms Joyce's "nearly paranoid disregard of the reader."

It is certainly true that under such circumstances, the reader finds it increasingly difficult to enter the novel as its *life*-informant or reality principle. He is kept at a distance by a *pattern* the remains unassimilable to the extent that it is the private object of the author. As the words of Joyce become more his own epiphanies and less his characters' they fail to provide intellective continuity in proportion as they revert to poetry. At the very best, expressive form can control only brief moments of the author's development (see Chapter 1, p. 17). But even what Kenneth Burke sees as the "onomatopoetic correspondence between form and theme" (*Counter-statement*) becomes too much the vocal imitation of rhythm and sound to allow symbolic translation of that sound; such prose is transmuted into melodic variations. The reader is left with either a series of puzzles or a discontinuous appreciation of esthetic moments—what R. M. Adams (*Surface and Symbol*) describes as moments of instantaneous and pure vision, an indefinite sequence of *objets trouvés*. There has been occasion to note with reference to the theories of Breton (Chapter 1, p. 42) that the found object represents a moment of the artist's vision within the nonstructuring of the phenomenal world. Adams' speculation confirms that, at this level, the novel has indeed become a *thing* of its author; another name must be found for the game played by the reader: as rebus-solver or detached admirer he is no longer a participant in the cooperative creation of a human experience through character and event.

At a certain point, Joyce changed from one kind of experimentation to another. Perhaps because of a progressive irritation with a world from which he felt increasingly alienated, or a megalomaniacal pleasure in following the verbal play of his mind through the vast storehouse of his own experience, Joyce moved from an exploration of his characters' inner world to that of his own, from a fictional phenomenology to simple phenomenological response. It remained for another author to follow Joyce's first path with the rigor of the scientist rather than with the protean gusto of the poet. That author was to be Alain Robbe-Grillet.

A literary critic before he achieved fame as a novelist, Robbe-Grillet has documented his theoretical beliefs at some length in articles, interviews, and essays that became vindicatory after the controversy stirred up by his second novel, *The Voyeur*, in 1955. In the process he reached two general conclusions: the first, that the object of any novel is to convey "reality"—the so-called *nouveau roman* being no different in that respect from any other; the second, that the novel itself is an object, of the kind already analyzed among the works of Kafka, Sartre, Joyce, and so forth. But in comparison to them Robbe-Grillet represents an extreme position born of a conviction that fiction must be an ever more accurate parcel of the phenomenal world with which it is concerned. It is not sufficient that the novel synthesize that world: rigorously confined to a description of phenomena, it must represent for its reader an ontic duplicate of its model. Robbe-Grillet shares with Kafka, the surrealists, and Sartre a heightened awareness of the object, which he believes to be, as they do, something alien and alienating, a refractory density. It will be recalled that Marcel's *madeleine* is typical of his world in that its immanence is in reality Marcel's: the *madeleine* does not make him aware of a *madeleine*, or of *madeleines* in general; it makes him aware of a part of himself—the indwelling past. Marcel's object is friable; the warm tea dissolves it into a landscape.

The Sartrean object is of quite another kind: no matter how desperate the hero's need to assimilate it, that object remains itself. Defying the human attempt to alter it into serpent, claw, or talon, the horsechestnut tree root remains a root, an incomprehensible entity that declares itself and its beholder to be forever distinct, planetary distances apart from each other and irrecusably alien. Since Robbe-Grillet refuses as a novelist to humanize perceptual datum through interpretation or any form of the Proustian catalysis, one might suppose that he would look with approval on Sartre's objects: they are, after all, independent performers whose role is to frustrate the assimilative urge of a human consciousness. Robbe-Grillet has himself referred to the Heideggerian *da-sein:* "All around us, defying our pack of animistic or domesticating adjectives,

things *are there.*" [6] There would seem to be, at first
glance, a remarkable similarity between both points of
view. However, since the absolute remains equally distant
from every human endeavor to grasp it, Robbe-Grillet
finds that Sartre falls far short of his intent and treats him
about as roughly as Sartre treated the object-assimilators
who preceded him. Robbe-Grillet does not find that Roquentin is very different from Marcel: Roquentin too ab-
sorbs his objects—or to use the critic's expression, he
"humanizes" them. Robbe-Grillet notes that in *Nausea*,
the object is generally perceived through touch, a more intimate sense than sight (he reminds his reader that one
fears contagion through touch rather than through sight).
When Sartre does rely on sight, he tends, according to his
critic, to fall back on the most deceptive quality of the object—its color. Robbe-Grillet quotes from *Nausea* the description of "Cousin Adolphe's braces, which can hardly
be distinguished against the blue of his shirt" ("Nature,
Humanism and Tragedy"), to show that color is the characteristic of the object most liable to fluctuations of light,
position, mood—and therefore the most likely to engage
the subjective response of the observer. He also questions
Sartre's use of sound and concludes that his objects, even
though meant to evidence their distance from man, are
viewed anthropocentrically: it is as if they mocked man,
but with man's own gestures. This anthropocentrism
Robbe-Grillet calls thinking "along with" the object, not
"about" it.

[6] "A Path for the Future Novel" (1956) reprinted in *For a New
Novel*; in that same collection, very nearly identical expressions
can be found in the essay on Beckett and others. Every essay by
Robbe-Grillet, unless otherwise identified, is from this collection.

Anthropocentrism puts man in the way of what he is examining. It supposes a transcendental system, that is to say, a constraint upon the impartiality of the eye; and, borrowing a concept from Roland Barthes, Robbe-Grillet believes that it derives from man's need to inform with his tragic vision the indifferent objects of his world. This is the humanistic prejudice, mistakenly endowing with human values that which cannot contain them. It is also the traditional mode of the novel, and in particular, the Balzacian novel—a pet aversion of *nouveau roman* theorists, who believe that the nineteenth-century author represents the only standard most readers are willing to accept.[7]

Still, it should not be assumed that any contemporary novel has it in its power to copy former models—even nineteenth-century ones: the reader's truths have changed; his response must be of a different sort. Moreover, if such a novel ever stated a truth or insight, that truth is known at present and no longer has value. The need for renewal is therefore constant, and there can never be a definitive form for the novel, no matter how exalted or promising a former mode: "to write like Joyce" or "return to classicism" is equally vain ("Le Réalisme, la psychologie et l'avenir du roman," in *Critique*, XII [July 1956]). It is only the reader who reads the new forms with a deliberately archaic eye who will be disappointed. Moreover, the novel cannot properly "signify"; in a world void of

---

[7] "The only conception of the novel that is current today is, in fact, that of Balzac" ("A Path for the Future Novel," *NNRF*, IV [July 1956]). But Balzac as bugaboo appears in nearly every essay —and frequently more than once. Note also Nathalie Sarraute (*L'Ere du soupçon*), who begins several of her arguments on the assumption that Balzac represents a widespread and fundamental view of fiction.

significance, it is nonsensical to require significance of the novel.[8]

The antihumanistic view of the novel which Robbe-Grillet defends is intended to free man outside the novel —to liberate human vision, allowing the assertion of the eye. In a discontinuous and nonsignificant world, the modern subject can be no more than his sight: man is "the eye that sees" ("New Novel, New Man"). Robbe-Grillet desires, instead of the subtly animistic object of Sartre, a monolith that is closed, hard, and separate from man; his novel will not provide the reader with information *about* "reality": it will be a part of that reality, a phenomenal catalyst that effects its change without being affected. "Information" can proceed only one way—from object to reader. The process of "humanization" reverses this direction: the unaffected reader informs his novel. The reader must "see" the landscape; he must not be told that it is "austere" or "calm" ("A Path for the Future Novel"). No human growth is otherwise conceivable.

This view of the novel imposes restrictions on the writer. The Balzacian author was a nimble god, moving in and out of his characters, on intimate terms with objects, granting his creatures free will only to the extent that it did not interfere with his control of plot. For the novel to be the pure object that Robbe-Grillet requires, the god's eye-view must be traded for a man's—a human eye not unlike the lens of a motion-picture camera that sees but

[8] Here, though Robbe-Grillet intends once again to reject Sartre, he echoes him: "The world is neither meaningful nor absurd. It quite simply *is*" ("A Path for the Future Novel"). He asserts further that as the middle classes began to lose their privileges which rested upon and insured a stable social structure, phenomenology and the sciences "were discovering the reign of the discontinuous" ("New Novel, New Man," 1961).

does not interpret. Beyond this objective viewer, there is
but the span of his vision—an *ascesis* that does away with
the author, whatever the manner of his former omniscience. The specialized role of the central character contrives a new kind of fictional person, the windowpane
hero, a transparency whose action will be neither described nor explained, whose only consciousness is perforce the reader's, the single sensitivity of the fictional
eye: "The time comes when this man's eye falls on certain
things, positively and emphatically. He sees them, but he
refuses to take possession of them" ("Nature, Humanism
and Tragedy").

The committed writer envisaged by Sartre cannot satisfy such an *ascesis*. If he is to be no more than a function
(as viewfinder, ocular aperture), he becomes a part of that
duality rejected by Sartre, a conscience that cannot enter
its own work, since he will have but a single commitment:
to preserve the impersonal integrity of his object. The object, the human gesture, asserts itself only as *presence*. It
does not derive its meaning from the implications of a system; its statement does not depend on an echo, whether
sentimental, Freudian, sociological, or metaphysical ("A
Path for the Future Novel"), and calls for a frugal style
void of affect and of soul-breeding words or figures, such
as "animistic or domesticating adjectives," the man-seeking
metaphor, and so on. Robbe-Grillet agrees with Nathalie
Sarraute (*L'Ere du soupçon*) that dialogue is the form
most consistently refractory to personalization and most
likely to resist soul through surface.

Robbe-Grillet acknowledges that absolute objectivity
cannot be attained; he urges it nevertheless as a goal and as
a reminder of the temptation for the "humanist" to sentimentalize and falsify through a promiscuous imposition of

his own sensitivity. Such steady vigilance against human intrusion would seem to jeopardize the humanity of the protagonists; this Robbe-Grillet denies. "Objectivity" he defines as a concentration on the object ("New Novel, New Man"): it precludes neither a human presence nor a human dilemma; it is simply a refusal to comment on that presence, to go beyond the description of what causes that dilemma. The postures of the characters are recognizably human, but each moment of the human gesture should be seen only discontinuously, as a prereflective instant of pure vision. (A collection of the author's word sketches is called *Instantanés*, a title conveying the sense of its English translation—"Snapshots"—as well as the immediacy of the vision that can account only for such arrested and fragmentary instants.) Robbe-Grillet refuses the "archaic myth of depth" derived from a belief in inherent "significances" and chooses instead a flat texture, which, whatever the author's craft, never constructs a "story": it is able to create only an unlinked sequence of objective moments and momentary objects. For Robbe-Grillet, that surface affords adventure enough; the object is apocalyptic only if it can be *seen*— as in a privileged moment when the veil of its meaning suddenly drops away.[9]

The reader enters the world of such a book with as few safeguards as he is vouchsafed in his own world; its people, its objects, its events will allow him no cue: he must decipher each as he encounters it. His trajectory is equally problematic; he finds himself adrift amidst characters who are a becoming, but with no teleological purpose. And

[9] The adventure starts exactly as does that of the surrealists, with an obsessive sense of *things*. But it stops short: for Robbe-Grillet, there are no derivative consequences; these are in the province of the reader, not of the author.

blurring the last boundaries between his world and theirs, the reader finds that these discontinuous characters enjoy no chronology of their own; time, otherwise nonexistent in the novel, has the only dimension that remains: the reader's.

A novel developed along these lines must be limited to a single consciousness. It cannot be an experience shared among several characters, as in *Troilus and Criseyde* or *La Princesse de Clèves*. Though its eye might conceivably scan a complex frieze, like that of *Don Quixote* or *Remembrance of Things Past*, the narrowness of its focus renders unlikely such an undertaking. Because it is the factual datum of a single consciousness, it cannot turn into the sort of speculation that creates another consciousness, such as Anny and the self-taught man, who, in *Nausea*, are creatures of Roquentin's meditation. Such a novel could move, like Joyce's, from one center of awareness to another. But since Robbe-Grillet has chosen to concentrate on the object of a given consciousness rather than on the consciousness itself, a multiplication of the sources of awareness becomes for him the problem of the object's multiple refraction.

Narrowing its concern to the nonspeculative datum of the eye, such a novel reverses the affective implications of Husserl's objective direction as propounded by Sartre; neither novelist will sentimentalize the object, but whereas the Sartrean consciousness is drawn toward an inherence, there is for Robbe-Grillet only the reader's response to stimuli that have no immanent properties. Object-creating and emotion-filled words having thus been eliminated, their incantatory spell is replaced by the incantatory spell of situations. As signs, words depend for their spell on prior assumptions by the reader—assumptions on which the merely situational statement cannot rely. But since it is the author who determines the choice and disposition of these situations, as he once determined the choice and disposition of his affective words, the author, even when he is self-absconding, remains a factor. Since he cannot be absent from his work, the extent of his presence must be determined either by the actual role he chooses to play in his story (as in the case of Cervantes in *Don Quixote*) or by manipulation that serves to disclose him rather than his tale; an instance of such manipulation is provided by Robbe-Grillet in his first published novel, *The Erasers* (1953).

The identifiable instances of the author's theory in *The Erasers* are in his manipulations of the object of his analysis, time, and the novel's pervasive mood—the hero's sense of *déjà vu*. There is a Prologue during which a gun is fired at a man, then the five chapters of the novel concerned with the intervening moment before the fatal bullet hits—twenty-four hours during which time stands still and certain human gestures, ultimately useless ones, are made. Throughout this curious elongation, with its echo moments, its false starts into an inexistent future, its reminiscences, the author has scattered bits of information with no apparent purpose but to provide the reader with a false track. At the simplest level, the story is that of an antigovernment gang whose mission is to "wipe out" (they may be viewed as "erasers") a number of backstage but important political figures in an unnamed country. On eight successive days, they have killed eight such figures, each day at the same hour. The novel relates the ninth of these attempts, the first one that is not immediately successful. The intended victim, an economist called Daniel Dupont, has been only slightly wounded by a member of the gang, a certain Garinati. In order to protect himself, Dupont takes into his confidence two close friends, his attending physician, Dr. Juard, and a businessman, Marchat: he will hide in Dr. Juard's clinic until a government car and chauffeur can remove him; meanwhile, for the benefit of the local police chief, Inspector Laurent, his corpse will have been supposedly claimed by officials in the capital city.

The government sends a special agent, Wallas, to take over the case from the local authorities—even though Wallas himself has not been told about the circumstances surrounding the feigned death of Dupont. Wallas is on trial: he is on his first assignment. He takes a room in the block where the murder is committed and, with the hostile cooperation of Laurent, begins his investigation. He uncovers a number of clues, but none sheds any significant light. At last, he receives through the mail a photograph of Dupont's house, on which an unknown hand has written an invitation for seven thirty that evening. Wallas determines to hide inside the house in order to discover the identity of his correspondent. Instead of the latter, Dupont himself shows up in search of documents which Marchat was too fearful to gather. Responding to a threatening gesture by Dupont, Wallas shoots and kills the supposed victim.

The consciousness of Wallas, which must serve as the reader's, since it confronts phenomena that will remain unexplained, is of a special kind—both by virtue of those phenomena and because of the nature of its perceptual faculties. The world within which it is placed has been deliberately tampered with. Moreover, Wallas is neither a neutral nor an accurate sensor: certain of his impressions are obsessive; his memory is untrustworthy; his inner and outward eyes are not always differentiable. And to the extent that he is an entity that can be comprehended externally, there occurs a strange suffusion of the outer world by the inner one.

Much of what was to have been simple perceptual evidence is in fact relatively sophisticated commentary, starting with the names of the streets that are reminders of Kafka: "rue des Arpenteurs," reminiscent of the surveyor of *The Castle*; "boulevard Circulaire," symbolic of the circular nature of Wallas' quest within a closed moment of time; "rue de Corinthe," emblematic of Oedipean bias, and so on. This part of the world does not belong to Wallas; it is the author's, and a parafictional sign to the reader. But the world that Wallas sees is itself hallucinated. For no stated reason, Wallas repeatedly attempts to purchase an undiscoverable eraser, the description of which sounds rather like that of an ordinary drawing eraser:

a soft, crumbly gum eraser that friction does not twist but reduces to dust; an eraser that cuts easily and whose cut surface is shiny and smooth, like mother-of-pearl. He has seen one such, a few months ago, at a friend's [. . .] . It looked like a yellowish cube, about an inch or two long, with the corners slightly rounded—maybe by use. The manufacturer's brand was printed on one side, but was too worn to be legible any more: only two of the middle letters were still clear: "di" [p. 126].

At one of the stationers' shops to which this recurrent quest takes him, there is a display window with a dummy dressed as a painter before an easel whose canvas shows a Greek temple. The backdrop is a greatly enlarged photograph of Dupont's house. At yet another stationer's, Wallas' visualization inverts the previous scene: the painter is amidst the ruins of Thebes, painting what turns out to be a photograph of Dupont's house. The visual reversal (painting and subject) is compounded through a process of visual metamorphosis (painting into photograph) whose effect is similar to that of the solarization, or positive-negative inversion, within frames of *Last Year at Marienbad* (1961). Such aberrations of the eye correspond to the aberrations of a world in which images of a house and its symbolic projection (the Greek temple) occur, not only as the result of the hero's obsessive concern, but also because of the author's style, which links moments sylleptically, allowing a single action or mood to flow through two events that are unrelated.

Lest it be argued that these aberrations are merely the hero's, time undergoes similar distortions that cannot be explained as the individual's. There is first the oracular wristwatch of Wallas that stops at seven thirty when Garinati first shoots Dupont, and starts at the same time twenty-four hours later, when Wallas kills him. But that wristwatch does not mark off distinct periods. The visual obsession of images is also the cyclical nature of time, which turns upon certain human gestures. One such gesture is the ascent of the stairs leading to the study of Dupont. Garinati rehearses the recollection and the anticipation of his action; its recurrence makes of it something out of time, an arrested moment to which time returns:

the actor suddenly stops, in the middle of a phrase . . . He knows it by heart, this role he plays every evening; but today he refuses to go any farther. Around him the other characters freeze, arm raised or leg half bent. The measure begun by the musicians goes on and on [p. 19].

The arrested wristwatch of Wallas does not arrest time. Rather it is the situation of such obsessive moments outside of time that allows the character to step into his projection of himself or permits another to perform a movement which his own has anticipated. Garinati's visions in the Prologue belong to moments that preceded the Prologue and to moments that precede Wallas: Garinati anticipates himself on one of the footbridges of the city while the nearby drawbridge opens to let a trawler pass, as he anticipates Wallas in a similar moment near the same bridge, or in moments on the flight of stairs leading to Dupont's study. The reader has been warned:

Soon unfortunately time will no longer be master. Wrapped in their aura of doubt and error, this day's events, however insignificant they may be, will in a few seconds begin their task, gradually encroaching upon the ideal order, cunningly introducing an occasional inversion, a discrepancy, a confusion, a warp, in order to accomplish their work: a day in early winter without plan, without direction, incomprehensible and monstrous [p. 7].

It is this mythologizing of moments through their arrest that enables Wallas to enter the world in which the gesture of an assassin will become his own, a necessary process only if one accepts that the hero has been fated to enact a long and complex coincidence. As unaccountable as Wallas' desire for a particular eraser, and the erotic moments that attend his quest, or the segments of time that catch him up in their cross-reflections, are reminders of the Oedipus myth that capriciously alter Wallas' landscape and impinge upon his actions. Window curtains in their embroidery, a chance statuette, a public monument —these and other objects turn into fugitive glimpses of the legend. Wallas, who has vague recollections of the city he visited as a child with his mother, remembers suddenly that they had come to look for his father. (And inevitably, after so much walking, his feet have swelled.) A drunkard asks him riddles that are a drunken parody of the sphinx's original question: "What animal is parricide in the morning, incestuous at noon, and blind at night?" The allusions are freely cast throughout and frequently sound like the author's private fun—it is most likely not fortuitously that Wallas catches sight of a newspaper headline that discloses: "The medium deceived her clients."

There is no reason why Wallas should be pursued by the shadow of Oedipus: he has made no sign to the gods. When once they wanted to show Laius that the very motions of his escape would be a part of his condemnation, the gods had a reason: it was Laius who had first addressed them; he had asked whether he would be happy. Gods may be perverse, but their godliness requires of them some minimal decorum: they do not speak until spoken to. But the shadow hovering over Wallas is that of an unmotivated coincidence: no matter how many curtains display an infant with shepherds, no matter how frequently a drunk hints at the name Apollo Loxios in his concern with the word "oblique" [10] (or suggests Oedipus himself as he mutters something that sounds like "foundling"), Wallas enters the criminal gesture of Garinati by accident—even if one assumes that Dupont is his long-lost father. Without a prior reason for the gods' interest, their presence would be doubtful. Wallas appears to be simply unlucky: he kills by mistake—the victim of one more coincidence, after all the others that have suggested their adventitious kinship with the myth.

---

[10] A somewhat obscure allusion for the reader who is unfamiliar with Lucian (*Zeus Tragoedus*). But the reference to the Greek satirist is significant: in both authors, the oracular wisdom is viewed problematically.

It is not an archaic myth that is caught in the cross-reflection of these temporal mirrors; it is the deceptiveness of a world in which time ceases to move according to a linear predictability and becomes erratic. The objective eye attempts to assert itself; it notes details with great precision; it is so keen, in fact, that the object of its vision becomes sharp—straight lines, flat planes, angular masses. But it can do no more; its world is subverted, and that subversion is the author's. Two objects in particular—two cubes —can be isolated to show the manner of the author's infringement. The first is the imagined eraser which has no function as an object, since, however intently it is visualized by Wallas, it is in fact twice a figment: inexistent in the objective world of Wallas, its being is more a function of the author's comments than of the hero's quest. In "Time and Description in Contemporary Narration," Robbe-Grillet defines a new purpose for novelistic description—"gommage":

It is no rare occurrence, in fact, in a modern novel, to find a description that starts from nothing. It doesn't begin by giving the reader a general picture, it seems to spring from a minute and unimportant detail, which is more like a geometrical point than anything else—a starting point—from which it invents lines, planes, and a whole architecture [. . .]. But the lines of the drawing go on accumulating, and it becomes overloaded; they contradict each other, and change places until the very construction of the image renders it more and more uncertain. A few more paragraphs, and when the description is complete, you discover that it hasn't left anything permanent behind it: in the end, it has become a twofold movement ["de création et de gommage"].[11]

[11] *For a New Novel*, pp. 145–146. "Gommage" is incorrectly rendered in the English translation as "getting stuck"; its idiomatic

The very central eraser that *is,* even though it *is not,* serves both as a critical term and a fictional instance of what the term denotes. It does not allow the reader to situate Wallas within an adventure that can be unified and comprehended by an external eye, but creates the evolving and dissolving moments of the hero's awareness that intend for the reader a similarly discontinuous experience.

However, if the eraser is in fact the middle letters "di," the author removes it from the reader's store of experienced and neutral objects in order to turn it into a wholly personal comment, a further digression that subverts even the reader's fragmented awareness of an episodic consciousness by suggesting that these fragments are not discontinuous after all but are indeed subsumed within the shadowy structure of the Greek myth.[12] The eraser is left with no more objective reality than a street named Corinth or rue des Arpenteurs. Thereafter, there is something pathetically vulgar in the erotic response of Wallas to the object of his desire which turns out to be such a completely literary creation, and one not of his own making.

The other cube, the vitrified mass that serves as a paperweight on Dupont's desk, evidences the same descent from object to argument in an even simpler way. It is first described as "A kind of cube, but slightly misshapen, a shiny

---

meaning is derived from *gommer:* to erase or rub out. Olga Bernal (*Alain Robbe-Grillet: Le Roman de l'absence*) interprets the author correctly when she terms *The Erasers* an effort to *rub out* the false fictional construct of the novel.

12 Or the amusement of the author who contrives it. Roudiez has pointed out, as Bruce Morrissette indicates (*Les Romans de Robbe-Grillet*), that "di" does not necessarily represent the middle part of "Œdipe," but may well be the "middle letters" of a French name whose commonness would make it even more applicable to a brand of erasers—Didier, for example.

block of gray lava, with its faces polished as though by wear, the edges softened, compact, apparently hard, heavy as gold, looking about as big around as a fist; a paper-weight?" (p. 21). It undergoes a metamorphosis: "The cube of vitrified stone, with its sharp edges and deadly corners, is lying harmlessly between the inkwell and the memo-pad" (p. 236). Once again, it might be possible to interpret this evolution of an object as a moment of the consciousness proposed to the reader—if indeed there were an object. But there is none: if "things *are there*" in defiance of "our pack of animistic or domesticating adjectives," then the "deadly corners" ("coins meurtriers") of the previously "softened" stone are only the bearers of the author's message. The object remains illusory, but the presence of its creator is very real.

The reader of *The Erasers* is solicited at two levels. At one of these, he encounters spatial and temporal objects that move in and out of their usual state of normalcy. Familiar things grow strange through phenomenological proximity. Time becomes an object equally strange as motion arrested and recurrent. But at the level where wrist-watches stop and start in response to otherworldly demands, where the circumstances of Oedipus suggest themselves with an insistence that is not born of necessity, the strangeness is of another kind—those intimations of inevitability, of mystery, perhaps of horror, do not result from constitutional factors but are reminders of an external and irrelevant world—a kind of Gothicism (an actual example of which can be found in the author's short story, "The Secret Room").

The world of *The Voyeur*, though the story is written in the third person, may well be the exclusive perception of Mathias. His circumstances are similar to those of Wallas: he returns to an island where he has been before—the place where he was born, according to one of his assertions. He is a door-to-door salesman of ladies' and gentlemen's wristwatches. On the island, a young girl has died a violent death, perhaps actually, in the past (from the start, Mathias has in his wallet a newspaper clipping relating such an incident), perhaps only within a local legend (a young girl was cast into the waves as a propitiatory victim in days gone by), perhaps during an hour that remains unaccounted for in Mathias' schedule. Inasmuch as Robbe-Grillet uses the same techniques as he does in *The Erasers*, situating his moments according to the recurrence of an obsession rather than the needs of a chronology or the determination of deliberate acts, the question of the hero's guilt remains in suspense. But whether or not Mathias is guilty, whether or not he has raped and killed a young girl, he is afraid. The reader is allowed to assume that Mathias was once rebuffed by a young girl and that his obsession is related in some way to that occurrence: the slapping sound of a wave triggers one of his early reminiscences, sends him back to the sadistic scene referred to in his clipping. But whether the criminal actor in that scene was once Mathias himself, or whether he merely enjoys a form of solitary sadism and fears discovery, cannot be determined at this point any more than it can be determined with reference to the murder on the island (if indeed that murder represents another occurrence). The reader is afforded only discontinuous and anachronic visions that are either purely fanciful or of a slightly modulated reality (a girl aboard the ferry, a movie poster, a print in a bedroom, a photograph, a frightened barmaid), which the fearful and erotic imagination of Mathias keeps conjuring.

What was the more or less gratuitous hallucination of moments or objects in *The Erasers,* or its merely Gothic gloss, can be interpreted as the contorting effects of fear in *The Voyeur.* Obsessional anticipations, the incriminating words of Julien,[13] Mathias' going over his tracks in search of evidence (cigaret butts, candy wrappings) that he might have left behind, or coming up time and again against the same fearsome corners of his mind—these can be understood as anguished or pathological motions. The very style of Robbe-Grillet may be seen as a contamination of the text by the aberration of its protagonist—the running together of zeugmatic or sylleptic moments through only the coincidence of a mood or action; the hypostatizing of time as repetition or cessation; the obsessive concern with a precision that not only determines the sharp vision already referred to, but, in an effort to avoid "animistic or domesticating adjectives," borrows from the sciences the terms of its measurements or those measurements themselves. All of these, each in its own way, may correspond to the sense that Mathias has of the world because of an abnormal perception.

It is in this light that must be viewed the figure 8, the

---

[13] Who is, according to Morrissette (*op. cit.*), the "voyeur" of the title (if indeed there is a "voyeur" at all, the novel having been projected originally as "Le Voyageur"—the usual designation of Mathias in the story). It should be noted that, in the absence of clearer bearings, even the testimony of Julien can be read as the workings of the hero's anxiety: Mathias has overheard the grandparents of Julien accusing the latter of Jacqueline's murder. It is not unusual for Mathias to inform a given object or topic with his anxiety: the ambiguous words of Julien may be no more than Mathias' fear of the incriminating form which Julien's self-exculpation might take. (Or again, this scene may simply rehearse the past, possibly in a self-dichotomizing of Mathias as his recollection of a former self.)

primary symbolic device of *The Voyeur*. The shape of the
8 recurs continually, in smoke rings, in the flight of birds,
in a man's gestures with his hands, in a sign along the
quay, etc. At first it operates in the curious way of other
thematic material in these novels—as mood, as *déjà-vu*.
But as the reader is able to speculate more extensively
about Mathias, the figure becomes a logical locus for the
fears and the erotic fantasies of Mathias. As reminders of
the wristwatches which he must sell (for a livelihood, or
out of a real or fancied need to establish an alibi), as visions of the cord binding the wrists of the victim, of the
criminal's handcuffs, and so on, the 8's that Mathias scrib-
bles on his agenda show the recurrence of his concerns,
while the figure repeated throughout the tale becomes for
the reader an obsessive pattern perhaps equivalent to the
obsessed mind of the hero.

Even so, the figure is repeated to the extent of becoming
occasionally little more than a sign of the virtuosity of the
author, for it can also represent infinity, according to
Morrissette (*Les Romans de Robbe-Grillet*), or the path
of Mathias across the island and his attempt to go back
over his tracks, or again, an anticipation of the new poster
which he finds on his return to the harbor: the advertise-
ment for a movie entitled *Monsieur X on the Double Cir-
cuit*.[14] The device serves a literary purpose as long as it
helps convey the content of a human consciousness. But as
an instance of the author's ingenuity, it merely proposes a

[14] In the original edition, the part of the voyager's schedule that is
not accounted for appears as a blank page between Parts I and II
and corresponds to the unnumbered page 88. Hopefully, this is
just an amusing coincidence—like that of the missing page 8 in the
novels of Robbe-Grillet published by the Editions de Minuit
whose numberings begin with page 9, following half of the first
signature.

game to the ingenuity of the reader. (Dante could play such games with his audience because they referred to intellectual and moral beliefs that existed before the poet's words, to a political and religious awareness whose symbols the poem did not create. And at least some of Joyce's mythology echoes in his readers as language and topography. But such games as are played in the books and movies of Robbe-Grillet are self-contained.)

The subsequent development of Robbe-Grillet's novels can be predicted in part through his transition from *The Erasers*, which has an object and a literary comment at its core, to the greater discretion apparent in *The Voyeur*, whose central motif does not disallow the expression of a character's perception. The rest of his novels to date can each be read as an account of moments of an obsessed or hallucinated awareness: the watchfulness of a suspicious and insistent eye (*Jealousy*, 1957); the fevered wanderings of a soldier in a strange city (*In the Labyrinth*, 1959); or a combination of these—an erotically inclined "I," a desperate quest through a nightmarish city, a drug-distorted vision affecting the eye that sees it, and so on (*La Maison de rendez-vous*, 1965). What were external devices in the first two novels become, in the later ones, elements of style—images, themes, the pattern of words. In *Jealousy*, which is the account of an obsessive inspection, the *eye* is both symbol and motor, the structure of the novel being determined by a single perception and its aberration; the reader "sees" only what the central consciousness sees, thinks it sees, or merely remembers. Its scrutiny is maniacal: jealousy is before all else an intensity of questioning; it detects the most trivial noise, the slightest motion, the tiniest of details—the crackling sound of an insect, the movement of the shadows throughout the day, the grain and texture of surfaces. Every act is contained within a beholding: "his behavior, nevertheless, does not pass unnoticed"; "once the eye is accustomed to the darkness, a paler form can be seen"; "it is relatively easy to count the trees"; "the slats of the blind are too sharply slanted to permit what is outside to be seen." [15] But jealousy requires the defeat of its questioning; the informing vision is frustrated whenever it encounters another eye: "she [. . .] absently stares"; "without raising her eyes"; "does not reveal the slightest expression"; and so forth. The eye is baffled, its vision discontinuous: the glass of some of the window panes is defective; the slats of the blind break up the field of vision.[16] But the true nature of that discontinuity derives from the insistency of a preoccupation: through the eye of a *jalousie* that sees, remembers, or imagines, the reader is repeatedly led back to a limited number of scenes—A... , the woman, writing a letter, looking at Frank, combing out her long black hair; Frank, the jungle neighbor and acquaintance, drinking an iced drink, killing a centipede against a wall, planning a ride to town with A... .

It is likewise as an eye that the reader responds to the

---

[15] Perhaps a last refuge of the author's playfulness is in the title: *La Jalousie* designates not only the state of the central consciousness but its framework and point of view—that of a jalousie, not an unlikely prop in a plantation house set amidst the jungle. (No attempt will be made here to interpret the recurrent count of banana clusters.)

[16] A device and prop that will find their way into the second of Robbe-Grillet's movies, *L'Immortelle* (1963)—whose camera directions are sometimes indicative of the manner in which the author constructs his novels: when the lens is to be directed from the heroine's point of view, Robbe-Grillet notes that her position "is comparable to that of a narrator in a modern novel [. . .] through the eyes of whom everything is seen."

awareness of the fictional eye. In the absence of structuring links, he is limited to simple impressions. His intermittent glance is too brief to elaborate a sense of *life:* he is left with a *pattern* of insights that never coalesce, fragmentary reminders of fragments. As noted, the reader interprets such a pattern retrospectively as the character's obsession or hallucination. But when the author allows a sylleptic echo between one moment of awareness and its unrelated sequent, he achieves more than characterization: when Robbe-Grillet alternates the sound of the centipede's mandibles and that of A... brushing her hair, without narrative transition, the reader persists momentarily in a former state of mind before he can adjust to the next scene; he thus comes to that scene as pure sense, and his apprehension is phenomenological before he can rationalize it. In *La Maison de rendez-vous,* the author allows a single mood to inform several different scenes by deriving from a recumbent female form the image of a woman on a couch, a drug addict in a poster, a carved figure on a ring, etc.

These wholly tentative moments of awareness may also serve to identify the author in the process of writing his novel, thus spanning in yet another way the distance between fiction and reality. Starting in *The Labyrinth* with the usual objects and figures (a bayonet, a picture on a wall, a pattern), the author uses the attempts of the soldier to situate his world as his own, in order to place experimentally the scenes he is writing (a false experimentation since the final form of the novel is that very tentativeness): the picture on the wall may be no more than an arrested grouping of characters in the room where it hangs; or the author may conversely abandon his characters in mid-motion, like the picture on the wall (the source of the ·first inspiration?). Or again, he may alter his perspective:

the soldier looking through the window sees himself in the street below. At such an impasse, a nonascribed voice breaks in to question or comment: "No. It was something else"; "It is probably here that the scene occurs"; "But this scene leads to nothing"; "No, no, no"; and so on (a technique which is picked up, sometimes verbatim, in *La Maison de rendez-vous*).

"Things are never definitely put to rights," says Lady Ava toward the end of *La Maison de rendez-vous;* it is one of the many utterances that do not achieve dialogue, a mere intermittence of the ear—as alien as the discontinuous eye. Such words provide no information relevant to the fiction, but the author invests them nevertheless with part of his commentary.[17] Lady Ava's sentence might be an epigraph for the novels of Robbe-Grillet. The reader does not understand exactly what Lady Ava is referring to: he is free to speculate that she is tired, or dying; or perhaps his hearer has not quite heard. But in fact, the reader has not understood her because he was intent upon a character, someone with an intelligible world to communicate. And there are no characters. The eye that sees, the passion that distorts are evident only in the perceived object, not in the perceiver: the deed may be visible, never the doer. If, because of a title or an identifiable emotion, the reader finds a way of subsuming his disjointed impressions, the responsibility for ascribing them to an informing consciousness may well be his alone. The capriciously cross-reflecting mirrors and the deliberately misleading games notwithstanding, this is the gift that Robbe-Grillet intended—a reader estranged, free from the familiarity and

---

[17] An analogous newspaper headline in *The Erasers* has already been mentioned: "The medium deceived her clients" is the author's fun, rather than fiction.

limitations of a humanizing eye. At a moment of the human quandary when life has lost its predetermined meaning, objects have ceased to be reassuring, identity has become problematical, and divine right and the natural mastery of man are at best speculative theories, Robbe-Grillet's is a novel for our times.

10

The Novel as Ritual:

Defoe's *Crusoe* and

Dostoevski's *Idiot*

—Trois livres, Messieurs, trois livres tiennent en face de la prison.

Il jeta autour de lui un coup d'œil ironique et amer:

—Robinson. Don Quichotte. L'Idiot.

—Et l'Evangile, dit une voix.

—Non.

MALRAUX, Les Noyers de l'Altenburg

More could be said about the experiment of Robbe-Grillet; considerably more has, but much of what has been said appears to revolve around two main questions: To what extent is the creation of an alien object possible? To what extent is the creation of an alienated reader desirable (or for that matter, possible)?

The intent of such an object is clear enough: modern "objectivity" is, no less than any other literary device, an attempt to neutralize the critic in the reader. If it were possible, the creation of a pure literacy object would achieve absolute *pattern*, undifferentiated from other phenomena, and could assume an undifferentiated acceptance by the reader. But it is evident that the *telling*, narrative or description, cannot relate such an object: no matter how "visual," the word is only a symbolic mediator—a sign. A word can be a visual object only within special circumstances (e.g., the typographical games of Sterne or the surrealists); but if *object* is what remains of the word when sense is not considered, that remainder is not its sight but its sound. It is as such a sound-object that the lyric poem enforces its meaning beyond that of its words as signs. It is noteworthy that although Robbe-Grillet refuses categories and experience as means of interpretation, he does not create his literary object through object-words: he accepts words as conventional signs, hoping that their symbolic equivalences will not spill over into the affective worlds of experience and feeling.

Even if one were to assume a word that might synthesize the object which it intends, the object read would still be of another kind for having been read. Its position in the phenomenal world would be first, and abnormally, its position within the self-contained world of the book; and its coming into being for the reader would still be determined by the peculiar awareness born of reading. The futility of looking for an object within the significance of a word seems therefore to be compounded by a literary ingenuity more and more intent on making that word what it can never be in fact.

If the word cannot secrete the object that will startle the reader into a nonliterary, and therefore noncritical, response (achieving the reader's most genuine acceptance at the moment of his most genuine surprise), what of the book itself? One will recall the experiment of Kafka through *The Trial,* whose tale synthesizes a phenomenal part of the world which has contrived, as fiction, the destruction of Joseph K.; or the diary of Roquentin, which, as the reader closes it, turns into the object upon whose making the experience of the fictional Roquentin was centered. These two instances of objectification have part of their process in common: each becomes an object retrospectively, after the reader is through with his reading; in each case, the reader's objective sense of the closed book is expressed within, and confirms, the fullest dimensions of his own world, its habitual phenomena, the accumulation of his own experience, and the peculiarities of his affectivity. Robbe-Grillet does not trust his reader that far: he wants to anticipate and insure such a post-reflective objectivity by preserving the book-as-object during its every moment, through a discontinuity that does not allow the flow of the telling to merge with the subjective experience of the reader. Some mention has already been made of the numerous essays of Robbe-Grillet (such as "A Path for the Future Novel" of 1956, and others written since then) in which he acknowledges the resistance of the average reader and a need to write deliberately in opposition to that reader's normal bent. In an article written for a *Dictionary* of contemporary literature (*Dictionnaire de littérature contemporaine* [Paris: Editions universitaires, 1962]) he refers to what he calls "common meanings" which, in the phenomenal world beyond the novel, may allow collective political action or a common moral interpretation; but he does not accept that these common meanings should be carried over from the phenomenal world into that of the novel: clearly, Robbe-Grillet requires a person able to assume a different set of responses when he becomes a reader. His reasons have been adequately documented: in his opinion, art does not go beyond presentation. It is in support of this belief that he marshals as witnesses other art forms that are primarily graphic, in particular the motion picture and painting.

Inasmuch as graphic arts depend for their appreciation primarily on the eye, an attempt to involve the mind jeopardizes the work's integrity if this additional aim requires modification of the elements whose organic balance was determined by the visual statement. But from Giotto to Rembrandt to Picasso, painters who have felt firmly in control of their canvas have not feared to add to the presentation on that canvas the representation of something external to it. In such cases, the vision of the painter is not recorded as an absolutely alien object but becomes, from the point of view of the one looking at the painting, a mediating commentary upon his own vision. It is this dialectic of response that Robbe-Grillet most frequently slights in evolving hierarchies of esthetic morality and in imposing the modes of one art form on another. When motion pictures add to graphic dimensions that develop in space a development in time, the connective and causal links that a spectator establishes as part of his normal mode become even more difficult to resist. A movie such as *L'Immortelle* may alienate its spectator periodically and purposely by reducing an imitation of life to an autonomous statement of the image, but that very reduction acknowledges the assimilative urge of the spectator who has assumed the other images, prior to their reduction, as *life*.

Moreover, words are not graphic in their usual acceptation. The theory of Robbe-Grillet repeats in another form the Aristotelian bias that saw every art form as imi-

tative. Robbe-Grillet allows confusion between the spatial
development of painting (or the space-time development
of motion pictures) and the peculiar modes of the word.
Furthermore, the belief that art can be no more than presentation supposes that its unique mode must be visual,
even when it is not visible—thus placing the reader in an
abnormal relation to the word. The word is a loose and ill-
definable stimulus because of its ambiguous nature as sign
and object: when Robbe-Grillet accepts what he terms
"common meanings" outside the novel, his very term for
"meanings" ("significations") refers to a complex of cultural and affective factors (meaning, sense, acceptation,
symbol) from which the word itself is inseparable.

It is normal that, as an author, Robbe-Grillet wishes to
leave the impress of his creation, requiring recognition of
its distinctiveness even as it is assimilated. This requirement
represents no more than a conscious assertion of its form
—an inevitable consequence of sophistication, once artifact
and reader can no longer assume each other naïvely, at
face value. But to what extent is it possible to maintain the
reader in a relation to the work of art that does not proceed beyond formal appreciation? Is it indeed possible for
the novel so to alienate the reader as to move him from an
appreciation of form ("I admire") to phenomenal belief
("it is real") through his utter acceptance of a surface, the
novel's absolute assertion of *pattern?* A distancing so radical in its effect supposes, in the absence of an entirely
different way of synthesizing the object, an entirely different reader.

The evolution of a humane art is a slow and continuing
process, as slow as the evolutionary process of the society,
the times, the artists of which it is evidence. When a tech-
nician synthesizes new forms in experimental isolation, his

art is inhuman: such "art" reflects a number of abstract considerations rather than the race and requires a similarly synthetic condition for its appreciation. Moreover, experimental analysis constructs only a skeletal art: fragmentation, detachment, destruction, play are passing devices for Cervantes and Proust, dialectical moments in the elaboration of the huge and complex friezes of a human panorama—whether in the world of men or of a single man. But an art form whose entire purpose is the use of these devices turns into an art of boredom and dehumanization. When it requires for its refusal of significance a reader who will inhibit his cultural response and his tragic nature, it becomes increasingly the poor and partial art of an impoverished age, of an impoverished artist bereft of lyricism, allegorical density, human commitment. Nor is it likely that a reader whose very instinct and metabolism require order, continuation, memory, and self-assertion will entertain as more than a passing fad an art so pathological in its form as to be able to frame only a pathological and aberrant vision.

Robbe-Grillet sees historical time as disuse and archaism, never as enrichment or as a necessary definition of human consciousness: the reader for whom old works retain a personal meaning is either stagnant or sentimental. He analyzes such vestiges as useless reminders of a moment passed, of a truth incapable of extension. And yet, even at a time when the author most concerned with the imitation of *life* conceives of a dialectical need for *pattern*, there endures through Defoe and Dostoevski a kind of novel so ingenuous that it implies in both author and reader a sense diametrically in contradiction with the theoretical ideals of Robbe-Grillet—a nearly primitive belief in the statement of life.

Alongside Rogers' *Cruising Voyage round the World,* *Robinson Crusoe* offers little in the way of sailing adventures (in contrast to the dispersiveness and diffusion of *The Farther Adventures*); a first shipwreck, two years in captivity, four years as a colonist in Brazil are passed over rapidly, as if Defoe were in a hurry to get the hero to his island, the preliminaries being, like the spinning around that starts a game of blindman's bluff, an effort to make the hero lose his bearings and remove the reader from the familiarity of beaten paths. If it is the island that centers the interest as a document of exotic fauna and flora, in the manner of those described by Rogers, Dampier, Knox, and so forth, Defoe's is tame and spiritless: with the exception of a stray penguin amidst the tropical lushness, little of what it has to offer is strange or even intriguing; its very lushness reminds Robinson of "a planted garden." It does not even contain the allegorical savages that are soon to people such literary Edens; it does feature briefly a few functional cannibals, but they use the island mainly to deposit Friday, whose astuteness in abstract discourse and theology seems to make of him largely a figure of stylistic relief—a means for the author to move from speculative monologue to relative concreteness and demonstration through dialogue. And lastly, if this is a tale about a hero (and Crusoe is Defoe's most heroic protagonist, both in the manner of his reversals, which he brings upon himself, and in his fortitude in confronting them), Robinson Crusoe is a singularly plodding hero.

The ultimate normalcy of this hero and the domestic nature of his exceptional circumstances are matched by the simplicity of the author's telling. The first-person narrative is so ingenuous as to require the author's belief in his own subterfuge, not unlike that of the "editor" of the

Preface, who believes "the thing to be a just history of fact." The narrative eye becomes briefly—for a fictional period of one year—the narrative "I" of a diary: that part of the narrative is like a magnifying glass applied to the details of the hero's daily life; it does not alter the narrative point of view, nor does it modify the reader's relation to the narrator (in fact, Defoe's transition from diary back to first-person narrative is scarcely noticeable). The observer has a Puritan eye and a Puritan conscience: he notes scrupulously the surfaces of his world and records only what he sees; the essential person and the essential object are presumably as their exterior shows them to be. As for his speculations, they are moral and given as such.

And yet, there appear to be two Robinson Crusoes. Several commentators have pointed out that the first one we meet is marked by "a radical perversity and impiety." [1] He is, at any rate, driven by a hunger to assert himself beyond the upper station of lower-class life described by his father as the most comfortable of social enclaves and the safest. To define this restlessness as mainly the urge of *homo economicus* (to cite Ian Watt's term and theory) would seem to miss the intensity of Crusoe's craving and attendant sin, which send him forth in defiance of family, social, and divine commandments—the usual guarantees of capitalist stability. The first Robinson Crusoe evades his father's wisdom, his mother's pleading; he shows poor ethical and business sense by selling into bondage his protégé Xury, whom he will need for his Brazilian plantation, and ultimately leaves his plantation to become a slave

[1] G. A. Starr, *Defoe and Spiritual Autobiography*, p. 79. See also J. Paul Hunter, *The Reluctant Pilgrim*, which reassesses *Robinson Crusoe* in order to show that it can be read, and must have been intended, as an orthodox Puritan document.

trader. He sounds less like an indefatigable businessman than like the Rimbaud of "Le Bateau ivre" crying out his need to burst the bonds of human finitude: "O que ma quille éclate! O que j'aille à la mer!" Such hungers are too great for the measure which society prescribes: the first part of the spiritual trajectory of Rimbaud and Robinson Crusoe requires that they leave the world of men.

This is the last of the visibly passionate Crusoe—a brief meteor. The Crusoe of the island is a different man: from the ashes of the prodigal and the rebel, there rises a strangely humble phoenix with the virtues of a Puritan conscience, the skills and patience of a painstaking craftsman. It is here that the drab heroism of the protagonist begins, of the definitive protagonist whose simplicity matches the simple expectations of the style that describes him. As a moral figure, Crusoe is the apodictic power of his acts; as the narrator, he believes in the apodictic power of his words. Words and purpose are modest, yet they will evidence another mode of the passionate hero—the passion of the man who must, in Malraux's expression, "get back to his fellow-men." It was a need to encompass and transcend that drove the first Robinson farther and farther away from his fellows until he was projected at last upon the vastness of uncharted seas; a need born of a more accurate understanding of his hunger now determines that he will laboriously return to the world he has abandoned. The accountant's figures, the calendar-maker's dates, the housekeeper's itemizing, the wealth of circumstantial description are Crusoe's steps back through the wilderness to the society of the 1650's. His belief in the apodictic value of the descriptions is his faith in his course and in the world toward which that course is set.

Ian Watt points out that by this time the novel is no

longer a true picture of life on a desert island—Defoe had, after all, access to authentic source material showing how castaways "harassed by fears and dogged by ecological degradation [. . .] sank more and more to the level of animals, lost the use of speech, went mad or died of inanition" (*The Rise of the Novel*, p. 83). But if Defoe has disregarded "the actual psychological effects of solitude" (p. 87), it is for a good reason—presumably because he is telling his reader something that goes beyond the concerns of eighteenth-century economics or tales of the sea, something that concerns the nature of man. Crusoe's shipwreck may have enabled him to identify correctly the source of his former craving as human solitude or human finitude—but the sense was in him long before he made any identification. He was born with questions before his particular God directed him to ask them; his Puritanism only confirmed his belief that the individual is cut adrift from a paternal God and that he is the one who must fashion within himself the only spiritual entity which he can state. When he is shipwrecked, Robinson Crusoe merely goes from an unformulated sense of the human quandary to its emblematic form. Crusoe becomes aware of his human limitation amidst men—his escape from the human condition seemed therefore to require escape from their world. His island teaches him that his awareness is a self-defining truth and that flight is consequently absurd: he must return to men and live out his lonesomeness fraternally, amidst the alienated children of God.

Defoe's narrative remains superficial and simple because of his conviction that he speaks of a human constant to a reader who cannot fail to recognize and accept it. The psychology is rudimentary; the linguistic manner (including the diary form, popular among Puritans in the seven-

teenth century) is current and colloquial, resorting to literature only in a nonliterary way.[2] Even the hero's mercantile concerns are far from incompatible with a Puritan's
world view. Such social and spiritual evidence is supposed
to inform the inventory of surfaces and the analysis of
mechanisms as it simultaneously reduces them to what
they are: allegorical shells.[3] Defoe reminded his readers of
that fact in his *Serious Reflections* (whose first essay is ap-
propriately "On Solitude") by assuming the identity of
Robinson and justifying that assumption: "It is as reasonable to represent one kind of imprisonment by another, as
it is to represent anything that exists by that which exists
not."

The other hero whose ingenuousness does not remove
him from the modern temper, presumably because that ingenuousness moves him "back to his fellow men," is Prince
Myshkin, Dostoevski's *Idiot*.[4] What kind of an idiot is
Myshkin? Nearly every character in *The Idiot* (and not
only the major ones) debates that question. The Prince
elicits sufficient animus to be called an idiot at one time or

[2] Gustaf L:son Lannert: "In RC the Holy Scripture is the only
book Defoe quotes or alludes to" (*An Investigation into the Language of Robinson Crusoe*, p. 14). See also Hunter, *op. cit.*
[3] As commentators on Robinson Crusoe have noted, the Puritan
does not write fiction, but the whole world is a moral allegory to
him.
[4] The first hero on Malraux's list (chronologically) is Don Quixote. Inasmuch as the deception of Cervantes is intended to make
the reader accept his hero, the trajectory of the Don from figure
mocked to victim of that mockery would certainly represent a return to humankind. But until the moment of that return, the presence of the author complicates the picture. (It is perhaps noteworthy that in the moments of the Don's travail, at the end of
each book, the author removes himself from the scene.)

another by nearly everyone but is nevertheless of such a kind as to cause the invective to be followed by a retraction in nearly every case. There are of course the semifactual intimations of gossip and Myshkin's own avowals: he has spent several years in Switzerland, under the care of Schneider, for what he himself describes as nearly total idiocy; in fact, he gauges the extent of his present recovery in part through his wonder at being able to speak Russian so well. But there is also the undeniable fact that he is epileptic. Epilepsy has the two fundamental requirements of sanctity: it is refractorily mysterious and it is frightening—since at least the days of Hippocrates, it has been the "sacred disease," through which a supernatural voice is heard in the one whom it seizes. (At the height of Myshkin's paroxysm, "it seems indeed as though it were someone else screaming from within the man" [II, 5]). From the start, Myshkin is beyond the world of men because of a special sign: "His eyes were large, blue and dreamy; there was something gentle, though heavy-looking in their expression, something of that strange look from which some people can recognize at the first glance a victim of epilepsy" (I, 1).

That "something gentle" in the Prince's expression indicates another of the major reasons for which he has been set apart from a humanity whom his isolation will serve to define. Dostoevski's letters and notes concerning *The Idiot* make clear what that reason is: as a character, Myshkin represents the end product of an attempt to depict "a truly perfect and noble man." There has been in the world but one figure of absolute beauty—Christ, whose very manifestation was a miracle. But, writes Dostoevski, "of all the noble figures in Christian literature, I reckon Don Quixote as the most perfect. But Don Quixote is noble only by being at the same time comic. [. . .] The reader feels sympathy and compassion with the Beautiful, derided and unconscious of its own worth." [5] Myshkin, the figure of non-evil, stands virtually alone in a world whose active forces are variously symbolized by the tarantula-like monster of which Ippolit has a vision, by death as the pale rider of Lebedyev's Apocalypse, ugliness overcoming beauty, darkness threatening the extinction of light. As against the memory of a paradise lost, this is the dynamic actuality of hell, a world of men and women possessed with a rage to have and to dominate—sexually, through money, through social or political power. Their strength and needs are incarnate in Rogozhin, the antinomic "double" of Myshkin (linked in the vision of Ippolit with the evil tarantula). [6]

To say that Rogozhin embodies the demonic power of Dostoevski's apocalyptic times is not to say that he is a morality figure, any more than others of the characters. The most evil of these people is saved from becoming a symbolic figure by an evident self-belief (wholly condoned by the author). It is in the violent nature of such pride that the narrative finds its motor force, developing as a consequence of the character of Nastasya Fillipovna, the girl first protected and later degraded by Totsky. Worldly and beautiful to the external eye, Nastasya suffers from an exacerbated pride that makes her deeply aware and resentful of what she considers to be her fall from grace. Acting

[5] Letter to his niece Sofia Alexandrovna, Geneva, January 1 [13], 1868. The translation used here is by Ethel C. Mayne.
[6] On Dostoevski's use of "doubles," see in addition to his own early *The Double* (1846), Dmitri Chizhevsky, "The Theme of the Double in Dostoevsky," reprinted in *Dostoevsky, A Collection of Essays*, ed. E. R. Wellek; also René Girard, *Dostoïevsky: Du double à l'unité*.

on impulse, she first humiliates and threatens Totsky and next chooses to cast her lot with Rogozhin instead of the outwardly more respectable Ganya, simply because fewer calculations enter into the former. Both men undoubtedly love Nastasya, but whereas the animal passion that Rogozhin feels for her is not clearly distinct from the rest of his nature, the love of Ganya does not free him of other desires—his craving to come into wealth, to advance socially, and so on. It is at the moment of Nastasya's choice that Myshkin interferes, sensing that the luminous part of Nastasya would be dimmed if she were to give herself to Rogozhin. What remains luminous in Nastasya recognizes in Myshkin a redemption of such magnitude that it cannot accept that redemption, being aware that saint and sinner cannot mix. Nastasya is undoubtedly fortified in her moral withdrawal by the parallel urgings of her pride that cannot submit to any possession: she senses that the impulse of Myshkin, though one of love, has been prompted by charity, a form of love less submissive than that born of desire, which, whatever its end, is fundamentally human in that it denotes first a need in the lover. The distance that separates Nastasya from Myshkin is in part that which separates man from God.

But having once glimpsed salvation, Nastasya cannot give up Myshkin any more than she can accept him: her flights toward Rogozhin are invariably followed by equally sudden withdrawals. In order to bring about a situation which she can contemplate only in moments of impulsive generosity, she turns to Aglaia Epanchin, whom the Prince has unaccountably singled out as an object of light in a world which he does not generally question but which forebodes gloom to the author. Writing to Aglaia in order to urge her to marry the Prince, Nastasya confirms, "He thought of you as 'light.' Those were his own words" (III, 10). And because, like Rogozhin, she belongs to a violent race, Nastasya turns from words to action: she breaks up the projected marriage between Aglaia and Yevgeny Pavlovich. But Aglaia is no less a creature of pride: she too is restive at the very thought of marriage. Her gradual inclination toward Myshkin develops in opposition to a constant irritation with herself and with the actions of Nastasya, which she interprets correctly as the result of torment and love. When she finally confronts her rival, a balance that was at best precarious is irretrievably upset.

Such is the world, such the people, from which Myshkin is twice isolated. Lacking either the driving energy of evil or a motor pride to give him direction, the Prince remains a figure unconscious of his alienation from the people to whom he must instinctively "get back." [7] His integration within the narrative fabric is no less problematic. The creature of unmitigated good must be corrupted to achieve such integration, and so lose his original definition, or he remains of a different kind, free of narrative bonds and dependent on the virtues of awe and admiration that establish the relation of the epic hero to a reader of good will. But the saint is not an epic hero; it is virtually impossible for him to elicit admiration through the practice of humility (a quandary for the Christian saint in particular, who must practice his very virtues with discretion lest they turn into something else). Even love, the most divine of attributes, becomes a dilemma within the realm of man:

---

[7] The clothes he wears are symbolic: "what was quite suitable and satisfactory in Italy turned out not quite sufficient for Russia" (I, 1); when he returned from Moscow, "his clothes were all new and had been cut by a good Moscow tailor. But there was something wrong even with his clothes" (II, 2).

Nastasya is right in sensing that a figure of universal love lacks the dimensions of anxiety and yearning that make the emotion human. In fact, the saint lacks many of the dimensions necessary to enter the world of men, and as the novel chronicles that world, he fits into it awkwardly. Meanwhile, his absolute virtue also defeats the author's schemes and stratagems, since there is every likelihood that these would contaminate a hero dependent for the definition of his sainthood on a rejection of guile.

These many difficulties suggest the comic possibility, especially as it is evident that Dostoevski had Don Quixote in mind while he was writing about Myshkin. Shortly after their first meeting, the Prince sends Aglaia a letter that comes as close to being a declaration of love as this figure of utter benevolence can make. She hides it in a book that turns out to be *Don Quixote;* when she discovers what she has done, she laughs. Later on, she applies the title "poor knight" to Myshkin—a reference to the poem by Pushkin, whose hero she analyzes as "a serious" Don Quixote. At the conclusion of the tale, when the not less perceptive Yevgeny sums up Myshkin's character, he once again uses the ways and ideals of the quixotic knight for his analogies. Yet Myshkin is not made of the same stuff as the Spanish hero, and Dostoevski is the first to sense it; in the already quoted letter to Sofia Alexandrovna he writes, after the enumeration of "Christian" masterpieces that begins with the "comic" *Don Quixote,* "I have not yet found anything similar to that" (though he has begun the second of the four parts). He already refers to his future book as *The Idiot,* a title Cervantes could not have given his: the Spanish hero is protected through structural complexities from this sort of affectionate directness. It is in such affection and directness that the comic possibility is dissipated. In the same letter to Sofia, Dostoevski interprets the comic nature of Don Quixote from a particular point of view: "The reader feels sympathy and compassion with the Beautiful, derided and unconscious of its own worth. The secret of humor consists precisely in this art of wakening the reader's sympathy." This interpretation has the hero alienated only through his fictional context (his own view of himself and the other characters' view of him) but does not envisage the separation of either the author or the reader, who are linked to Don Quixote through "sympathy." For Dostoevski, Cervantes' character is betrayed through his inability to match decorum to substance and by the inability of others to distinguish between surface and substance: neither circumstance suggests that the reality of his substance is doubted by author or reader, both of whom see the man rather than the comic object. On these terms, Myshkin is of course a figure much like Don Quixote: he acts virtuously but is not conscious of that virtue and makes no effort to relate it to other humans; as a result, his encounters turn to disasters of a painful kind—as would Don Quixote's if he were not an object (at least until such time as Cervantes chooses to let his hero *feel*, so as to mark off one form of telling from another).

Myshkin keeps stumbling over the bloody roots of reality in their most trivial as well as in their most tragic forms. One need but note the fixed star by which the knight sets his course: Dulcinea is hardly the "lumen coeli" of Pushkin's poem; to the extent that she is real, she embodies the coarsest of realities: she tends pigs. But Don Quixote's world is secure in proportion as it is distant from externally objective criteria: it remains visionary and hence within his control. Myshkin, on the other hand, is the attendant, not of one, but of two ladies, and both exist as forces sufficiently real to affect him: they compel him to acknowledge the impossibility of utter benevolence by making him a participant in the final tragedy which he tried to prevent.

Unable to attain a comic dimension because of the author's belief in him, Myshkin faces a dilemma that cannot be resolved whenever his absolute definition confronts in others the human non-absolute which was meant to be his focus and justification: his "rage of goodness"[8] becomes what Murray Krieger has termed "the curse of saintliness."[9] The way out of this impasse is ultimately to alter Myshkin as a dramatic figure: instead of the simple statement of good whose emblem was Christ radiant, he ends up as the dialectical figure that catches his eye in the house of Rogozhin—in a painting by Holbein "of our Saviour who had just been taken from the cross" (II, 4)—a man upon whose flesh the marks of suffering are still visible, a mediator between an idea and its necessary corruption in human terms. It is through this act of mediation that Myshkin accomplishes his journey from Switzerland back to Russia, from a dehumanized concept "back to his fellow-men."

Rejection of the comic mode and of Christlike perfection for the sake of human immediacy as rendered through the vision of Holbein supposes the rejection of a complicated relationship between author and reader. *The Idiot* is an unambiguous instance of *life:* the candid assumption of a human truth by the author and his confidence in the reader leave little scope for the devising of *pattern.* Dosto-

[8] The expression is R. P. Blackmur's (*Eleven Essays in the European Novel*).
[9] In an article so titled (in *Dostoevsky,* ed. R. Wellek).

evski moves in and out of his tale in pursuit of a guileless
dialogue with his reader and characters. He introduces the
fourth part through an extended aside. In Cervantes, such
an aside would have represented terrain expressly mined
for the reader, but Dostoevski intends no such deception;
he does not question his characters (whom he assumes to
be real to the extent that his remarks about them are ingenuous) any more than he questions his own relation, as
commentator, to his fiction or to the reader who presumably accepts the comments with equal candor. Nor is this
the sole instance of Dostoevski's mingling in his fiction: his
narrative pleasure is as great as Ivolgin's; in IV, iv, *both*
create a Napoleonic legend that arises mainly out of the
joy of storytelling. At other times, as in IV, ix, he steps
back from his story, pretexting a need for clarity, but
actually in order to change from formal to informal narration. At times, he warns the reader that the episode will
be amusing (as in IV, ix) and is confident that the reader
will be amused. A few pages later, he engages in rhetorical
questions, the answers to which are perfectly well known
to him and to his reader, while at other times, he plays at
being an accurately informed commentator; these are
merely ways of dwelling affectionately on the unquestioned reality of his characters, whose world and his own
are so indissolubly one.

The very "doubles" of Dostoevski are simply that—
doubles: two instances of *life* with different attributes;
their action remains natural even when their intent is
supernatural. In *The Double*, their greatest claim to an
otherworldliness is that they look alike; in *The Idiot*,
Myshkin and Rogozhin are linked only through the normal consequences of their mutual attraction after fate has
brought them together in a railway carriage. As a matter

of fact, Lebedyev is in the same compartment, and he too will henceforth gravitate toward the Prince. Everyone is drawn to Myshkin, for he has about him the charisma of the saint. If he is able to move beyond that charismatic vesture into a human bond with Rogozhin, it is because the author never doubted that his essence was human and never expected his reader to doubt.

Man is born naked. From the randomness of his jeopardy, he seeks the elements of a constant that will make the vagrancies of the threat predictable. That constant, whether magical object or ritual incantation, is both a sacred form of the indwelling menace and an object tamed because in that form the threat remains within his grasp. At the center of every ritual there is an object, a menace in portable form—the stone of Mecca, a thorn of the Crown, a rabbit's foot, a black ewe. At the moment of man's reaction to fear, the random manifestation of the threat is synthesized into something more than the mere shape of human anxiety. If that fear remains attached to objects that have not been properly sanctified, it is termed superstition; educated fear appreciates the magic object and is aware of its virtue. But whatever the degree of education, awe cannot be removed from the object of worship without utterly changing the nature of worship: even a god of love and mildness threatens. The one responding to the ritual and the ritual object remains in his response as ambiguous as they: without the residual darkness implicit in the very nature of wonderment, superstition and control are equally unthinkable—but residual darkness remains in every assertion of control.

The high priest of these mysteries is likewise ambiguous: *sacred* and *sullied* derive from a common etymon;

the high priest is both. Because he begins beyond human boundaries, he is separate from men; he is eccentric; his path is unlike the common path. He is dangerous and wonderful, as are dangerous and wonderful the magic objects of his craft. But he exists for man nevertheless. He is alone, a mediator between two worlds, and his role changes him; he is unique and pure. (Priests are shorn of the dead or defiling parts of their bodies, of hair, fingernails, etc.; they are especially anointed; their clothing is consecrated to the sole use of their office; they live under a sexual interdict that either privileges them or removes from them the act of carnal intercourse with the impure.) But that purity is alien to the health and normalcy of the working day, which proclaims the officiant sullied even as he is pure.

In a world addressed to the dissipation of mystery, mystery ceases to be a collective concern. If it persists, it is as a personal question, perhaps as the private vision that dwells on the enduring incompleteness of man even within an ever more fully explained structure. As the magical object loses the power to gather around it large segments of the collectivity, the artifact—the creation of the artist—tends to replace it and becomes the concern of a few. The artifact is an occult object only because it remains beyond the understanding of many and transmutes an awareness for some—but its attributes do not include the immanence of a threat: it is more esthetic than incantational. A large part of this writing has been devoted to showing how, over a period of time, the artist has attempted to make of that object something that exists more and more for its own sake, and ultimately, an occasion of mere phenomenological perception, a phenomenal sample as alien and as familiar as any other within the phenomenal world. But the reason for that effort has been stated also: it develops against a resistance to belief by a reader increasingly determined to turn into an object what was meant to be a medium between him and his world through the operative magic of mimesis. Socially conscious critics have traced all parts of this evolutionary process to the unsatisfactory evolution of society: for Lukács and Goldmann, the novel comes about as the result of nonconceptualized dissatisfaction within society and for that reason will always suppose in one form or another an alienated hero. (Lukács goes so far as to point out that a hero who is conceived as isolated beyond the power of society to effect or affect that isolation represents an instance of poor ontology); for others, like Adorno (as for Robbe-Grillet), the disappearance of realism from the modern novel derives from social alienation: what once contrived an unsatisfactory hero now contrives an unsatisfactory form.[10] These views suggest that the novel's content and form are determined by the modes of a society that might equally as well resolve questions which the ritual attempts only to synthesize as a result of a sense of limitation. The left-wing critic represents an optimistic view of man, at variance with the belief out of which ritual is born—the assumption that man's reach must fall short of his desire and vision.

To the extent that every sign must send the reader back to his experience and his lore, the novel remains inextricably a part of the reader's being. It is against this necessary condition that his sophistication reacts, but that reaction acknowledges the temptation of belief, a need to sense his

---

[10] The views here referred to appear especially in the following: György Lukács, *The Meaning of Contemporary Realism;* Lucien Goldmann, *Pour une sociologie du roman;* Theodor W. Adorno, *Noten zur Literatur.*

existence in his reassertion of the human quandary. His strength is limited; his capacity can be ascertained, his life-span predicted; but there remains as well the boundless extension of his imagination, which defines his freedom and his bondage as it strains toward absolutes that have no correspondence in his reality, as it instinctively rejects his finitude the very moment it becomes aware of that finitude. The literature that reflects him as he is thus magnified in his aspiration and his defeat is a ritual that rehearses for him the awesomeness and the intensity of being, the paean that rhythms the soaring of his hope and the dirge that gives a cadence to his grief—the systolic modulations of his self-awareness.

His officiant is the soiled and sacred poet, able to find words for his vision but aware of his most ignominious mysteries. The three authors mentioned by Malraux—Cervantes, Defoe, Dostoevski—those who plotted the path of a man back to his fellow men, were all symbolically set apart from men: each was imprisoned. And each came close to human corruption. Their writing records what was most vulgar and most sublime in their experience and justifies it all because man is all of it. In Defoe and Dostoevski, nontranscended cares of a most trivial nature are closely bound up with cares of the soul, as can be seen in the characters' concern with money—Robinson's, of course, but even Myshkin's when he comes between Nastasya and Rogozhin. Everyday preoccupations and beliefs of Defoe are transferred as such to his hero: his recollections of Newgate ("It is [. . .] reasonable to represent one kind of imprisonment by another"), his trust in providential dreams, his mercantile and Puritan ethics are indistinguishably consigned to his own memoirs and Robinson's, transcribed by an identical hand—an unmediated identity of form and content that prompted Riesman to call *Robinson Crusoe* "the ancestor of the comic book" (*The Lonely Crowd*, 1950). The fictional world of Dostoevski is equally real: the day Rogozhin enters the life of Nastasya, she reads about Mazurin, the actual murderer whose crime Rogozhin will copy in killing her (see C. Motchoulski: *Dostoïevski*). Myshkin's epilepsy is the author's, and the face that haunts Myshkin, the face of the man about to be executed, is Dostoevski's own. The critic in the mid-twentieth century may discover in such writing what Krieger calls "existential psychoanalysis" ("The Curse of Saintliness"), but to the author it was no more than existential awareness.

Robinson Crusoe and *The Idiot* are not reread because of the complexities of a critic's interpretations: they are reread because of their simplicity. They are the rote through which the reader experiences once again the awareness that he is alone yet cannot live alone, that he needs to love and still will lose his love, that he cannot accept death though he will surely die. And as he reads, the reader recounts himself as desire, as striving, as loss. When new experiments in literature achieve greater insights, when society has resolved such paradoxes, then it will be time for simple works like these to die.

Books Cited

Adams, Robert Martin. *Strains of Discord: Studies in Literary Openness*. Ithaca, N.Y.: Cornell University Press, 1958.
——. *Surface and Symbol: The Consistency of James Joyce's Ulysses*. New York: Oxford University Press, 1962.
Adorno, Theodor W. *Noten zur Literatur*. 2 vols. Berlin: Suhrkamp, 1958–1961.
Alberti, Leon Battista. *Della pittura*. Edited by Luigi Mallé. Florence: Sansoni, 1950.
Amadís de Gaula. Edited by Edwin B. Place. Madrid: Instituto "Miguel de Cervantes," 1959–1965.
André le Chapelain. *The Art of Courtly Love (De Amore)*. Translated by John Jay Parry. New York: F. Ungar, 1957.
Antonio de Lofraso. See Frasso, Antonio de lo.
Aragon, Louis. *Le Paysan de Paris*. Paris: Gallimard, 1926.
Aristotle. *Aristotle's Theory of Poetry and Fine Art, with a Critical Text and Translation of the Poetics*. Translated by Samuel Henry Butcher. New York: Dover, 1951.
Auerbach, Erich. *Mimesis: The Representation of Reality in Western Literature*. Garden City, N.Y.: Doubleday, 1957.
Balzac, Honoré de. *Eugénie Grandet*. Edited by Pierre-Georges Castex. Paris: Garnier, 1965.
Baudelaire, Charles. "Correspondances," in *Œuvres complètes*. Edited by Y. G. Le Dantec. Paris: Gallimard, 1961.
Benoît de Sainte-Maure. *Le Roman de Troie*. Edited by Léo-

pold Constans. 6 Vols. Paris: Firmin Didot, 1904–1912.

Bernal, Olga. *Alain Robbe-Grillet: Le Roman de l'absence.* Paris: Gallimard, 1964.

Bersani, Leo. *Marcel Proust: The Fictions of Life and Art.* New York: Oxford University Press, 1965.

Blackmur, R. P. *Eleven Essays in the European Novel.* New York: Harcourt Brace, 1964.

Blanchot, Maurice. *L'Espace littéraire.* Paris: Gallimard, 1955.

Boccaccio, Giovanni. *Decameron.* Edited by Vittore Branca. 2 vols. Florence: Le Monnier, 1960. Translated into French by Jean Bourciez, *Le Décaméron* (Paris: Garnier, 1963).

——. *Il Filostrato & Il Ninfale fiesolano.* Edited by Vincenzo Pernicone. Bari, Italy: Laterza, 1937.

Boethius, Anicius Manlius Severinus. *De consolatione philosophiae.* Translation by Chaucer, edited by Richard Morris. London: Trübner, 1868.

Boileau-Despréaux, Nicolas. *L'Art poétique: Commenté par Boileau et par ses contemporains.* Edited by P. V. Delaporte, S.J. 3 vols. Lille, France: Desclée de Brouwer, 1888.

Booth, Wayne C. *The Rhetoric of Fiction.* Chicago: University of Chicago Press, 1961.

Bourciez, Jean. See Boccaccio.

Brasillach, Robert. *Portraits.* Paris: Plon, 1935.

Breton, André. *Nadja.* Paris: Gallimard, 1928.

——. *Position politique du surréalisme.* Paris: Sagittaire, 1935.

Brod, Max. *Franz Kafka: A Biography.* Translated by G. Humphreys Roberts and Richard Winston. New York: Schocken, 1963.

Bronson, B. H., and others. *Studies in the Comic.* Berkeley: University of California Press, 1941.

Budgen, Frank. *James Joyce and the Making of Ulysses.* Second edition. Bloomington: Indiana University Press, 1960.

Burke, Kenneth, *Counter-statement.* Second edition. Los Altos, Calif.: Hermes, 1953.

Butor, Michel, *Les Œuvres d'art imaginaires chez Proust.* London: University of London Athlone Press, 1964.

——. *Répertoire: Etudes et Conférences, 1948–59*. Paris: Editions de Minuit, 1960.

Camus, Albert. *Caligula*, in *Théâtre, Récits, Nouvelles*. Edited by Roger Quilliot. Paris: Gallimard, 1962.

——. *Le Mythe de Sisyphe*. Paris: Gallimard, 1942. Translated by Justin O'Brien, *The Myth of Sisyphus and Other Essays* (New York: Knopf, 1955).

Capellanus, Andreas. See André le Chapelain.

Cascales, Francisco de. *Tablas poéticas*. Madrid: A. de Sancha, 1779.

Castelvetro, Lodovico. *Poetica d'Aristotele vulgarizzata et sposta per Lodovico Castelvetro*. Basel: Pietro de Sedabonis, 1576.

Cervantes Saavedra, Miguel de. *La Casa de los Celos y Selvas de Ardenia*, in *Teatro completo de Miguel de Cervantes Saavedra*. 3 vols. Madrid: Hernando, 1896–1897.

——. *El Ingenioso Hidalgo Don Quijote de la Mancha*. Edited by Don Diego Clemencín. 6 vols. Madrid: Aguado, 1833–1839. Translated by John Ormsby, *The Ingenious Gentleman Don Quixote of La Mancha* (New York: Knopf, 1926). Translated by Samuel Putnam, *Don Quixote de la Mancha* (2 vols.; New York: Viking Press, 1949).

——. *Exemplary Novels* and *Galatea*, in *The Complete Works of Miguel de Cervantes Saavedra*. Edited by James Fitzmaurice-Kelly. Glasgow: Gowans and Gray, 1901–1903.

La Chanson de Roland. Edited by T. Atkinson Jenkins. Revised edition. New York: D. C. Heath, 1929.

Chaucer, Geoffrey. *The Works of Geoffrey Chaucer*. Edited by F. N. Robinson. Boston: Houghton Mifflin, 1957.

——. See also Boethius.

Chernowitz, Maurice Eugene. *Proust and Painting*. New York: International University Press, 1945.

Chrétien de Troyes. *Cligès; Le Chevalier de la Charrette (Lancelot); Le Chevalier au Lion (Yvain)*, in *Romans*. Edited by Mario Roques. 4 vols. Paris: Champion, 1952–1960.

Clancier, Georges-Emmanuel. *Les Incertains*. Paris: Seghers, 1965.

Corneille, Pierre. *L'Illusion comique*. Edited by Robert Garapon. Paris: Didier, 1957.

Dampier, William. *A New Voyage round the World*. Fifth edition. London: James Knapton, 1703.

Dante Alighieri. *The Divine Comedy*. Original with English translation by John D. Sinclair. 3 vols. New York: Oxford University Press, 1961.

———. *Vita Nuova and Canzoniere of Dante Alighieri*. Translated by Thomas Okey. London: Dent and Sons, 1930.

Defoe, Daniel. *Robinson Crusoe* (including *Farther Adventures* and *Serious Reflections*); *A Journal of the Plague Year; Moll Flanders*. Shakespeare Head Edition. Oxford: Basil Blackwell, 1927–1928.

Dentan, Michel. *Humour et création littéraire dans l'œuvre de Kafka*. Geneva: Droz, 1961.

Dictionnaire de l'Académie. First edition. Paris, 1964.

Dostoevski, Fyodor M. *The Double: A Poem of St. Petersburg*. Translated by George Bird. Bloomington: Indiana University Press, 1958.

———. *The Idiot*. Translated by Constance Garnett. New York: Macmillan, 1951.

———. *Letters of Fyodor Michailovitch Dostoevsky to his Family and Friends*. Translated by Ethel Colburn Mayne. New York: Macmillan, 1917.

Ducasse, Isidore Lucien. *Les Chants de Maldoror*, in *Œuvres complètes*. Paris: Corti, 1961.

Dujardin, Edouard. *Les Lauriers sont coupés*. Paris: Librairie de la Revue Indépendante, 1888.

———. *Le Monologue intérieur: Son apparition, ses origines, sa place dans l'œuvre de James Joyce*. Paris: Messein, 1931.

Dunlop, John Colin. *History of Prose Fiction*. 2 vols. London: G. Bell, 1888.

Enéas, roman du XIIᵉ siècle. Edited by J.-J. Salverda de Grave. Paris: Champion, 1925–1929.

Ercilla y Zúñiga, Alonso de. *La Araucana*. Barcelona: Iberia, 1962.

Fernández de Avellaneda, Alonso. *El Ingenioso Hidalgo D. Quijote de la Mancha*. Barcelona: D. Cortezo, 1884.

Feuillerat, Albert. *Comment Marcel Proust a composé son roman*. New Haven: Yale University Press, 1934.

Fletcher, Angus John Stewart. *Allegory: The Theory of a Symbolic Mode*. Ithaca, N.Y.: Cornell University Press, 1964.

Flores, Angel, editor. *The Kafka Problem*. New York: Octagon Books, 1963.

Flores, Angel, and M. J. Bernardete, editors. *Cervantes across the Centuries*. New York: Dryden Press, 1948.

Folengo, Teofilo. *Baldus*, in *Le Maccheronee*. Edited by Alessandro Luzio. Bari, Italy: Laterza, 1911.

Frasso, Antonio de lo. *Los Diez Libros de fortuna de amor*. Barcelona: Pedro Malo, 1573.

Garshin, Vsevolod M. "Four Days," in *The Signal and Other Stories*. Translated by Rowland Smith. New York: Knopf, 1917.

Girard, René. *Dostoïevski: Du double à l'unité*. Paris: Plon, 1963.

——. *Mensonge romantique et vérité romanesque*. Paris: Grasset, 1961. Translated by Yvonne Freccero, *Deceit, Desire and the Novel* (Baltimore: Johns Hopkins Press, 1965).

Goldmann, Lucien. *Pour un sociologie du roman*. Paris: Gallimard, 1964.

Les Grandes et Inestimables Chronicques de l'énorme géant Gargantua, in Huntington Brown, *The Tale of Gargantua and King Arthur*. Cambridge: Harvard University Press, 1932.

Grossvogel, David I. *The Self-conscious Stage in Modern French Drama*. New York: Columbia University Press, 1958.

Guillaume de Machaut. *Le Paradis d'amour*, in *Poésies lyriques*. Edited by V. Chichmaref. 2 vols. Paris: Champion, 1907–1909.

Harrap's Standard French and English Dictionary. Edited by J. E. Mansion. 2 vols. London: George G. Harrap, 1958–1959.

Horace (Quintus Horatius Flaccus). *Satires, Epistles, Ars Poetica*. (Loeb Classical Library.) Cambridge: Harvard University Press, 1961.

Huizinga, Johan. *The Waning of the Middle Ages: A Study of the Forms of Life, Thought and Art in France and the Netherlands in the XIVth and XVth Centuries*. Garden City, N.Y.: Doubleday, 1954.

Hunter, J. Paul. *The Reluctant Pilgrim: Defoe's Emblematic Method and Quest for Form in Robinson Crusoe*. Baltimore: Johns Hopkins Press, 1966.

Jakubec, Joël. *Kafka contre l'absurde*. Lausanne: Cahiers de la Renaissance Vaudoise, 1962.

Jameson, Fredric. *Sartre: The Origins of a Style*. New Haven: Yale University Press, 1961.

Jean de Meung and Guillaume de Lorris. *Le Roman de la rose*. Paris: Champion, 1965.

Joyce, James. *Dubliners*. New York: Modern Library, 1954.

——. *Finnegans Wake*. New York: Viking Press, 1959.

——. *A Portrait of the Artist as a Young Man*. New York: Viking Press, 1944.

——. *Ulysses*. New York: Random House, 1946.

Kafka, Franz. *Amerika*. Translated by Edwin Muir. New York: New Directions, 1946.

——. *The Castle*. Translated by Willa and Edwin Muir. Definitive edition. New York: Knopf, 1954.

——. *Dearest Father: Stories and Other Writings* (includes "Reflexions" and "Wedding Preparations in the Country"). Translated by Ernst Kaiser and Eithne Wilkins. New York: Schocken, 1954.

———. *The Diaries of Franz Kafka*. Edited by Max Brod. Translated by Joseph Kresh. 2 vols. New York: Schocken, 1948–1949.

———. *Die Erzählungen* (includes "Small Fable"). Frankfort: Fischer, 1965.

———. *The Penal Colony* (includes "A Country Doctor"; "In the Penal Colony"; "The Judgment"; "The Metamorphosis"; "The Worries of a Family Man"). Translated by Willa and Edwin Muir. New York: Schocken, 1948.

———. *The Trial*. Translated by Willa and Edwin Muir. Definitive edition. New York: Knopf, 1957.

Kettle, Arnold. *An Introduction to the English Novel*. 2 vols. London: Hutchinson's University Press, 1951–1953.

Kirby, Thomas Austin. *Chaucer's Troilus: A Study in Courtly Love*. Gloucester, Mass.: P. Smith, 1958.

Knox, Robert. *An Historical Relation of Ceylon*. Glasgow: MacLehose, 1911.

Laclos, Pierre Ambroise François Choderlos de. *Les Liaisons dangereuses*. Edited by Edouard Maynial. 2 vols. Paris: Belles Lettres, 1956.

Lafayette, Marie-Madeleine Pioche de la Vergne, Comtesse de. *La Princesse de Clèves*. Edited by Emile Magne. With "Extraits de Valincour." Paris: Droz, 1946.

Lannert, Gustaf L:son. *An Investigation into the Language of Robinson Crusoe as Compared with That of Other 18ᵗʰ Century Works*. Uppsala, Sweden: SVEA, 1910.

Lautréamont. See Ducasse, Isidore Lucien.

Lazar, Moshé. *Amour courtois et fin' amors dans la littérature du XIIᵉ siècle*. Paris: Klincksieck, 1964.

Lefebvre, Henri. *Rabelais*. Paris: Editeurs français réunis, 1955.

Lefranc, Abel Jules Maurice. *Rabelais*. Paris: Albin Michel, 1953.

Lesser, Simon O. *Fiction and the Unconscious*. Boston: Beacon Press, 1957.

Levin, Harry. *Contexts of Criticism*. Cambridge: Harvard University Press, 1957.

———. *James Joyce: A Critical Introduction*. London: Faber and Faber, 1960.

Lewis, D. B. Wyndham. See Rabelais.

Litz, A. Walton. *The Art of James Joyce: Method and Design in Ulysses and Finnegans Wake*. New York: Oxford University Press, 1964.

López Pinciano, Alonzo. *Filosophía antigua poética*. Edited by Alfredo Carballo. Madrid: Instituto "Miguel de Cervantes," 1953.

Lucian of Samosata. *Zeus Tragoedus*. (Loeb Classical Library.) Cambridge: Harvard University Press, 1960.

Lukács, György. *The Meaning of Contemporary Realism*. Translated by John and Necke Mander. London: Merlin Press, 1963.

Madariaga, Salvador de. *Don Quixote: An Introductory Essay in Psychology*. London: Oxford University Press, 1961.

Magny, Claude-Edmonde. *Les Sandales d'Empédocle: Essai sur les limites de la littérature*. Neuchâtel, Swit.: Baconnière, 1945.

Maistre Pierre Pathelin. Edited by Richard T. Holbrook. Paris: Champion, 1956.

Malraux, André. *Les Noyers de l'Altenburg*. Paris: Gallimard, 1948. Translated by A. W. Fielding, *The Walnut Trees of Altenburg* (London: J. Lehmann, 1952).

Martorell, Juan. *Tirant lo Blanch*. New York: Hispanic Society of America, 1904.

Menéndez Pidal, Ramón. *La Chanson de Roland et la tradition épique des Francs*. Translated by I.-M. Cluzel. Paris: Picard, 1960.

Moeller, Charles, *Littérature du XX^{ieme} siècle et christianisme*. 4 vols. Tournai, Belg.: Casterman, 1953–60.

Monnier, G.-F. *Etude psychopathologique sur l'écrivain Franz Kafka*. Bordeaux: Faculté de Médecine et de Pharmacie, 1951.

Monnin-Hornung, Juliette. *Proust et la peinture*. Geneva: Droz, 1951.

Morrissette, Bruce. *Les Romans de Robbe-Grillet*. Paris: Editions de Minuit, 1963.

Moss, Howard. *The Magic Lantern of Marcel Proust*. New York: Macmillan, 1962.

Motchoulski, C. *Dostoïevski: L'Homme et l'œuvre*. Translated by Gustave Welter. Paris: Payot, 1963.

Novak, Maximillian E. *Defoe and the Nature of Man*. London: Oxford University Press, 1963.

Oliveros de Castilla, in *La Historia delos nobles caualleros Oliueros de Castilla y Artus Dalgarbe*. New York: De Vinne, 1902.

Ong, Walter J., S.J. *The Barbarian Within and Other Fugitive Essays and Studies*. New York: Macmillan, 1962.

Ortega y Gasset, José. *The Dehumanization of Art and Notes on the Novel*. Translated by Helen Weyl. Princeton: Princeton University Press, 1948.

Painter, George D. *Proust:* Vol. I, *The Early Years;* Vol. II, *The Later Years*. Boston: Little Brown, 1959–1965.

Palmerin de Inglaterra, in Adolfo Bonilla y San Martin, *Libros de caballerías*. Madrid: Bailly-Bailliére, 1907–1908.

Pathelin. See *Maistre Pierre Pathelin*.

Pausanias. *Description of Greece*. Translated by J. G. Frazer. 6 vols. New York: Macmillan, 1898.

Petit de Julleville, Louis, *Histoire de la langue et de la littérature française des origines à 1900*. Paris: A. Colin, 1896–1899.

Piper, William B. *Laurence Sterne*. New York: Twayne, 1965.

Plotinus. *Enneads*. Translated by S. MacKenna and B. S. Page. London: Faber and Faber, 1962.

Politzer, Heinz. *Franz Kafka: Parable and Paradox*. Revised edition. Ithaca, N.Y.: Cornell University Press, 1966.

Poulet, Georges. *L'Espace proustien*. Paris: Gallimard, 1963.

Pound, Ezra Loomis. *Literary Essays of Ezra Pound*. Edited by T. S. Eliot. Norfolk, Conn.: New Directions, 1954.

Proust Marcel. *A la recherche du temps perdu*. Edited by Pierre Clarac and André Ferré. 3 vols. Paris: Gallimard,

1954. Translated by C. K. Scott Moncrieff and Frederick A. Blossom, *Remembrance of Things Past*. 2 vols. (New York: Random House, 1941).

——. *La Bible d'Amiens*. (Translation of John Ruskin, *The Bible of Amiens*.) Paris: Collection d'Auteurs Etrangers, 1904.

——. *Jean Santeuil*. 3 vols. Paris: Gallimard, 1952. Translated by Gerard Hopkins (New York: Simon and Schuster, 1955).

Pseudo-Villon. *The Free Meals of François Villon (Les Repues franches)*. Edited and translated by Lewis Wharton. London: Fortune Press, n.d.

Pulci, Luigi. *Il Morgante*. Edited by Raffaello Ramat. Milan: Rizzoli, 1961.

Queneau, Raymond. *Pierrot mon ami*. Paris: Gallimard, 1943.

Rabelais, François. *Pantagruel* and *Gargantua*, in *Œuvres complètes*. Edited by Jean Plattard. 5 vols. Paris: Belles Lettres, 1948–1959. Translated by Thomas Urquhart and Peter Motteux, *Gargantua and Pantagruel;* Introduction by D. B. Wyndham Lewis (New York: Dutton, 1929).

Racine, Jean Baptiste. *Andromaque* and *Phèdre*, in *Théâtre complet de Racine*. Edited by Maurice Rat. Paris: Garnier, 1953.

Les Repues franches. See Pseudo-Villon.

Riesman, David, with Nathan Glazer and Reuel Denney. *The Lonely Crowd: A Study of the Changing American Character*. New Haven: Yale University Press, 1950.

Riley, Edward Calverley. *Cervantes's Theory of the Novel*. Oxford: Clarendon Press, 1962.

Robbe-Grillet, Alain. *L'Année dernière à Marienbad*. Paris: Editions de Minuit, 1961. Translated by Richard Howard, *Last Year at Marienbad* (New York: Grove Press, 1962).

——. *Dans le labyrinthe*. Paris: Editions de Minuit, 1959. Translated by Richard Howard, *In the Labyrinth* (New York: Grove Press, 1960).

——. *Les Gommes*. Paris: *Editions de Minuit*, 1953. Translated by Richard Howard, *The Erasers* (New York: Grove Press, 1964).

——. *L'Immortelle*. Paris: Editions de Minuit, 1963.

——. *Instantanés*. Paris: Editions de Minuit, 1962. Translated by Barbara Wright, *Snapshots and Towards a New Novel* (includes "The Secret Room" [London: Calder and Boyars, 1965]).

——. *La Jalousie*. Paris: Editions de Minuit, 1957. Translated by Richard Howard, *Jealousy* (New York: Grove Press, 1959).

——. *La Maison de rendez-vous*. Paris: Editions de Minuit, 1965.

——. *Pour un nouveau roman*. Paris: Editions de Minuit, 1963. Translated by Richard Howard, *For a New Novel* (includes "Nature, Humanism and Tragedy"; "New Novel, New Man"; "A Path for the Future Novel"; "Time and Description in Contemporary Narration" [New York: Grove Press, 1965]).

——. *Le Voyeur*. Paris: Editions de Minuit, 1955. Translated by Richard Howard, *The Voyeur* (New York: Grove Press, 1958).

Rogers, Woodes. *A Cruising Voyage round the World*. London: A. Bell and B. Lintot, 1718.

Le Roman d'Enéas. See *Enéas, roman du XIIᵉ siècle*.

Le Roman de Thèbes. Edited by Léopold Constans. Paris: Firmin Didot, 1890.

Rougemont, Denis de. *Love Declared: Essays on the Myths of Love*. Translated by Richard Howard. New York: Pantheon, 1963.

Ruskin, John. See Proust.

Sainte-Beuve, Charles Augustin. *Portraits de femmes*. Paris: Garnier, 1884.

Sand, George. *François le Champi*. Paris: Calmann-Lévy, 1928.

Sarraute, Nathalie. *L'Ere du soupçon*. Paris: Gallimard, 1956.

Sartre, Jean-Paul. *Les Chemins de la liberté* (*L'Age de raison, Le Sursis, La Mort dans l'âme*). Paris: Gallimard, 1945–

1949. Translated as *The Roads to Freedom* (*The Age of Reason, The Reprieve, Troubled Sleep* [New York: Knopf, 1947–1951].

——. *L'Etre et le néant: Essai d'ontologie phénoménologique.* Paris: Gallimard, 1943. Translated by Hazel E. Barnes, *Being and Nothingness.* (New York: Philosophical Library, 1956).

——. *Huis-clos.* Paris: Gallimard, 1945. Translated by Stuart Gilbert, *No Exit* (New York: Knopf, 1946).

——. *L'Imaginaire: Psychologie phénoménologique de l'imagination.* Paris: Gallimard, 1940. Translated as *The Psychology of Imagination* (New York: Philosophical Library, 1948).

——. *Le Mur.* Paris: Gallimard, 1939. Translated by Lloyd Alexander, *The Wall and Other Stories* (Norfolk, Conn.: New Directions, 1948).

——. *La Nausée.* Paris: Gallimard, 1938. Translated by Lloyd Alexander, *Nausea* (Norfolk, Conn.: New Directions, 1959).

——. *Qu'est-ce que la littérature?* Paris: Gallimard, 1948. Translated by Bernard Frechtman, *What Is Literature?* (New York: Philosophical Library, 1949).

——. *Situations.* 4 vols. Paris: Gallimard, 1947–1964. *Situations* I and III translated by Annette Michelson (New York: Philosophical Library, 1957). *Situations* II is devoted mainly to *What Is Literature? Situations* IV translated by Benita Eisler (New York: Braziller, 1965).

Shattuck, Roger. *Proust's Binoculars.* New York: Random House, 1963.

Soulier, Jean Pierre. *Lautréamont: Génie ou maladie mentale?* Geneva: Droz, 1964.

Spitzer, Leo. *Stilstudien.* 2 vols. Munich: Hueber, 1928.

Starr, G. A. *Defoe and Spiritual Autobiography.* Princeton: Princeton University Press, 1965.

Statius, Publius Papinius. *Thebaid,* in *Statius.* (Loeb Classical Library.) London: Heinemann, 1928.

Sterne, Laurence. *The Writings of Laurence Sterne.* 7 vols. Boston: Houghton, Mifflin, 1926–1927.

——. *Tristram Shandy.* Edited by James A. Work. New York: Odyssey Press, 1940.

Tirant lo Blanch. See Martorell, Juan.

Traill, H. D. *Sterne.* New York: Harpers, 1887.

Ullmann, Stephen. *The Image in the Modern French Novel.* Cambridge: Cambridge University Press, 1960.

——. *Style in the French Novel.* New York: Barnes and Noble, 1964.

Valincour, Jean Baptiste Henri du Trousset de. *Lettres à la marquise ***.* See Lafayette.

Van Ghent, Dorothy. *The English Novel.* New York: Rinehart, 1953.

Voltaire, François Marie Arouet de. *Le Siècle de Louis XIV.* Paris: Hachette, 1919.

Watt, Ian. *The Rise of the Novel.* Berkeley: University of California Press, 1957.

Wellek, René, editor. *Dostoevsky: A Collection of Critical Essays.* Englewood Cliffs, N.J.: Prentice-Hall, 1962.

Woolf, Virginia. *The Second Common Reader.* New York: Harcourt, Brace, 1932.

Young, Karl. *The Origin and Development of the Story of Troilus and Criseyde.* London: Kegan Paul, 1908.

Zola, Emile. *La Terre.* Paris: Charpentier. 1887.

Index

Date Due

Demco 38-297